Investing in ETFs

FOR

DUMMIES®

A Wiley Brand

Investing in ETFs

FOR DUMMIES®

A Wiley Brand

by Russell Wild

FOR DUMMIES®

A Wiley Brand

Investing in ETFs For Dummies®

Published by: **John Wiley & Sons, Inc.,** 111 River Street, Hoboken, NJ 07030-5774, www.wiley.com

Copyright © 2016 by John Wiley & Sons, Inc., Hoboken, New Jersey

Published simultaneously in Canada

Contents at a Glance

Introduction *1*

Part I: Getting Started with ETFs *5*

Chapter 1: The (Sort of Still) New Kid on the Block 7

Chapter 2: Getting to Know the Players 29

Part II: Getting to Know ETFs *51*

Chapter 3: Large Growth and Large Value 53

Chapter 4: Small Growth and Small Value 73

Chapter 5: Going Global: ETFs Without Borders 85

Chapter 6: Sector Investing and Specialized Stocks 105

Chapter 7: For Your Interest: The World of Bond ETFs 123

Chapter 8: REITs, Commodities, and Active ETFs 143

**Part III: Customizing and Optimizing
Your ETF Portfolio** *161*

Chapter 9: Sample ETF Portfolio Menus 163

Chapter 10: Understanding Risk and Return 185

Chapter 11: Exercising Patience and Learning Exceptions 205

Part IV: The Part of Tens *227*

Chapter 12: Ten FAQs about ETFs 229

Chapter 13: Ten Mistakes Most Investors
(Even Smart Ones) Make 235

Index *241*

Table of Contents

Introduction... **1**

About This Book 1
Icons Used in This Book.. 3
Beyond the Book... 4
Where to Go from Here 4

Part I: Getting Started with ETFs 5

Chapter 1: The (Sort of Still) New Kid on the Block 7

What the Heck Is an ETF, Anyway?.. 8
Choosing between the classic and
the new indexes 9
Preferring ETFs over individual stocks..................... 11
Distinguishing ETFs from mutual funds..................... 12
Why the Big Boys Prefer ETFs... 13
Trading in large lots 13
Savoring the versatility.................................... 14
Why Individual Investors Are Learning to Love ETFs 14
The cost advantage: How low can you go?.............. 14
Uncle Sam's loss, your gain............................... 17
What you see is what you get 19
Getting the Professional Edge 20
Consider a few impressive numbers...................... 21
You can do what they do!................................. 22
Passive versus Active Investing: Your Choice 22
The index advantage 22
The allure of active management 24
Measuring keeps getting tougher 24
Do ETFs Belong in Your Life? 25
Calculating commissions................................. 25
Moving money in a flash.................................. 26
Understanding tracking error 26
Making a sometimes tricky choice 26

Chapter 2: Getting to Know the Players 29

Creating an Account for Your ETFs.................................... 30
Answering a zillion questions 30
Placing an order to buy.................................. 31

But wait just a moment! 33
Trading ETFs like a pro 33
Introducing the Shops 34
What to look for 34
A price structure like no other................................ 35
The Vanguard Group..................................... 36
Fidelity Investments 37
Charles Schwab.................................... 37
T. Rowe Price 38
TD Ameritrade.................................... 38
Other brokerage houses 39
Presenting the Suppliers 40
It's okay to mix and match — with caution.............. 40
BlackRock iShares 41
Vanguard ETFs 42
State Street Global Advisers (SSgA) SPDRs 43
Invesco PowerShares 44
WisdomTree 45
Guggenheim.................................... 45
ProShares.................................... 46
Other suppliers 47
Familiarizing Yourself with the Indexers 47
Standard & Poor's.................................... 47
Dow Jones................................ 48
MSCI.................................... 48
Russell................................ 49
Barclays 49

Part II: Getting to Know ETFs.......................... 51

Chapter 3: Large Growth and Large Value 53
Utilizing the Monsters of Money-Making:
Large-Growth Stocks.......................... 54
Style review 55
Looking into Stocks Big and Brawny 57
Contrary to all appearances 57
Let history serve as only a rough guide 58
Large Cap ETF Options Galore.............................. 58
Strictly large cap or blend? 59
Blended options for large cap exposure................... 60
Strictly large growth.................................. 62
ETFs I wouldn't go out of my way to own.................. 64
Large Value: Counterintuitive Cash Cows 65

Looking for the Best Value Buys 67
Taking the index route 68
Making an ETF selection 68

Chapter 4: Small Growth and Small Value 73

Harnessing Small Growth with Sweet Start-Ups 74
Your Choices for Small Growth 75
Small cap blend funds 76
Strictly small cap growth funds 78
Opting for Small Value: Diminutive Dazzlers 80
Latching on for fun and profit 81
Keeping your balance 82

Chapter 5: Going Global: ETFs Without Borders 85

The Ups and Downs of Different Markets
around the World 86
Low correlation is the name of the game 87
Remember what happened to Japan 88
Finding Your Best Mix of Domestic and International 88
Not too high 89
Not too low 90
Just right 91
Not All Foreign Nations — or Stocks — Are
Created Equal 92
Choosing the Best International ETFs for Your
Portfolio 93
Four brands to choose from 94
All the world's your apple: ETFs that
cover the planet 95
European stock ETFs 96
Pacific region stock ETFs 98
Emerging-market stock ETFs 99
iShares value and growth 101
WisdomTree currency hedged funds 102
Small cap international 103

Chapter 6: Sector Investing and
Specialized Stocks 105

Selecting Stocks by Sector, Not Style 106
Calculating your optimal mix 107
Seeking risk adjustment with high and
low volatility sectors 107
Knowing where the style grid comes through 108
Seeking low correlations for
added diversification 108

Sector Choices by the Dozen.. 109
Specialized Stock ETFs: Investing for a Better World 110
 Tracking the history of SRI performance................. 111
 Your growing number of choices for
 social investing... 111
Dividend Funds: The Search for Steady Money 112
 Your high dividend ETF options............................. 112
 Promise of riches or smoke and mirrors?............. 113
Investing in Initial Public Offerings........................... 116
 The roller coaster of recent IPO performance........ 117
 Taking a broader look at IPOs................................. 117
Funds That (Supposedly) Thrive When
 the Market Takes a Dive.............................. 118
Funds That Double the Thrill of Investing
 (for Better or Worse)....................................... 119
All-in-One ETFs: For the Ultimate Lazy Portfolio 120
 Getting worldwide exposure to
 stocks and bonds...................................... 121
 Russell's average review for the average
 reader on an average day 122

**Chapter 7: For Your Interest: The World
of Bond ETFs 123**

Tracing the Track Record of Bonds.................................... 124
 Portfolio protection when you need it most........... 125
 History may or may not repeat............................... 126
Tapping into Bonds in Various Ways 126
 Finding strength in numbers 127
 Considering bond fund costs 128
Sampling a Basic Bond-ETF Menu.................................... 129
 Tapping the Treasurys: Uncle Sam's IOUs 130
 Bread at $10 a loaf? Getting inflation
 protection in a flash.................................... 132
 Banking on business: Corporate bond ETFs 133
 The whole shebang: Investing in the entire
 U.S. bond market.................................... 135
Moving Beyond Basics into Municipal and
 Foreign Bonds.. 137
 Municipals for mostly tax-free income 137
 Foreign bonds for fixed-income diversification....... 138
 Emerging-market bonds: High risk, high return 140

Chapter 8: REITs, Commodities, and Active ETFs 143

Real Estate Investment Trusts (REITs) 144
Why REITs should be in your portfolio 144
Calculating a proper REIT allocation 146
Picking REIT ETFs for your portfolio........................ 147
All That Glitters: Gold, Silver, and Other Commodities.... 148
Gold, gold, gold!... 149
Silver: The second metal... 151
Oil and gas: Truly volatile commodities 152
Playing the commodity market indirectly:
A (somewhat) safer approach............................... 155
Going Active with ETFs 158

Part III: Customizing and Optimizing
Your ETF Portfolio 161

Chapter 9: Sample ETF Portfolio Menus 163

So, How Much Risk Can You Handle and
Still Sleep at Night? 164
A few things that just don't matter.......................... 164
The irony of risk and return...................................... 166
The 20x rule... 166
Other risk/return considerations 168
The limitations of risk questionnaires 168
Keys to Optimal Investing.. 169
Incorporating Modern Portfolio Theory.................. 170
Minimizing your costs.. 170
Striving for tax efficiency.. 171
Timing your investments (just a touch).................. 171
Finding the Perfect Portfolio Fit.. 172
Considering the simplest of the simple 173
Racing toward riches 174
Sticking to the middle of the road 175
Taking the safer road 176
Aiming for Economic Self-Sufficiency in Your
Golden Years 178
Taking the basic steps 179
Choosing the right vessels 179
Curing the 401(k) Blues.. 182

Chapter 10: Understanding Risk and Return......185

Risk Is Not Just a Board Game............................ 186
    The trade-off of all trade-offs (safety
    versus return) 187
    So just how risky are ETFs?................................ 187
Smart Risk, Foolish Risk.. 188
How Risk Is Measured 190
    Standard deviation: The king of all risk
    measurement tools...................................... 191
    Beta: Assessing price swings in relation
    to the market.. 193
    The Sharpe, Treynor, and Sortino ratios:
    Measures of what you get for your risk............... 194
Meet Modern Portfolio Theory 196
    Tasting the extreme positivity of
    negative correlation 196
    Settling for limited correlation..................... 198
    Reaching for the elusive Efficient Frontier.............. 199
Mixing and Matching Your Stock ETFs 200
    Filling in your style box................................ 201
    Buying by industry sector 202
    Don't slice and dice your portfolio to death............ 203

Chapter 11: Exercising Patience and Learning Exceptions.........................205

The Tale of the Average Investor (A Tragicomedy
    in One Act)... 206
    Returns that fall way short of the indexes 207
    ETFs can make failure even easier!..................... 208
    The lure of quick riches................................ 209
    Caveat emptor: ETF-trading websites
    for suckers... 209
Patience Pays, Literally 211
Exceptions to the Rule (Ain't There Always) 212
    Rebalancing to keep your portfolio fit.................. 213
    Contemplating tactical asset allocation................. 216
    Investing the SweetSpot way............................ 219
    Revamping your portfolio with life changes:
    Marriage, divorce, and babies............................ 221
Are Options an Option for You?.............................. 224

Part IV: The Part of Tens...................................... 227

Chapter 12: Ten FAQs about ETFs.................229

Are ETFs Appropriate for Individual Investors? 229
Are ETFs Risky? 230
Do I Need a Financial Professional to Set Up and
Monitor an ETF Portfolio? 230
How Much Money Do I Need to Invest in ETFs?................ 231
With Hundreds of ETFs to Choose from,
Where Do I Start? 232
Where Is the Best Place for Me to Buy ETFs?................... 232
Is There an Especially Good or Bad Time
to Buy ETFs? 233
Do ETFs Have Any Disadvantages? 233
Does It Matter Which Exchange My ETF
Is Traded On? 234
Which ETFs Are Best in My IRA, and
Which Are Best in My Taxable Account? 234

Chapter 13: Ten Mistakes Most Investors
(Even Smart Ones) Make......................235

Paying Too Much for an Investment................................. 235
Failing to Properly Diversify 236
Taking on Inappropriate Risks 236
Selling Out When the Going Gets Tough 236
Paying Too Much Attention to Recent Performance........ 237
Not Saving Enough for Retirement 237
Having Unrealistic Expectations of Market Returns.......... 238
Discounting the Damaging Effect of Inflation 238
Not Following the IRS's Rules 239
Failing to Incorporate Investments into a
Broader Financial Plan 239

Index.. 241

Introduction

*E*very month, it seems, Wall Street comes up with some newfangled investment idea. The array of financial products (replete with 164-page prospectuses) is now so dizzying that the old lumpy mattress is starting to look like a more comfortable place to stash the cash. But there is one relatively new product out there definitely worth looking at. It's something of a cross between an index mutual fund and a stock, and it's called an *exchange-traded fund,* or ETF.

Just as computers and fax machines were used by big institutions before they caught on with individual consumers, so it was with ETFs. They were first embraced by institutional traders — investment banks, hedge funds, and insurance firms — because, among other things, they allow for the quick juggling of massive holdings. Big traders like that sort of thing. Personally, playing hot potato with my money is not my idea of fun. But all the same, over the past several years, I've invested most of my own savings in ETFs, and I've suggested to many of my clients that they do the same.

I'm not alone in my appreciation of ETFs. They have grown exponentially in the past few years, and they will surely continue to grow and gain influence. While I can't claim that my purchases and my recommendations of ETFs account for much of the growing $2 trillion+ ETF market, I'm happy to be a (very) small part of it. After you've read this book, you may decide to become part of it as well, if you haven't already.

About This Book

As with any other investment, you're looking for a certain payoff in reading this book. In an abstract sense, the payoff will come in your achieving a thorough understanding and appreciation of a powerful financial tool called an exchange-traded fund. The more concrete payoff will come when you apply this understanding to improve your investment results.

What makes me think ETFs can help you make money?

> ✔ **ETFs are intelligent.** Most financial experts agree that playing with individual stocks can be hazardous to one's wealth. Anything from an accounting scandal to the CEO's sudden angina attack can send a single stock spiraling downward. That's why it makes sense for the average investor to own lots of stocks — or bonds — through ETFs or mutual funds.

> ✔ **ETFs are cheap.** At least 250 ETFs charge annual management expenses of 0.20 percent or lower, and 60 of them charge 0.10 percent a year or less. The average actively managed mutual fund, in contrast, charges 1.25 percent a year. Index mutual funds generally cost a tad more than their ETF cousins. Such cost differences, while appearing small on paper, can make a huge impact on your returns over time.

> ✔ **ETFs are tax-smart.** Because of the clever way ETFs are structured, the taxes you pay on any growth are minimal.

> ✔ **ETFs are open books.** Quite unlike mutual funds, an nearly all ETFs' holdings are readily visible. If this afternoon, for example, I were to buy 100 shares of the ETF called the SPDR (pronounced "spider") S&P 500, I would know that exactly 4.02 percent of my money was invested in Apple, Inc, 2.07 percent in the Microsoft Corporation, and 1.94 percent in Exxon Mobil Corp. You don't get that kind of detail when you buy most mutual funds. Mutual fund managers, like stage magicians, are often reluctant to reveal their secrets. In the investment game, the more you know, the lower the odds you will get sawed in half.

If the book you're now reading were like some (but certainly not all) mutual funds, it would be largely unintelligible and expensive. (It might be doubly expensive if you tried to resell the book within 90 days!) Luckily, this book is more like an ETF. Here's how:

> ✔ *Investing in ETFs For Dummies* **is intelligent.** I don't try to convince you that ETFs are your best investment choice, and I certainly don't tell you that ETFs will make you rich. Instead, I lay out facts and figures and summarize some hard academic findings, and I let you draw your own conclusions.

✔ *Investing in ETFs For Dummies* **is cheap.** Hey, top-notch investment advice for just the price of this one small book (plus or minus any discounts, shipping, and tax). Where else are you going to get that kind of deal? *And* should you come to the conclusion after reading this book that ETFs belong in your portfolio, you'll likely get your money (plus any shipping costs and tax) back — in the form of lower fees and tax efficiency — in no time at all.

✔ *Investing in ETFs For Dummies* **is tax-smart.** Yes, the money you spent for this book, as all other outlays you make for investment advice, may be deducted from your federal income taxes (provided you itemize your deductions). Go for it!

✔ *Investing in ETFs For Dummies* **is an open book.** We've already established that!

If you've ever read a *For Dummies* book, you have an idea of what you're about to embark on. This is not a book you need to read from front to back. Feel free to jump about and glean whatever information you think will be of most use. There is no quiz at the end. You don't have to commit it all to memory.

Icons Used in This Book

Throughout the book, you find little globular pieces of art in the margins called *icons.* These admittedly cutesy but handy tools give you a heads-up that certain types of information are in the neighborhood.

Although this is a how-to book, you also find plenty of whys and wherefores. Any paragraph accompanied by this icon, however, is guaranteed pure, 100 percent, unadulterated how-to.

The world of investments offers pitfalls galore. Wherever you see the bomb, know that there is a risk of you losing money — maybe even Big Money — if you skip the passage.

Read twice! This icon indicates that something important is being said and is really worth putting to memory.

If you don't really care about the difference between standard deviation and beta, or the historical correlation between U.S. value stocks and REITs, feel free to skip or skim the paragraphs with this icon.

 The world of Wall Street is full of people who make money at other people's expense. Where you see the pig face, know that I'm about to point out an instance where someone will likely be sticking a hand deep in your pocket.

Beyond the Book

In addition to all the material you find in the book you're reading right now, this product also comes with some access-anywhere goodies on the web. Check out the Cheat Sheet at `www.dummies.com/cheatsheet/investinginetfs` for helpful insights and pointers on utilizing ETFs successfully. You also get some additional articles that would have kept this book from fitting into a portable size at `www.dummies.com/extras/investinginetfs`.

Where to Go from Here

Where would you like to go from here? If you wish, start at the beginning. If you're interested only in stock ETFs, hey, no one says that you can't jump right to Chapter 6. Bond ETFs? Go ahead and jump to Chapter 7. It's entirely your call.

Part I
Getting Started with ETFs

In this part . . .

- ✔ Find out how ETFs work, and how they're different from other investment options.

- ✔ Look into the plusses and minuses of ETFs to determine whether they're a good fit for you.

- ✔ Get the pieces into position for ETF investing, from starting an account to finding a broker.

- ✔ Understand the indexers and exchanges.

Chapter 1

The (Sort of Still) New Kid on the Block

In This Chapter

▶ Distinguishing what makes ETFs unique

▶ Appreciating ETFs' special attributes

▶ Understanding that ETFs aren't perfect

▶ Taking a look at who is making the most use of ETFs, and how

▶ Asking whether ETFs are for you

*T*here are, no doubt, a good number of pinstriped ladies and gentlemen in and around Wall Street who froth heavily at the mouth when they hear the words *exchange-traded fund*. In a world of very pricey investment products and very well paid investment-product salespeople, ETFs are the ultimate killjoys.

Since their arrival on the investment scene in the early 1990s, more than 2,300 ETFs have been created, and ETF assets have grown faster than those of any other investment product. That's a good thing. ETFs enable the average investor to avoid shelling out fat commissions or paying layers of ongoing, unnecessary fees. And they've saved investors oodles and oodles in taxes.

Hallelujah.

What the Heck Is an ETF, Anyway?

Banking your retirement on stocks is risky enough; banking your retirement on any individual stock, or even a handful of stocks, is Evel Knievel-jumping-the-Snake-River investing. Banking on individual bonds is typically less risky (maybe Evel Knievel jumping a creek), but the same general principle holds. There is safety in numbers. That's why teenage boys and girls huddle together in corners at school dances. That's why gnus graze in groups. That's why smart stock and bond investors grab onto ETFs.

Just as a deed shows that you have ownership of a house, and a share of common stock certifies ownership in a company, a share of an ETF represents ownership (most typically) in a basket of company stocks. To buy or sell an ETF, you place an order with a broker, generally (and preferably, for cost reasons) online, although you can also place an order by phone. The price of an ETF changes throughout the trading day, which is to say from 9:30 a.m. to 4:00 p.m. New York City time, going up or going down with the market value of the securities it holds. (Sometimes there can be a little sway — times when the price of an ETF doesn't exactly track the value of the securities it holds — but that situation is rarely serious, at least not with ETFs from the better purveyors.)

Originally, ETFs were developed to mirror various indexes:

- ✔ The SPDR S&P 500 (ticker SPY) represents stocks from the S&P (Standard & Poor's) 500, an index of the 500 largest companies in the United States.

- ✔ The DIAMONDS Trust Series 1 (ticker DIA) represents the 30 underlying stocks of the Dow Jones Industrial Average index.

- ✔ The NASDAQ-100 Trust Series 1, which was renamed the PowerShares QQQ Trust Series 1 (ticker QQQ), represents the 100 stocks of the NASDAQ-100 index.

The component companies in an ETF's portfolio usually represent a certain index or segment of the market, such as large U.S. value stocks, small growth stocks, or micro cap stocks. (If you're not 100 percent clear on the difference between *value* and *growth,* or what a micro cap is, rest assured that I define these and other key terms in Part II.)

Sometimes, the stock market is broken up into industry sectors, such as technology, industrials, and consumer discretionary. ETFs exist that mirror each sector.

Regardless of which securities an ETF represents, and regardless of what index those securities are a part of, your fortunes as an ETF holder are tied, either directly or in some leveraged fashion, to the value of the underlying securities. If the price of Exxon Mobil Corporation stock, U.S. Treasury bonds, gold bullion, or British Pound futures goes up, so does the value of your ETF. If the price of gold tumbles, your portfolio (if you hold a gold ETF) may lose some glitter. If GE stock pays a dividend, you are due a certain amount of that dividend — *unless* you happen to have bought into a leveraged or inverse ETF.

As I discuss in Chapter 6, some ETFs allow for leveraging, so that if the underlying security rises in value, your ETF shares rise doubly or triply. If the security falls in value, well, you lose according to the same multiple. Other ETFs allow you not only to leverage but also to *reverse* leverage, so that you stand to make money if the underlying security falls in value (and of course lose if the underlying security increases in value). I'm not a big fan of leveraged and inverse ETFs, for reasons I make clear in Chapter 6.

Choosing between the classic and the new indexes

Some of the ETF providers (Vanguard, iShares, Schwab) tend to use traditional indexes, such as those I mention in the previous section. Others (Invesco PowerShares, WisdomTree, Guggenheim) tend to develop their own indexes.

For example, if you were to buy 100 shares of an ETF called the iShares S&P 500 Growth Index Fund (IVW), you'd be buying into a traditional index (large U.S. growth companies). At about $117.30 a share (at this writing), you'd plunk down $11,170 for a portfolio of stocks that would include shares of Apple, Microsoft Corp., Walt Disney, Facebook, Amazon, and Johnson & Johnson. If you wanted to know the exact breakdown, the iShares prospectus found on the iShares website (or any number of financial websites, such as http://finance.yahoo.com) would tell you specific percentages: Apple, 7.48 percent; Microsoft Corp., 4.10 percent; Walt Disney, 1.75; and so on.

Many ETFs represent shares in companies that form foreign indexes. If, for example, you were to own 100 shares of the iShares MSCI Japan Index Fund (EWJ), with a market value of about $13.30 per share as of this writing, your $1,330 would buy you a stake in large Japanese companies such as Toyota Motor, Honda Motor, Mitsubishi, and Softbank Corp. Chapter 5 is devoted entirely to international ETFs.

Both IVW and EWJ mirror standard indexes: IVW mirrors the S&P 500 Growth Index, and EWJ mirrors the MSCI Japan Index. If, however, you purchase 100 shares of the PowerShares Dynamic Large Cap Growth Portfolio (PWB), you'll buy roughly $3,100 worth of a portfolio of stocks that mirror a very unconventional index — one created by the PowerShares family of exchange-traded funds. The large U.S. growth companies in the PowerShares index don't include Apple, Microsoft, or Amazon, but rather companies like Schlumberger N.V., Bristol-Myers Squibb, and MasterCard Incorporated. Invesco PowerShares refers to its custom indexes as "enhanced."

A big controversy in the world of ETFs is whether the newfangled, customized indexes offered by companies like Invesco PowerShares make any sense. Most financial professionals are skeptical of anything that's new. Those of us who have been around for a while have seen too many "exciting" new investment ideas crash and burn. But I, for one, try to keep an open mind.

Another big controversy is whether you may be better off with an even newer style of ETFs — those that follow no indexes at all but rather are "actively" managed. I prefer index investing to active investing, but that's not to say that active investing, carefully pursued, has no role to play. More on that topic later in this chapter and throughout the book.

Other ETFs — a distinct but growing minority — represent holdings in assets other than stocks, most notably bonds and commodities (gold, silver, oil, and such). And then there are exchange-traded notes (ETNs), which allow you to venture even further into the world of alternative investments — or speculations — such as currency futures. I discuss these products in Part II of the book.

Preferring ETFs over individual stocks

Okay, why buy a basket of stocks rather than an individual stock? Quick answer: You'll sleep better.

You may recall that in August 2010, HP CEO Mark Hurd suddenly resigned over a sex scandal. The stock plummeted, and HP shareholders lost billions. A few years before that, the always fashionable Martha Stewart was convicted of obstruction of justice and lying to investigators in an insider-trading case involving a small company called ImClone. Within hours, shares in Stewart's namesake firm, Martha Stewart Living Omnimedia, tumbled 23 percent.

Those sorts of things — sometimes much worse — happen every day in the world of stocks.

A company I'll call ABC Pharmaceutical sees its stock shoot up by 68 percent because the firm just earned an important patent for a new diet pill; a month later, the stock falls by 84 percent because a study in the *New England Journal of Medicine* found that the new diet pill causes people to hallucinate and think they're Ghandi — or Martha Stewart.

Compared to the world of individual stocks, the stock market as a whole is as smooth as a morning lake. Heck, a daily rise or fall in the Dow of more than a percent or two (well, 2 or 3 percent these days) is generally considered a pretty big deal.

If you, like me, are not especially keen on roller coasters, then you are advised to put your nest egg into not one stock, not two, but many. If you have a few million sitting around, hey, you'll have no problem diversifying — maybe individual stocks are for you. But for most of us commoners, the only way to effectively diversify is with ETFs or mutual funds.

Distinguishing ETFs from mutual funds

So what is the difference between an ETF and a mutual fund? After all, mutual funds also represent baskets of stocks or bonds. The two, however, are not twins. They're not even siblings. Cousins are more like it. Here are some of the big differences between ETFs and mutual funds:

- ✔ ETFs are bought and sold just like stocks (through a brokerage house, either by phone or online), and their prices change throughout the trading day. Mutual fund orders can be made during the day, but the actual trading doesn't occur until after the markets close.

- ✔ ETFs tend to represent indexes — market segments — and the managers of the ETFs tend to do very little trading of securities in the ETF. (The ETFs are *passively* managed.) Most mutual funds are actively managed.

- ✔ Although they may require you to pay small trading fees, ETFs usually wind up costing you less than mutual funds because the ongoing management fees are typically much less, and there is never a *load* (an entrance and/ or exit fee, sometime an exorbitant one) as you find with many mutual funds.

- ✔ Because of low portfolio turnover and also the way ETFs are structured, ETFs generally declare much less in taxable capital gains than mutual funds.

Table 1-1 provides a quick look at some ways that investing in ETFs differs from investing in mutual funds and individual stocks.

Table 1-1   ETFs Versus Mutual Funds Versus Individual Stocks

	ETFs	Mutual Funds	Individual Stocks
Priced, bought, and sold throughout the day?	Yes	No	Yes
Offer some investment diversification?	Yes	Yes	No
Is there a minimum investment?	No	Yes	No
Purchased through a broker or online brokerage?	Yes	Yes	Yes
Do you pay a fee or commission to make a trade?	Typically	Sometimes	Yes
Can that fee or commission be more than a few dollars?	No	Yes	No
Can you buy/sell options?	Sometimes	No	Sometimes
Indexed (passively managed)?	Typically	Atypically	No
Can you make money or lose money?	Yes	Yes	You bet

Why the Big Boys Prefer ETFs

When ETFs were first introduced, they were primarily of interest to institutional traders — insurance companies, hedge fund people, banks — who often have investment needs considerably more complicated than yours and mine. In this section, I explain why ETFs appeal to the largest investors.

Trading in large lots

Prior to the introduction of ETFs, a trader had no way to buy or sell instantaneously, in one fell swoop, hundreds of stocks or bonds. Because they trade both during market hours and, in some cases, after market hours, ETFs made that possible.

Institutional investors also found other things to like about ETFs. For example, ETFs are often used to put cash to productive use quickly or to fill gaps in a portfolio by allowing immediate exposure to an industry sector or geographic region.

Savoring the versatility

Unlike mutual funds, ETFs can also be purchased with limit, market, or stop-loss orders, taking away the uncertainty involved with placing a buy order for a mutual fund and not knowing what price you're going to get until several hours after the market closes.

And because many ETFs can be sold short, they provide an important means of risk management. If, for example, the stock market takes a dive, *shorting* ETFs — selling them now at a locked-in price with an agreement to purchase them back (cheaper, you hope) later on — may help keep a portfolio afloat. For that reason, ETFs have become a darling of hedge fund managers who offer the promise of investments that won't tank should the stock market tank. See Chapter 11 for more on this topic.

Why Individual Investors Are Learning to Love ETFs

Clients I've worked with are often amazed that I can put them into a financial product that will cost them a fraction in expenses compared to what they are currently paying. Low costs are probably what I love the most about ETFs. But I also love their tax efficiency, their transparency (you know what you're buying), and the long track record of success for indexed investments.

The cost advantage: How low can you go?

In the world of actively managed mutual funds (which is to say most mutual funds), the average annual management fee, according to Morningstar, is 1.25 percent of the account balance. That may not sound like a lot, but don't be misled. A well-balanced portfolio with both stocks and bonds may return, say, 6 percent over time. In that case, paying 1.25 percent to a third party means that you've just lowered your total investment returns by more than one-fifth. In a bad year, when your investments earn, say, 1.25 percent, you've just lowered your investment returns to *zero*. And in a *very* bad year . . . you don't need me to do the math.

I'm astounded at what some mutual funds charge. Whereas the average is 1.25 percent, I've seen charges 10 times that amount. Crazy. Investing in such a fund is tossing money to the wind. Yet people do it. The chances of your winding up ahead after paying such high fees are next to nil. Paying a *load* (an entrance and/or exit fee) that can total as much as 8.50 percent is just as nutty. Yet people do it.

In the world of index funds, the expenses are much lower, with index mutual funds averaging 0.87 percent and ETFs averaging 0.53 percent, although many of the more traditional indexed ETFs cost no more than 0.20 percent a year in management fees. A good number — 122 at last count — are 0.10 percent or less. Some are so low as to be negligible.

Numerous studies have shown that low-cost funds have a huge advantage over higher-cost funds. One study by Morningstar looked at stock returns over a five-year period. In almost every category of stock mutual fund, low-cost funds beat the pants off high-cost funds. Do you think that by paying high fees you're getting better fund management? Hardly. The Morningstar study found, for example, that among mutual funds that hold large blend stocks (*blend* meaning a combination of value and growth . . . an S&P 500 fund would be a blend fund, for example), the annualized gain was 8.75 percent for those funds in the costliest quartile of funds; the gain for the least costly quartile was 9.89 percent.

Why ETFs are cheaper

The management companies that bring us ETFs, such as BlackRock, Inc., and Invesco PowerShares, are presumably not doing so for their health. No, they're making a good profit. One reason they can offer ETFs so cheaply compared to mutual funds is that their expenses are much less. When you buy an ETF, you go through a brokerage house, not BlackRock or Invesco PowerShares. That brokerage house

(Merrill Lynch, Fidelity, TD Ameritrade) does all the necessary paperwork and bookkeeping on the purchase. If you have any questions about your money, you'll likely call Schwab, not BlackRock. So unlike a mutual fund company, which must maintain telephone operators, bookkeepers, and a mailroom, the providers of ETFs can operate almost entirely in cyberspace.

ETFs that are linked to indexes do have to pay some kind of fee to Dow Jones or MSCI or whoever created the index. But that fee is *nothing* compared to the exorbitant salaries that mutual funds pay their stock pickers, er, market analysts.

An unfair race

Active mutual funds really don't have much chance of beating passive index funds — whether mutual funds or ETFs — over the long run, at least not as a group. (There are individual exceptions, but it's virtually impossible to identify them before the fact.) Someone once described the contest as a race in which the active mutual funds are "running with lead boots." Why? In addition to the management fees that eat up much of any gains, there are also the trading costs. Yes, when mutual funds trade stocks or bonds, they pay a spread and a small cut to the stock exchange, just like you and I do. That cost is passed on to you, and it's on top of the annual management fees previously discussed.

It's been estimated that annual turnover costs for active mutual funds typically run about 0.8 percent. And active mutual fund managers must constantly keep some cash on hand for all those trades. Having cash on hand costs money, too: The opportunity cost is estimated to be in the neighborhood of 0.4 percent.

So you take the 1.25 percent average management fee, and the 0.8 percent hidden trading costs, and the 0.4 percent opportunity cost, and you can see where the lead boots come in. Add taxes to the equation, and while some actively managed mutual funds may do better than ETFs for a few years, over the long haul I wouldn't bank on many of them coming out ahead.

Uncle Sam's loss, your gain

Alas, unless your money is in a tax-advantaged retirement account, making money in the markets means that you have to fork something over to Uncle Sam at year's end. That's true, of course, whether you invest in individual securities or funds. But before there were ETFs, individual securities had a big advantage over funds in that you were required to pay capital gains taxes only when you actually enjoyed a capital gain. With mutual funds, that isn't so. The fund itself may realize a capital gain by selling off an appreciated stock. You pay the capital gains tax regardless of whether you sell anything and regardless of whether the share price of the mutual fund increased or decreased since the time you bought it.

There have been times (pick a bad year for the market — 2000, 2008 . . .) when many mutual fund investors lost a considerable amount in the market yet had to pay capital gains taxes at the end of the year. Talk about adding insult to injury! One study found that over the course of time, taxes have wiped out approximately 2 full percentage points in returns for investors in the highest tax brackets.

In the world of ETFs, such losses are very unlikely to happen. Because most ETFs are index-based, they generally have little turnover to create capital gains. To boot, ETFs are structured in a way that largely insulates shareholders from capital gains that result when mutual funds are forced to sell in order to free up cash to pay off shareholders who cash in their chips.

No tax calories

The structure of ETFs makes them different from mutual funds. Actually, ETFs are legally structured in three different ways: as exchange-traded open-end mutual funds, exchange-traded unit investment trusts, and exchange-traded grantor trusts. The differences are subtle, and I elaborate on them somewhat in Chapter 3 and throughout Part II. For now, I want to focus on one seminal difference between ETFs and mutual funds, which boils down to an extremely clever setup whereby ETF shares, which represent stock holdings, can be traded without any actual trading of stocks. In a way it's like fat-free potato chips (remember Olestra?), which have no fat calories because the fat just passes through your body.

Market makers and croupiers

In the world of ETFs, we don't have croupiers, but we have market makers. *Market makers* are people who work at the stock exchanges and create (like magic!) ETF shares. Each ETF share represents a portion of a portfolio of stocks, sort of like poker chips represent a pile of cash. As an ETF grows, so does the number of shares. Concurrently (once a day), new stocks are added to a portfolio that mirrors the ETF.

When an ETF investor sells shares, those shares are bought by a market maker who turns around and sells them to another ETF investor. By contrast, with mutual funds, if one person sells, the mutual fund must sell off shares of the underlying stock to pay off the shareholder. If stocks sold in the mutual fund are being sold for more than the original purchase price, the shareholders left behind are stuck paying a capital gains tax. In some years, that amount can be substantial.

In the world of ETFs, no such thing has happened or is likely to happen, at least not with the vast majority of ETFs, which are index funds. Because index funds trade infrequently, and because of ETFs' poker-chip structure, ETF investors rarely see a bill from Uncle Sam for any capital gains tax. That's not a guarantee that there will never be capital gains on any index ETF, but if there ever are, they are sure to be minor.

The actively managed ETFs — currently a very small fraction of the ETF market, but almost certain to grow — may present a somewhat different story. They are going to be, no doubt, less tax friendly than index ETFs but more tax friendly than actively managed mutual funds. Exactly where will they fall on the spectrum? It may take another year or two (or three) before we really know.

Tax efficient does not mean tax-free. Although you won't pay capital gains taxes, you will pay taxes on any dividends issued by your stock ETFs, and stock ETFs are just as likely to issue dividends as are mutual funds. In addition, if you sell your ETFs and they are in a taxable account, you have to pay capital gains tax (15 to 20 percent) if the ETFs have appreciated in value since the time you bought them. But hey — at least you get to decide when to take a gain, and when you do, it's an actual gain.

ETFs that invest in taxable bonds and throw off taxable bond interest are not likely to be very much more tax friendly than taxable-bond mutual funds.

ETFs that invest in actual commodities, holding real silver or gold, tax you at the "collectible" rate of 28 percent. And ETFs that tap into derivatives (such as commodity futures) and currencies sometimes bring with them very complex (and costly) tax issues.

Taxes on earnings — be they dividends or interest or money made on currency swaps — aren't an issue if your money is held in a tax-advantaged account, such as a Roth IRA.

What you see is what you get

A key to building a successful portfolio, right up there with low costs and tax efficiency, is diversification. You cannot diversify optimally unless you know exactly what's in your portfolio. In a rather infamous example, when tech stocks (some more than others) started to go belly up in 2000, holders of Janus mutual funds got clobbered. That's because they learned after the fact that their three or four Janus mutual funds, which gave the illusion of diversification, were actually holding many of the same stocks.

Style drift: An epidemic

With a mutual fund, you often have little idea of what stocks the fund manager is holding. In fact, you may not even know what *kinds* of stocks he is holding. Or even if he is holding stocks! I'm talking here about *style drift*, which occurs when a mutual fund manager advertises his fund as aggressive, but over time it becomes conservative, and vice versa. I'm talking about the mutual fund manager who says he loves large value but invests in large growth or small value.

One classic case of style drift cost investors in the all-popular Fidelity Magellan Fund bundle. The year was 1996, and then fund manager Jeffrey Vinik reduced the stock holdings in his "stock" mutual fund to 70 percent. He had 30 percent of the fund's assets in bonds or short-term securities. He was betting that the market was going to sour, and he was planning to fully invest in stocks after it did. He was dead wrong. Instead, the market continued to soar, bonds took a dive, Fidelity Magellan seriously underperformed, and Vinik was out.

One study by the Association of Investment Management concluded that a full 40 percent of actively managed mutual funds are not what they say they are. Some funds bounce around in style so much that an investor would have almost no idea where her money was.

ETFs are the cure

When you buy an indexed ETF, you get complete transparency. You know exactly what you are buying. No matter what the ETF, you can see in the prospectus or on the ETF provider's website (or on any number of independent financial websites) a complete picture of the ETF's holdings. See, for example, http://finance.yahoo.com. If I go and type the letters *IYE* (the ticker symbol for the iShares Dow Jones U.S Energy Sector ETF) in the box on the top of the page, and then click the *Holdings* link on the left, I can see in an instant what my holdings are.

You simply can't get that information on most actively managed mutual funds. Or if you can, the information is both stale and subject to change without notice.

Transparency also discourages dishonesty

The scandals that have rocked the mutual fund world over the years have left the world of ETFs untouched. There's not a whole lot of manipulation that a fund manager can do when his picks are tied to an index. And because ETFs trade throughout the day, with the price flashing across thousands of computer screens worldwide, there is no room to take advantage of the "stale" pricing that occurs after the markets close and mutual fund orders are settled. All in all, ETF investors are much less likely ever to get bamboozled than are investors in active mutual funds.

Getting the Professional Edge

I don't know about you, but when I take the kids bowling and — as happens on very rare occasion — I bowl a strike, I feel as if a miracle of biblical proportions has occurred. And then I turn on the television, stumble upon a professional bowling tournament, and see guys for whom *not* bowling a strike is a rare occurrence. The difference between amateur and professional bowlers is huge. The difference between investment amateurs and investment professionals can be just as huge. But you can close much of that gap with ETFs.

Consider a few impressive numbers

By investment professionals, rest assured I'm not talking about stockbrokers or variable-annuity salesmen, or my barber, who always has a stock recommendation for me. I'm talking about the managers of foundations, endowments, and pension funds with $1 billion or more in invested assets. By amateurs, I'm talking about the average U.S. investor with a few assorted and sundry mutual funds in his 401(k).

Let's compare the two: During the 20-year period 1990 through 2009, the U.S. stock market, as measured by the S&P 500 Index, provided an annual rate of return of 8.2 percent. Yet the average stock mutual fund investor, according to a study by Dalbar, earned an annual rate of 3.2 percent over that same period, just barely keeping up with the inflation rate of 2.8 percent a year. Bond-fund investors did much worse. Why the pitiful returns? There are several reasons, but two main ones:

- ✔ Mutual fund investors pay too much for their investments.

- ✔ They jump into hot funds in hot sectors when they're hot and jump out when those funds or sectors turn cold. (In other words, they are constantly buying high and selling low.)

Professionals tend not to do either of those things. To give you an idea of the difference between amateurs and professionals, consider this: For that very same 20-year period in which the average stock mutual fund investor earned 3.2 percent, and the average bond mutual fund investor earned 1 percent, the multibillion-dollar stock-and-bond-and-real-estate California Public Employees' Retirement System (CALPERS) pension fund, the largest in the nation, earned nearly 8 percent a year.

You can do what they do!

Professional managers, you see, don't pay high expenses. They don't jump in and out of funds. They know that they need to diversify. They tend to buy indexes. They know exactly what they own. And they know that asset allocation, not stock picking, is what drives long-term investment results. In short, they do all the things that an ETF portfolio can do for you. So do it. Well, maybe . . . but first read the rest of this chapter!

Passive versus Active Investing: Your Choice

Surely, you've sensed by now my preference for index funds over actively managed funds. Until recently, all ETFs were index funds. And in the past few years, most index funds have been ETFs.

On March 25, 2008, Bear Stearns introduced an actively managed ETF: the Current Yield ETF (YYY). As fate would have it, Bear Stearns was just about to go under, and when it did, the first actively managed ETF went with it. Prophetic? Perhaps. In the years since, about 130 actively managed ETFs, from 29 providers, have hit the street, with quite modest commercial success. But time will tell. . . .

I don't think this development is necessarily a bad thing, but I'm not frothing at the mouth to invest in actively managed ETFs, either.

In the next few sections, I look at a few of the pros and cons.

The index advantage

The superior returns of indexed mutual funds and ETFs over actively managed funds have had much to do with the popularity of ETFs to date. Index funds (which buy and hold a fixed collection of stocks or bonds) consistently outperform actively managed funds. One study done by Fulcrum Financial tracked mutual fund performance over ten years and found that 81 percent of value funds underperformed the indexes, as did 63 percent of growth funds. And that is just one of many, many studies that present similar results.

Here are some reasons that index funds (both mutual funds and ETFs) are hard to beat:

- ✔ They typically carry much lower management fees, sales loads, or redemption charges.

- ✔ Hidden costs — trading costs and spread costs — are much lower when turnover is low.

- ✔ They don't have cash sitting around idle (as the manager waits for what he thinks is the right time to enter the market).

- ✔ They are more — sometimes much more — tax efficient.

- ✔ They are more "transparent" — you know exactly what securities you are investing in.

Perhaps the greatest testament to the success of index funds is how many allegedly actively managed funds are actually index funds in (a very expensive) disguise. I'm talking about closet index funds. According to a report in *Investment News*, a newspaper for financial advisers, the number of actively managed stock funds that are closet index funds has tripled over the past several years. As a result, many investors are paying high (active) management fees for investment results that could be achieved with low-cost ETFs.

R squared is a measurement of how much of a fund's performance can be attributed to the performance of an index. It can range from 0.00 to 1.00. An R squared of 1.00 indicates *perfect correlation:* When a fund goes up, it's because the index was up — every time; when the fund falls, it's because the index fell — every time. An R squared of 0.00 indicates no such correlation. This measurement is used to assess tracking errors and to identify closet index funds.

According to Morningstar data as interpreted by *Investment News,* nearly 28 percent of all large cap funds carry a three-year R squared of 0.95 or higher relative to the S&P 500 stock index. That kind of number makes them closet index funds. And if you look at the entire mutual fund industry, it is apparent that the triumph of indexing is becoming well known.

Recently, the average large cap fund had an R squared of almost 0.90. That number is up from 0.74 only a decade or so ago.

The allure of active management

Speaking in broad generalities, actively managed mutual funds have been no friend to the small investor. Their dominance remains a testament to people's ignorance of the facts and the enormous amount of money spent on (often deceptive) advertising and PR that give investors the false impression that buying this fund or that fund will lead to instant wealth. The media often plays into this nonsense with splashy headlines, designed to sell magazine copies or attract viewers, that promise to reveal which funds or managers are currently the best.

Still, active management can make sense — and that may be especially true when some of the best aspects of active management are brought to the ETF market. Some managers actually do have the ability to "beat the markets" — they are just few and far between, and the increased costs of active management often nullify any and all advantages these market-beaters have. If those costs can be minimized, and if you can find such a manager, you may wind up ahead of the game. Active management in ETF form may also be both more efficient and more transparent than it is in mutual fund form.

And finally, with some kinds of investments, such as commodities and possibly bonds, active management may simply make better sense in certain cases. I talk about these scenarios in Part III.

Measuring keeps getting tougher

Unfortunately, the old-style "active versus passive" studies that consistently gave passive (index) investing two thumbs up are getting harder and harder to do. What exactly qualifies as an "index" fund anymore, now that many ETFs are set up to track indexes that, in and of themselves, were created to outperform "the market" (traditional indexes)? And whereas index investing once promised a very solid cost savings, some of the newer ETFs, with their newfangled indexes, are charging more than some actively managed funds. Future studies are likely to become muddier and muddier.

 Here's my advice: Give a big benefit of the doubt to index funds as the ones that will serve you the best in the long run. If you want to go with an actively managed fund, follow these guidelines:

- ✔ Keep your costs low.

- ✔ Don't believe that a manager can beat the market unless that manager has done so consistently for years, and for reasons that you can understand. (That is, avoid "Madoff" risk!)

- ✔ Pick a fund company that you trust.

- ✔ Don't go overboard! Mix an index fund or two in with your active fund(s).

- ✔ All things being equal, you may want to choose an ETF over a mutual fund. But the last section of this chapter can help you to determine that. Ready?

Do ETFs Belong in Your Life?

Okay, so on the plus side of ETFs we have ultra-low management expenses, super tax efficiency, transparency, and a lot of fancy trading opportunities, such as shorting, if you are so inclined. What about the negatives? In the sections that follow, I walk you through some other facts about ETFs that you should consider before parting with your precious dollars.

Calculating commissions

I talk a lot more about commissions when I compare and contrast various brokerage houses in Chapter 2, but I want to give you a heads-up here: You may have to pay a commission every time you buy and sell an ETF.

Here's the good news: Trading commissions for stocks and ETFs (it's the same commission for either) have been dropping faster than the price of desktop computers. What once would have cost you a bundle, now — if you trade online, which you definitely should — is really pin money, perhaps as low as $4 a trade, and sometimes nothing at all. However, you can't simply ignore trading commissions. They aren't always that low, and even $4 a pop can add up. In most cases, you shouldn't agonize over the cost of trading ETFs; merely keep an eye on them.

Moving money in a flash

The fact that ETFs can be traded throughout the day like stocks makes them, unlike mutual funds, fair game for day-traders and institutional wheeler-dealers. For the rest of us common folk, there isn't much about the way that ETFs are bought and sold that makes them especially valuable. Indeed, the ability to trade throughout the day may make you more apt to do so, perhaps selling or buying on impulse. As I discuss in detail in Chapter 11, impulsive investing, although it can get your endorphins pumping, is generally not a profitable way to proceed.

Understanding tracking error

At times, the value of the securities held by the ETF may trade above or below the index it follows. This situation is called *tracking error*. At times, an ETF may also sell at a price that is a tad higher or lower than what that price should be, given the prices of all the securities held by the ETF. This situation is called selling at a *premium* (when the price of the ETF rides above the value of the securities) or selling at a *discount* (when the price of the ETF drops below the value of the securities). Both foreign-stock funds and bond funds are more likely to run off track, either experiencing tracking error or selling at a premium or discount. But the better funds do not run off track to any alarming degree.

In Chapter 2, I offer a few trading tricks for minimizing "off track" ETF investing, but for now, let me say that it is not something to worry about if you are a buy-and-hold ETF investor — the kind of investor I want you to become.

Making a sometimes tricky choice

In Parts II and III of this book, I give you lots of detailed information about how to construct a portfolio that meets your

needs. Here, I just want to whet your appetite with
very basic examples of decisions you may be facin

Say you have a choice between investing in an index mutual
fund that charges 0.15 percent a year and an ETF that tracks
the same index and charges the same amount. Or say you are
trying to choose between an actively managed mutual fund
and an ETF with the very same manager managing the very
same kind of investment, with the same costs. What should
you invest in?

If your money is in a taxable account, go with the ETF, provided you are investing at least a few thousand dollars and
you plan to keep your money invested for at least several
years. If you're investing less, and/or if you think you may
need to tap the money anytime soon, you may be better off
with the index mutual fund that won't charge you commissions to buy and sell shares.

But say you have, oh, $5,000 to invest in your IRA. (All IRA
money is taxed as income when you withdraw it in retirement,
and therefore the tax efficiency of securities held within an
IRA isn't an issue.) An ETF charges you a management fee
of 0.15 percent a year, and a comparable index mutual fund
charges 0.35, but buying and selling the ETF will cost you
$7.95 at either end. Now what should you do?

The math isn't difficult. The difference between 0.15 and
0.35 (0.20 percent) of $5,000 is $10. It will take you less than
one year to recoup your trading fee of $7.95. If you factor in
the cost of selling (another $7.95), it will take you 1.6 years
to recoup your trading costs. At that point, the ETF will be
your lower-cost tortoise, and the mutual fund your higher-
cost hare.

In general, building an entire portfolio out of ETFs usually
makes sense starting in the ballpark of $50,000. Anything less
than that, and you are most likely better off with mutual funds
or a mix of mutual funds and ETFs. The exception would be,
say, a portfolio of all Vanguard ETFs held at Vanguard, where
there would be no trading fees. Or a portfolio of all Schwab
ETFs held at Schwab, with the same deal. In these cases,
the ETF portfolio may make sense for even the smallest of
accounts.

If you have a trigger finger, and you are the kind of person who is likely to jump to trade every time there's a blip in the market, you would be well advised to go with mutual funds (that don't impose short-term redemption fees). You're less likely to shoot yourself in the foot!

The index mutual fund trap

Some brokerage houses, such as Vanguard and Fidelity, offer wonderful low-cost index mutual funds. But a problem with them is that you either can't buy them at other financial "supermarkets" (such as Charles Schwab or T. Rowe Price), or you have to pay a substantial fee to get into them. So building an entire portfolio of index mutual funds can be tough. If you want both Fidelity and Vanguard funds, you may be forced to pay high fees or to open up separate accounts at different supermarkets, which means extra paperwork and hassle. With ETFs, you can buy them anywhere, sell them anywhere, and keep them — even if they are ETFs from several different providers — all parked in the same brokerage house. I know of no major discount brokerage house that now charges more than $10 to make an online ETF trade.

Chapter 2

Getting to Know the Players

● ●

In This Chapter

▶ Setting up an account for your ETFs

▶ Meeting the brokerage houses

▶ Finding out who supplies ETFs to the brokers

▶ Introducing the indexers

▶ Distinguishing between the exchanges

● ●

I love to shop on Christmas Eve. It's the only time the entire year when men — husbands and boyfriends who finally realize that they need to buy a gift, quickly — outnumber women at the mall. I see these hulking figures, some in bright orange hunting jackets, walking the halls of the Lehigh Valley Mall, looking themselves like scared prey. "Where's the lingerie?" they ask, eyes to the ground.

Sometimes, when I suggest to a client that he buy a few ETFs for his portfolio, I see the same look of dire trepidation. I need to reassure him that buying ETFs isn't that difficult. In this chapter, I want to do the same for you.

This chapter is something of a shopper's guide to ETFs — a mall directory, if you will. I don't suggest which specific ETFs to buy (I will, I will — but that's for later chapters). Instead, I show you where to find the brokerage houses that allow you to buy and sell ETFs; the financial institutions that create ETFs; the indexes on which the financial institutions base their ETFs; and the exchanges where millions of ETF shares are bought, sold, and borrowed each day.

Creating an Account for Your ETFs

You — you personally — can't just buy a share of an ETF as you would buy, say, a negligee. You need someone to actually buy it for you and hold it for you. That someone is a broker, sometimes referred to as a *brokerage house* or a *broker-dealer*. Some broker-dealers, the really big ones, are sort of like financial department stores or supermarkets where you can buy ETFs, mutual funds, individual stocks and bonds, or fancier investment products like puts and calls. You'll recognize, I'm sure, the names of such financial department stores: Fidelity, Vanguard, Schwab, TD Ameritrade, and T. Rowe Price.

ETFs are usually traded just as stocks are traded. Same commissions. Mostly the same rules. Same hours (generally 9:30 a.m. to 4:00 p.m., Manhattan Island time). Through your brokerage house, you can buy 1 share, 2 shares, or 10,000 shares. Here's one difference between ETFs and stocks: Although people today rarely do it, you can sometimes purchase stocks directly from a company, and you may even get a pretty certificate saying you own the stock. (I *think* some companies still do that!) Not so with ETFs. Call BlackRock or State Street and ask to buy a share of an ETF, and they will tell you to go find yourself a broker. Ask for a certificate, and . . . well, don't even bother.

The first step, then, prior to beginning your ETF shopping expedition, is to find a brokerage house, preferably a financial department store where you can keep all your various investments. It makes life a lot easier to have everything in one place, to get one statement every month, and to see all your investments on one computer screen.

Answering a zillion questions

The first question you have to answer when opening an account is whether it will be a retirement account or a non-retirement account. If you want a retirement account, you need to specify what kind (IRA? Roth IRA? SEP?). A non-retirement account is a simpler animal. You don't need to know any special tax rules, and your money isn't committed for any time period unless you happen to stick something like a CD into the account.

The next question you have to answer is whether you want to open a *margin* account or a *cash* account. A margin account is somewhat similar to a checking account with overdraft protection. It means that you can borrow from the account or make purchases of securities (such as ETFs, but generally not mutual funds) without actually having any cash to pay for them on the spot. Cool, huh?

Unless you have a gambling addiction, go with margin. You never know when you may need a quick (and, compared to credit cards, inexpensive) and potentially tax-deductible loan. If you think you may have a gambling addiction, however, read the sidebar "Don't margin your house away!"

You're also asked questions about beneficiaries and titling (or registration), such as whether you want your joint account set up with rights of survivorship. I'll just say one quick word about naming your beneficiaries: Be certain that who you name is who you want to receive your money if you die.

Beneficiary designations supersede your will. In other words, if your will says that all your ETFs go to your brother, and your beneficiary designation on your account names someone else, your brother loses; all the ETFs in your account will go to someone else.

Finally, you're asked all kinds of personal questions about your employment, your wealth, and your risk tolerance. Don't sweat them! Federal securities regulations require brokerage houses to know something about their clients. Honestly, I don't think anyone ever looks at the personal section of the forms. I've never heard any representative of any brokerage house so much as whisper any of the information included in those personal questions.

Placing an order to buy

After your account is in place, which should take only a few days, you're ready to buy your first ETF. Most brokerage houses give you a choice: Call in your order, or do it yourself online. Calling is typically much more expensive, as it requires the direct assistance of an actual person. Being the savvy investor that you are, you're not going to throw money away, so place all your orders online! If you need help, a representative of the brokerage house will walk you through the process step-by-step — for free!

Keep in mind when trading ETFs that the trading fees charged by the brokerage, although usually not all that much, can nibble seriously into your holdings. Even if you work with a brokerage house that waives charges for trading particular ETFs, there will still be a small cost called the *spread* that you don't readily see. The spread is where you may lose a penny or two or three to middlemen working behind the scenes of each trade. Spreads can nibble at your portfolio just as the more visible fees do. Here's how to avoid getting nibbled:

✔ **Don't trade often.** Buy and hold, more or less (see Chapter 11). Yes, I know that a number of headlines since 2008 have declared that "buy and hold is dead." That's nonsense. Don't believe it. "Buy and hold," by the way, doesn't mean you *never* trade. But if you're making more than a few trades every few months, that's too much.

✔ **Know your percentages.** In general, don't bother with ETFs if the trade is going to cost you anything more than one-half of one percent. In other words, if making the trade is going to cost you $8 (a typical amount for an online trade), you want to invest at least $1,600 at a pop. If you have only $1,000 to invest, or less, you are often better off purchasing a no-load mutual fund, preferably an index fund, or waiting until you've accumulated enough cash to make a larger investment. Alternatively, you might choose a no-commission ETF, even if it's slightly less attractive than the ETF you'd have to pay a commission for. You may swap for the better alternative down the road, especially if you are funding a retirement account where swapping will have no tax consequences.

✔ **Be a savvy shopper.** Keep the cost of your individual trades to a minimum by shopping brokerage houses for the lowest fees, placing all your orders online, and arguing for the best deals. Yes, you can often negotiate with these people for better deals, especially if you have substantial bucks. Also know that many brokerage houses offer special incentives for new clients: Move more than $100,000 in assets and get your first 50 trades for free, or that sort of thing. Always ask.

But wait just a moment!

 Please don't be so enthralled by anything you read in this book that you rush out, open a brokerage account, and sell your existing mutual funds or stocks and bonds to buy ETFs. Rash investment decisions almost always wind up being mistakes. Remember that whenever you sell a security, you may face serious tax consequences. If you decide to sell certain mutual funds, annuities, or life insurance policies, there may also be nasty surrender charges. If you're unsure whether selling your present holdings would make for a financial hit on the chin, talk to your accountant or financial planner.

Trading ETFs like a pro

If you're familiar with trading stocks, you already know how to trade ETFs. If you aren't, don't sweat it. Although there are all kinds of fancy trades you could make, and we'll touch on a few later, I'm going to ask you now to familiarize yourself with only the two most basic kinds of trades: *market orders* and *limit orders.*

- ✔ **A market order** to buy tells the broker that you want to buy. Period. After the order is placed, you will have bought your ETF shares . . . at whatever price someone out there was willing to sell you those shares.

- ✔ **A limit order** to buy asks you to name a price above which you walk away and go home. No purchase will be made. (A limit order to sell asks you to name a price below which you will not sell. No sale will be made.)

Market orders are fairly easy. As long as you are buying a domestic ETF that isn't too exotic (the kind of ETFs I'll be recommending throughout this book); as long as you aren't trading when the market is going crazy; as long as you aren't trading right when the market opens or closes (9:30 a.m. and 4:00 p.m., Manhattan time weekdays), you should be just fine.

A limit order may be a better option if you are placing a purchase for an ETF where the "bid" and the "ask" price may differ by more than a few pennies (indicating the middlemen are out to get you), or where there may be more than a negligible difference between the market price of the ETF and the net asset value of the securities it is holding. This would include foreign-stock ETFs, junk-bond ETFs, and any other ETFs that trade not that many shares — especially on a day when the market seems jumpy. The risk with limit orders is that you may not get your price, and so the order may not go through.

To execute a limit order without risk that you'll miss out on your purchase, place the order slightly above the last sale. If your ETF's last sale was for $10 a share, you may offer $10.01. If you're buying 100 shares, you may have just blown a whole dollar, but you'll have your purchase in hand.

Introducing the Shops

I've read that the motorcycle industry boasts one of the highest levels of consumer loyalty in the United States. A Harley man would *never* be caught dead on a Yamaha. Not being a motorcyclist, I have no idea why that is. In the world of brokerage houses, after someone has a portfolio in place at a house such as Fidelity, Vanguard, or Schwab, that client is often very hesitant to switch. I know *exactly* why that is: Moving your account can sometimes be a big, costly, and time-consuming hassle. So, whether you're a Harley man or a Yamaha mama, if you have money to invest, it behooves you to spend some serious time researching brokerage houses and to choose the one that will work best for you. Perhaps I can help.

What to look for

Here's what you want from any broker who is going to be holding your ETFs:

- ✔ Reasonable prices
- ✔ Freebies, including free trades on certain ETFs
- ✔ Good service, meaning they answer the phone without putting you through answering-system hell, and they have evening and weekend hours
- ✔ A user-friendly website
- ✔ Good advice, if you think you're going to need advice

Can you lose your ETFs if your brokerage house collapses?

Brokerage houses, as part of their registration process with the federal government, are automatically insured through the Securities Investor Protection Corporation (SIPC). Each individual investor's securities are protected up to $500,000 should the brokerage house go belly up. Almost all larger brokerage houses carry supplemental insurance that protects customers' account balances beyond the half-million that SIPC covers.

TD Ameritrade, for example, has insurance through Lloyd's of London that protects each customer's account up to $150 million.

Note: Neither SIPC coverage nor any kind of supplemental insurance will protect the value of your account from a market downfall! For additional information on SIPC, you can order a free brochure by calling 1-800-934-4448, or check out its website at www.sipc.org.

✔ A service center near you, if you like doing business with real people

✔ Incentives for opening an account, usually a certain number of fee-free trades

✔ Financial strength

Financial strength really isn't as important as it may sound because all brokerage houses carry insurance. Still, a brokerage house that collapses under you can be a problem, and it may take time to recoup your money. See the sidebar "Can you lose your ETFs if your brokerage house collapses?"

I give you my take on some of the major brokerage houses in just a moment, but I first want to talk a bit about prices, which can be downright devilish to compare and contrast.

A price structure like no other

Comparing the prices at brokerage houses is anything but easy. At Vanguard, for example, you'll pay from $2 to $7 per ETF trade, depending on how much money you have with Vanguard. But if you are trading a Vanguard ETF at Vanguard, you'll pay nothing for the trade. At TD Ameritrade, there are

100 ETFs that you can buy and pay nothing for the trade. But beware! If you don't hold on to them for a full 30 days, you'll be assessed a $20 charge. At ShareBuilder, you can pay only $4 a trade, but you need to commit to a schedule of regular trades that occur only on Tuesdays. (That's right, only on Tuesdays.) This is *not* easy business.

It would take me many pages to relay to you the complicated price structures of the various brokerage houses. I'll pass. Instead, in the following sections, I give you a short summary of the pricing and then leave you to do some legwork. Always look at the entire brokerage package. That includes not only the price of trades but total account fees. You need to do some comparing and contrasting on your own, but with the tools I give you in the following sections, it shouldn't take an eternity.

The Vanguard Group

I mention Vanguard frequently in this book for a number of reasons. For one, I like Vanguard because of its leadership role in the world of index investing. Vanguard is also both an investment house that serves as a custodian of ETFs and is itself a provider of ETFs. (That's also true of Schwab and soon will be true of T. Rowe Price, too.) And — perhaps most important to the theme of this book — Vanguard's ETFs are top-notch products. But more on that in a few pages. Right now, I'm here to discuss Vanguard as a shop where you can buy and hold your ETFs.

Incidentally, buying and holding Vanguard ETFs at Vanguard offers an advantage over buying and holding those ETFs elsewhere, in that you won't pay any fees to trade. But Vanguard ETFs can be held at any brokerage, and typically the trading charges will be minimal, so Vanguard the shop and Vanguard the ETF supplier should be assessed separately.

As for Vanguard the shop, the trading commissions (that apply to ETFs other than Vanguard's own) are reasonable— $2 to $7 a trade, depending on the size of your Vanguard account — and the service is middle of the road (and better than that if you have big bucks with the company). What really shines about Vanguard is, well, two things . . . first, its broad array of top-rated index mutual funds. I know, I know, this is a book about ETFs. But index mutual funds and ETFs are close cousins, and sometimes it makes sense to have both in a portfolio. (More on that subject in Chapter 9.)

 If you do wish to hold Vanguard index mutual funds alongside your ETFs, Vanguard is an awfully logical place to hold them because you can buy and sell Vanguard funds, provided you don't do it often, at no charge. At Fidelity, in contrast, buying any Vanguard mutual fund will typically cost you $75.

Fidelity Investments

I like this brokerage house a lot. In fact, I house my own ETFs at Fidelity. The service, at least for me, is fabulous. (Okay, I admit it, my clients and I have a fair amount of money there.) Unlike most other brokerage houses, the phone reps at Fidelity are available 24/7.

The cost of trading at Fidelity is very competitive. Like Vanguard, Fidelity also has some excellent low-cost index funds of its own, which you may wish to keep alongside your ETF portfolio. And the Fidelity website has some really good tools — some of the best available — for analyzing your portfolio and researching new investments.

At present, 70 of BlackRock's iShares ETFs can be traded at Fidelity with no fees. Ditto for Fidelity's own 14 ETFs. All other ETFs will cost you $7.95 to trade. Fidelity, however, is quite liberal in granting free trades to new customers. Although the policy changes from time to time, recent clients of mine who have opened up fresh accounts at Fidelity were given 100 free trades . . . enough to last a very good while.

Charles Schwab

"Invest with Chuck" Schwab offers a lineup of 13 low-cost, sensible ETFs of its own creation, and they trade free if you open an account with this brokerage. All other ETFs cost $8.95 per online trade.

Whenever I've had occasion to do business with "Chuck's" staff, I find them friendly and knowledgeable. I just wish I could forgive Chuck for investing — and losing — so much of its clients' money in the mortgage crisis of 2008, and then admitting no wrong and making no restitution until being strong-armed by the court. (For those familiar with the case, I'm referring to Schwab's YieldPlus Fund debacle.)

T. Rowe Price

This Baltimore-based shop has several claims to fame, including its bend-over-backwards friendliness to small investors and its plethora of really fine financial tools, especially for retirement planning, available to all customers at no cost. The price of trading is a wee bit higher than average for a discount broker. ETFs cost $9.95 to $19.95 per online trade, depending on how much money you have invested and how often you trade.

The service at this firm is excellent (reps tend to be very chummy). If you decide that part of your portfolio should be in mutual funds, you can do a lot worse than going with T. Rowe Price's lineup of entirely load-free funds.

TD Ameritrade

For a number of years, TD Waterhouse and Ameritrade were known as the discount kings of the brokerage biz. They merged several years ago to form TD Ameritrade. The trading prices at TD are just about middle of the pack. Although I've never had occasion to work with TD, the service is reputedly quite high. The website has a very clean and crisp feel to it. On the down side (in my opinion, of course), the TD culture and many of the articles on the website promote frequent trading, as opposed to, say, Vanguard, where the culture is decidedly more buy-and-hold. (The same two philosophies exist among different providers of ETFs, as I discuss shortly.)

At the moment, this firm is offering commission-free online trades on 100 ETFs (certain iShares, Vanguard products, SPDRs, and PowerShares funds), BUT you must hold them for at least 30 days or you'll need to cough up $20 per trade. All other ETFs cost $10 per online trade. In 2010, the firm acquired online futures brokerage *thinkorswim,* where ETFs trade for $5 and no-load mutual funds trade fee-free.

Other brokerage houses

The houses I discuss in the previous sections aren't the only players in town. Here are a few more to consider:

- ✔ **Scottrade:** 800-619-7283; www.scottrade.com. Like TD Ameritrade (I suppose the "trade" in both names is something of a giveaway), the culture at Scottrade doesn't seem to promote wise investor behavior. The home page of the website, for example, is filled with offers for the latest apps to allow you to make trades from your cell phone.

- ✔ **eTrade:** 800-387-2331; www.etrade.com. Not only can you house your ETFs here, but you can refinance the mortgage on your house, as well.

- ✔ **TIAA-CREF:** 800-927-3059; www.tiaa-cref.org. A good company, but I can't work with them directly because I'm not a teacher. This brokerage house works only with people who have chalk under their fingernails. (If you're married to such a person, you qualify too.)

- ✔ **Folio Investing:** 888-973-7890; www.folioinvesting. com. This is a very different kind of brokerage house, where you pay a flat rate ($29 a month) and then perhaps a nominal trading charge. It also offers prefab, ready-to-go ETF portfolios for the laziest investors. (I comment on these portfolio options in Chapter 9.)

- ✔ **TradeKing:** 877-495-5464; www.tradeking.com. Despite the somewhat hokey name, this newcomer to the industry is offering the lowest trading prices — $5 per ETF trade, regardless of whether that's online or by phone — and customer service is reportedly excellent.

- ✔ **Capital One Investing/ShareBuilder:** 800-747-2537; www. capitaloneinvesting.com. At $6.95 a trade, or even less if you're willing to pay a monthly fee and commit to regular trades, it's hard to beat ShareBuilder on price. At present, they'll also throw in a $600 bonus for opening an account with at least $125,000.

Presenting the Suppliers

There are dozens and dozens of mutual fund providers. Some of the firms may offer just one fund, and they sometimes give the impression that the entire business is run out of someone's garage. Not so with ETFs. Fewer providers exist (currently 79), they tend to be larger companies, and the top four providers (BlackRock, Vanguard, State Street, and Invesco PowerShares) control 85 percent of the market. Why is that? In large measure it's because ETFs' management fees are so low that a company can't profit unless it enjoys the economies of scale and multiple income streams that come from offering a bevy of ETFs.

It's okay to mix and match — with caution

I want to emphasize that while picking a single brokerage house to manage your accounts makes enormous sense, there is no reason that you can't own ETFs from different sources. Like your favorite sports team or clothing store, each supplier of ETFs has its own personality. A portfolio with a combination of BlackRock, Vanguard, and State Street ETFs can work just fine. In fact, I recommend *not* wedding yourself to a single ETF supplier but being flexible and picking the best ETFs to meet your needs in each area of your portfolio.

(Note that brokerage houses typically don't sell every available mutual fund. But I've never heard of a brokerage house limiting which ETFs it will sell. The reason is simple: When you buy or sell an ETF, you pay a trading fee directly to the brokerage house. The more ETFs it can offer, the merrier.)

 When mixing and matching ETFs, I would just caution that you don't want holes in your portfolio, and you don't want overlap. Mixing and matching, say, a total U.S. stock fund from one ETF provider with a European stock fund of another provider would be just fine because there's virtually no chance for either overlap or gaps. However, I would recommend that in putting together, say, a U.S. value and a U.S. growth fund, or a U.S. large cap and a U.S. small cap fund, in the hopes of building a well-rounded portfolio, you may want to choose ETFs from the same ETF provider, using the same index providers

(Russell, Morningstar, S&P, and so on). That's because each indexer uses slightly (and sometimes not so slightly) different definitions of "value," "growth, "large," and "small." So mixing and matching funds from different providers may be less than ideal. More on this topic in Chapter 9.

All ETFs (and mutual funds) sold in the United States must be approved by the U.S. Securities and Exchange Commission. Other countries have their equivalent governmental regulatory authorities. None of the ETFs listed in this section or in Part II of this book are sold beyond the borders of the United States. Some of the ETF providers mentioned — particularly BlackRock — do sell ETFs in other countries, but they go by different names (*iShares* in Canada are known as *iUnits*), and they likely have different structures.

BlackRock iShares

With 316 ETFs for sale and $8,225 billion in ETF assets (about 38 percent of the U.S. ETF market), iShares is the undisputed market leader. The firm behind iShares, BlackRock, Inc., merged in 2009 with Barclays Global Investors, the mega-corporation that is now one of the largest investment banks in the world. Through its iShares, BlackRock offers by far the broadest selection of any ETF provider. You can buy iShares that track the major S&P indexes for growth and value, large cap and small cap stocks. Other iShares equity ETFs track the major Russell and Morningstar indexes. You can also find industry-sector iShares ETFs from technology and healthcare to financial services and software.

In the international arena, you can buy an iShares ETF to track either an intercontinental index, such as the MSCI EAFE (Europe, Australia, and the Far East), or much narrower markets, such as the Malaysian or Brazilian stock markets. iShares also offer a broad array of fixed-income (bond) ETFs, with six offerings ranging from long-term conventional Treasury bonds and inflation-protected securities (TIPS) to corporate bonds and foreign bonds.

Management fees vary from a low of 0.07 percent for the plain-vanilla large cap U.S. stock funds, such as the iShares S&P 500 (IVV), to a high of 0.94 percent for the much more exotically flavored iShares S&P India Nifty 50 Index (INDY).

Russell's review: You can't go too wrong with iShares. My only beef is with the price of some of the international funds where BlackRock has enjoyed a monopoly thus far. On the other hand, the firm has done an outstanding job of tracking indexes and offering variety. It also has done a good job of maintaining tax efficiency. I caution you, however, not to get sucked into the iShares candy store. Some of the ETFs track very small markets and market segments and clearly don't belong in most people's portfolios. I suggest that you think twice, for example, before making the iShares MSCI All Peru Capped Index Fund (EPU) a major part of your portfolio.

For more information, call 800-474-2737 or visit www.ishares.com.

Vanguard ETFs

It goes without saying that these people know something about index investing. In 1976, Vanguard launched the first index-based mutual fund for the retail investor, the Vanguard Index Trust 500 Portfolio. (Wells Fargo already had an index fund, but it was available only to endowments and other institutions.) In 2001, Vanguard launched its first ETF. Why Vanguard wasn't exactly in the ETF vanguard is anyone's guess, but by the time Vanguard ETFs were introduced to the market, iShares (then under Barclays) had already taken a solid lead. But Vanguard ETFs, due largely to their incredibly low costs, are quickly moving up. As of this writing, 67 Vanguard ETFs held $470 billion in assets, making Vanguard the second-largest — and fastest growing — ETF provider.

How low is low cost? The lowest-cost Vanguard ETFs — such as the Vanguard S&P 500 ETF (VOO) and the Vanguard Total Stock Market ETF (VTI) — will set you back 0.05 percent in total management expenses per year. (That's a mere 50 cents per $1,000 invested.) The average expense ratio for Vanguard ETFs is 0.16 percent, making them the cheapest to own in the major leagues.

Russell's review: I *love* Vanguard's low costs. Who wouldn't? (Although relative newcomer to the industry Schwab offers ETFs with fees just a bit lower.) Vanguard's lineup of ETFs, in line with Vanguard's corporate personality, is sensible and direct. The company uses reasonable indexes, tracks them well, and takes the utmost care to avoid capital gains taxes and make certain that all dividends paid are "qualified" dividends subject to a lower tax rate.

For more information, call 877-662-7447 or visit www. vanguard.com.

State Street Global Advisers (SSgA) SPDRs

State Street's flagship ETF, the first ETF on the U.S. market, is the SPDR S&P 500 (SPY). It boasts almost $72 billion in net assets. That's as big as an ETF gets. I suspect that status will change over time, but for now, SSgA's pet spider gives it a firm perch as the third-largest provider of ETFs. State Street's ETFs follow traditional indexes, carry reasonable fees, and are varied enough to allow for a very well-diversified port-folio, at least on the domestic equity side. All told, SSgA's 145 U.S.-based ETFs hold about $417 billion in assets.

Russell's review: The management expenses — 0.30 percent on average — are reasonable, and I like the variety of funds, from which, if you were so inclined, you could build an entire portfolio. The Select Sector SPDRs offer a very efficient way of investing in various industry sectors (if that's your thing). The websites are topnotch, and the SPDRs website in particular — www.spdrs.com — offers some fabulous portfolio-construction tools, such as the *Correlation Tracker,* which allows you to find ETFs that best complement your existing portfolio.

One drawback to SSgA's offerings is the legal structure of some of its ETFs. The oldest ETFs, such as SPY, are set up as unit investment trusts rather than open-end funds as most of the newer ETFs are. That means the older funds can't reinvest dividends on a regular basis, creating a cash drag that can bring down long-term total returns by a smidgen and a half. (It's hard to actually measure the impact.)

For more information, call 866-787-2257 or visit www. streettracks.net or www.spdrs.com.

Invesco PowerShares

Invesco PowerShares, number four in size and number three in number of ETF offerings, hesitates to call its 140 ETFs "actively managed" and instead refers to them as "dynamic" or "intelligent" or "smart beta" funds. The ETFs track a custom-made indexes, which, according to Invesco PowerShares, "quantitatively chooses stocks for their capital appreciation potential, evaluating and selecting stocks based on multiple valuation criteria, rather than simply by market cap alone."

"Multiple valuation criteria." Hmmm. That means potential high turnover and some added trading expenses. It also means that if you choose PowerShares ETFs to build your portfolio, you are no longer a true index investor, which (judging by historical data) may put you at something of a disadvantage.

The company has been quite innovative in its offerings of market-sector ETFs. Examples of this innovation include the Water Resources ETF (PHO), which allows you to invest in a "group of companies that focus on the provision of potable water," and the WilderHill Clean Energy Fund (PBW), which allows you to invest in "companies that focus on greener and generally renewable sources of energy." Another example is the KBW Property & Casualty Insurance Portfolio (KBWP). If you want to slice and dice your portfolio a gadzillion different ways, this lineup of ETFs will let you do just that.

Russell's review: I'm hesitant to embrace PowerShares' newish indexes without a longer track record. But nothing about the PowerShares alternative indexes scares me too much, either. Thus far, the firm has been very good at avoiding capital gains taxes, and the funds, while costing more than most ETFs, are still cheap when compared to actively managed mutual funds. Some of the market segments created by PowerShares, such as those mentioned in the previous paragraph, are intriguing, especially if they prove over time to show limited correlation to the rest of the stock market. Still, Water Resources should not make up the whale's share of anyone's portfolio.

For more information, call 800-983-0903 or visit www.powershares.com.

WisdomTree

WisdomTree Investments out of New York, with some fairly big-gun backers, issued 20 ETFs in June 2006. It has since launched 50 more but has closed 10 of the original lot. WisdomTree changed the investment objectives, strategies, and fund names of many of its ETFs.

Like Invesco PowerShares, WisdomTree does not like conventional cap-weighted indexes but prefers to create its own, using weightings based on earnings or dividends. Dividends, in fact, are something of a fetish of WisdomTree's. You can buy the WisdomTree LargeCap Dividend Fund (DLN), the WisdomTree SmallCap Dividend Fund (DES), or the WisdomTree International Dividend Top 100 Fund (DOO).

Russell's review: DOO? WisdomTree? It sounds like a remedial reading course for middle-school students. WisdomTree seems to be still finding itself. I'm seek maturity in my financial associations. And where does this dividend fetish come from? I hope for this company's sake that dividend investing proves profitable moving forward, but I'm far from certain that it will. More on that subject in Chapter 6.

For more information, call 866-909-9473 or visit www. wisdomtree.com.

Guggenheim

With its takeover of Rydex SGI in 2011, Guggenheim became eighth among U.S.-based ETF providers, but has lost some market share since. It is an interesting company with an unusual mix of products. Many of its ETFs are largely designed for people who are unhappy buying the usual indexes and want to take something of a gamble on a particular equity style, such as large growth stocks. For such an investor, Guggenheim offers its customized S&P 500/ Citigroup Pure Growth ETF. Using a proprietary seven factors to determine which stocks among the S&P 500 are the most "growthy," the firm bundles them into a package that promises purity for the gung-ho growth investor. The company does the same for you on the other side if you are a gung-ho value investor.

Perhaps the most intriguing of all of Guggenheim's investment products, the firm offers a lineup of "equal weight" ETFs, which, just like it sounds, offers you an opportunity to invest in various market segments with all company stocks represented in equal allocations (as opposed to the more traditional market capitalization–weighted method of allocation).

Russell's review: With an average annual management fee of about 0.50 percent, Guggenheim funds are pricier than those of the ETF majors. As for the "pure" funds, I find them intriguing, especially given their performance in the past several years. The S&P 500 Pure Value ETF (RPV), for example, has outclocked more traditional value stocks by about one percent a year over the past five years.

For more information, call 800-345-7999 or visit www. guggenheimfunds.com.

ProShares

ProShares offers some interesting investment strategies. The Short QQQ ProShares (PSQ) allows you to *short* the NASDAQ 100: If the NASDAQ goes down 5 percent tomorrow, your ETF will go up (more or less) 5 percent. Of course, the inverse is true, as well. Other ProShares offerings allow you to short the Dow, the S&P 500, or the S&P MidCap 400, among other indexes. The Ultra ProShares lineup of ETFs allow you to move with the market at double the speed. Ultra QQQ ProShares (QLD), for example, is designed to rise 10 percent when the NASDAQ 100 goes up 5 percent (and, of course, to fall 10 percent when the NASDAQ 100 goes down 5 percent). All these percentages are rough approximations. In the real world, you're going to profit less and risk more.

Russell's review: I'm not too hot on shorting and leveraging strategies, especially as these ETFs employ them, which is to say on a daily returns basis. In short, selling short is akin to market timing, and market timing, while loads of fun, isn't often profitable. As for the less-than-double-your-money, more-than-double-your-risk ProShares Ultra ETFs, well . . . excuse me while I take a minute to scratch my head and try to figure out the logic in that. See my discussion of both strategies in Chapter 6.

For more information, call 866-776-5125 or visit www. proshares.com.

Other suppliers

Fidelity Investments is the number one or number two U.S. brokerage house, running neck-and-neck with Vanguard the past couple of years. However, it produces but a modest line-up of 15 (rather plain-vanilla sector) ETFs. For more information, visit www.fidelity.com.

Similar discount-brokerage giant Charles Schwab (www. schwab.com) introduced its own ETFs in recent years; Schwab, evidently going after the iShares/SPDRs/Vanguard market, now has 71 very low-cost ETFs. Also, PIMCO (www. pimcoetfs.com), the mutual fund leader (especially in fixed-income investments), has launched 15 bond ETFs, with talk of launching more.

About 70 other suppliers of ETFs exist, mostly smaller companies with only a handful of offerings, and a small share of the market. Many will be gone in the years to come.

Familiarizing Yourself with the Indexers

At the core of every ETF is an index. The index is the blueprint on which the ETF is based. Some ETF providers use old, established indexes. Others create their own, often in conjunction with seasoned indexers. (That association helps them get approval from the SEC.) As a rule, for an ETF to be any good, it has to be based on a solid index. On the other hand, a solid index doesn't guarantee a good ETF because other things, like costs and tax efficiency, matter as well. That being said, I turn now to the five indexers that create and re-create the indexes on which most ETFs are based.

Standard & Poor's

Owned by publishing powerhouse McGraw-Hill, Standard & Poor's is perhaps best known for its credit-rating services.

The company also maintains hundreds of indexes, including the S&P 500 (the one you're most likely to see flashed across your television screen on the business channel). Over $1 trillion in investors' assets are directly tied to S&P indexes — more than all other indexes combined.

More ETFs are based on S&P indexes than any other, by far. Those include the iShares broad-based domestic and international ETFs, the Sector SPDRs that track various market segments, most Vanguard U.S. ETFs, the Invesco PowerShares industry-sector funds, and the Guggenheim equal-weight ETFs. For more information, visit www. standardandpoors.com.

Dow Jones

If there were an index for the price of unsalted peanuts in Portugal, Dow Jones would be its purveyor. The company, aside from publishing *The Wall Street Journal* and *Barron's,* develops, maintains, and licenses more than 3,000 market indexes. Those indexes include the world's best-known stock indicator, the Dow Jones Industrial Average, which, in my opinion, should have long ago gone the way of the Edsel.

The iShares industry and sector ETFs are based on Dow Jones indexes, as are at least some of the ETFs issued by State Street, ProShares, Deutsche Bank, and Charles Schwab. For more information, visit www.djindexes.com.

MSCI

With indexes of all kinds — stocks, bonds, hedge funds, U.S. and international securities — MSCI (formerly Morgan Stanley Capital International), although not quite a household name, has been gaining ground as the indexer of choice for many ETF providers.

MSCI indexes are the backbone of the international Vanguard ETFs, as well as many of the iShares global-industry funds and single-country ETFs. For more information, visit www. msci.com.

Russell

The largest 1,000 U.S. stocks make up the Russell 1000 index, although it remains relatively obscure because the Dow Industrial and the S&P 500 hog the spotlight when it comes to measuring large cap performance. The next 2,000 largest stocks on the U.S. market are in the Russell 2000. And the Russell 1000 plus the Russell 2000 make up the Russell 3000. Those are Russell's more popular indexes, but it has plenty of others as well.

A dozen of the iShares domestic ETFs are based on Russell indexes, as are seven of Vanguard's U.S. offerings. ProShares and Direxion also use Russell indexes. For more information, visit www.russell.com.

Barclays

Lehman Brothers for years was the leading indexer in the world of fixed income investments. The firm was acquired by Barclays Capital in 2008 (just as Barclays was leaving the ETF business), and thus the long-famous Lehman Brothers Aggregate Bond Index, the closest thing the fixed-income world has to the S&P 500, is now called the Barclays Capital Aggregate Bond Index.

BlackRock's iShares, SPDRs, Vanguard, and Van Eck all use Barclays Capital indexes for their fixed-income ETFs. Considering that the implosion of Lehman Brothers prior to its takeover by Barclays signaled the beginning of the financial crisis in 2008, a name change for these indexes seems understandable. For more information, visit https://ecommerce.barcap.com/indices/index.dxml.

Part II
Getting to Know ETFs

	Bargain-Basement (Value) Stocks	In-Between Priced Stocks	Hot and Pricey (Growth) Stocks	
				Big Companies
				In-Between Sized Companies
				Little Companies

For an article on optimizing your ETFs portfolio, visit
www.dummies.com/extras/investinginetfs.

In this part . . .

- ✔ Know what to expect from large- and small-growth stocks — the behemoths and the start-ups — so that you can appropriately utilize both.

- ✔ Satisfy your wanderlust (sorta) by delving into the world of international investing.

- ✔ Discover how to specialize with sector and style investing.

- ✔ Get the details you need to get into the bond game with ETFs.

- ✔ Go down further specialized ETF roads, like real estate investment trusts and commodities.

Chapter 3

Large Growth and Large Value

In This Chapter

▶ Sizing up the size factor in stock investing

▶ Recognizing ETFs that fit the style bill

▶ Choosing the best options for your portfolio

▶ Weighing value against growth for performance and risk

▶ Recognizing ETFs that fit the value bill

*W*hy would slower-growing companies (the dandelions of the corporate world) historically reward investors better than faster-growing (daisy) companies? Welcome to the shoulder-shrugging world of value investing.

Large growth stocks may feel exciting — sexy, even — but consider this: In the past 86 years, large value stocks have enjoyed an annualized growth rate of 11.1 percent, versus roughly 10.6 percent for large growth stocks — with roughly the same standard deviation (volatility). And thanks to ETFs, investing in value has never been easier.

In this chapter, I explain not only the role that both large growth and large value stocks play in your portfolio, but I also run through considerations for utilizing them and good ETF options to consider.

Utilizing the Monsters of Money-Making: Large-Growth Stocks

Mr. CEO, the one who shows his pearly whites on the cover of business magazines, makes it to newsstands because his company has a *total market capitalization* (the value of all its outstanding stock) of at least $5 billion, earnings have been growing and growing fast, the company has a secure niche within its industry, and many people envision the Borg-like corporation eventually taking over the universe. Think Google, Apple, Facebook, Amazon.

In the sections that follow, I explain what role such behemoths should play in your portfolio. But before getting into the meat of the matter, take a quick glance at Figure 3-1. It shows where large growth stocks fit into a well-diversified stock portfolio. (Find out more about this style box or grid, which divides a stock portfolio into large cap and small cap, value and growth, in Chapter 10.)

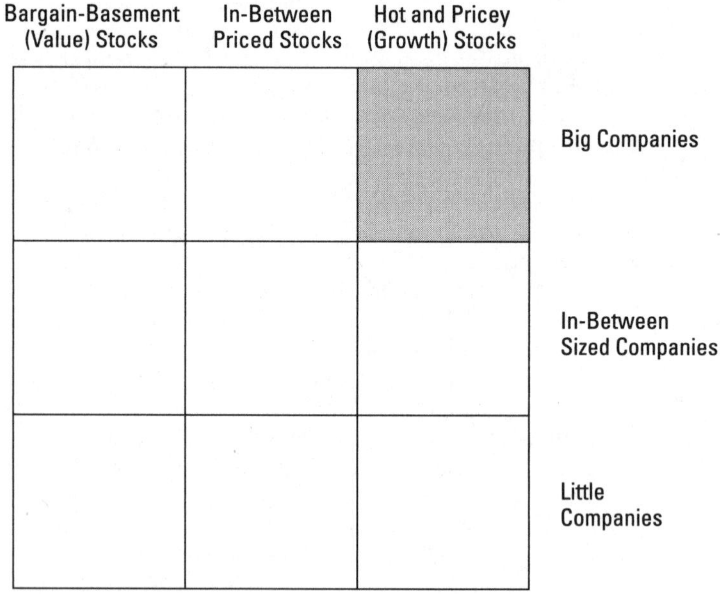

Bargain-Basement (Value) Stocks	In-Between Priced Stocks	Hot and Pricey (Growth) Stocks	
			Big Companies
			In-Between Sized Companies
			Little Companies

© John Wiley & Sons, Inc.

Figure 3-1: The place of large growth stocks in the grid.

Style review

In Chapter 10, I note that one approach to building a portfolio involves investing in different styles of stocks: large cap, mid cap, small cap, value, and growth. How did the whole business of style investing get started? Hard to say. Benjamin Graham, the "Dean of Wall Street," the "Father of Value Investing," who wrote several oft-quoted books in the 1930s and 1940s, didn't give us the popular style grid that you see in Figure 3-1. But Mr. Graham certainly helped provide the tools of fundamental analysis whereby more contemporary brains could figure things out.

In the early 1980s, studies out of the University of Chicago began to quantify the differences between large caps and small caps, and in 1992, two economists named Eugene Fama and Kenneth French delivered the seminal paper on the differences between value and growth stocks.

What makes large cap large?

Capitalization or *cap* refers to the combined value of all shares of a company's stock. The lines dividing large cap, mid cap, and small cap are sometimes as blurry as the line between, say, *Rubenesque* and *fat.* The distinction is largely in the eyes of the beholder.

If you took a poll, however, I think you would find that the following divisions are generally accepted:

- ✔ **Large caps:** Companies with more than $5 billion in capitalization

- ✔ **Mid caps:** Companies with $1 billion to $5 billion in capitalization

- ✔ **Small caps:** Companies with $250 million to $1 billion in capitalization

Anything from $50 million to $250 million would usually be deemed a *micro cap.* And your local pizza shop, if it were to go public, might be called a *nano cap (con aglio).* There are no nano cap ETFs. For all the other categories, there are ETFs to your heart's content.

How does growth differ from value?

Many different criteria are used to determine whether a stock or basket of stocks (such as an ETF) qualifies as *growth* or *value.* But perhaps the most important measure is the ratio of price to earnings: the *P/E ratio,* sometimes referred to as the *multiple.*

The P/E ratio is the price of a stock divided by its earnings per share. For example, suppose McDummy Corporation stock is currently selling for $40 a share. And suppose that the company earned $2 last year for every share of stock outstanding. McDummy's P/E ratio would be 20. (The S&P 500 currently has a P/E of about 19, but that ratio changes frequently.)

The higher the P/E, the more investors have been willing to pay for the company's earnings. Or to put it in terms of growth and value:

- ✔ The higher the P/E, the more *growthy* the company: Either the company is growing fast, or investors have high hopes (realistic or foolish) for future growth.

- ✔ The lower the P/E, the more *valuey* the company. The business world doesn't see this company as a mover and shaker.

Each ETF carries a P/E reflecting the collective P/E of its holdings and giving you an indication of just how growthy or valuey that ETF is. A growth ETF is filled with companies that look like they are taking over the planet. A value ETF is filled with companies that seem to be meandering along but whose stock can be purchased for what looks like a bargain price.

Putting these terms to use

Today, most investment pros develop their portfolios with at least some consideration given to the cap size and growth or value orientation of their stock holdings. Why? Because study after study shows that, in fact, a portfolio's performance is inexorably linked to where that portfolio falls in the style grid. A mutual fund that holds all large growth stocks, for example, will generally (but certainly not always) rise or fall with the rise or fall of that asset class.

Some research shows that perhaps 90 to 95 percent of a mutual fund's or ETF's performance may be attributable to its asset class alone. In other words, any large cap growth fund will tend to perform similarly to other large cap growth funds. Any small cap value fund will tend to perform similarly to other small cap value funds. And so on. That's why the financial press's weekly wrap-ups of top-performing funds will typically list a bunch of funds that mirror each other very closely. (That being the case, why not enjoy the low cost and tax efficiency of the ETF or index mutual fund?)

Looking into Stocks Big and Brawny

Large growth companies grab nearly all the headlines, for sure. The pundits are forever singing their praises — or trumpeting their faults when the growth trajectory starts to level off. Either way, you'll hear about it; the northeast corner of the style grid includes the most recognizable names in the corporate world. If you're seeking employment, I strongly urge you to latch on to one of these companies; your future will likely be bright. But do large growth stocks necessarily make the best investments?

Er, no.

Contrary to all appearances . . .

Over the course of the last 86 years, large growth stocks have seen an annualized return rate (not accounting for inflation) of about 10.6 percent. Not too bad. But that compares to 11.1 percent for large value stocks, with no greater volatility. Theories abound as to why large growth stocks haven't done as well as value stocks. Value stocks pay greater dividends, say some. Value stocks really *are* riskier; they just don't look it, argue others.

The theory that makes the most sense, in my opinion, is that growth stocks are simply hampered by their own immense popularity. Because growth companies grab all the headlines, because investors *think* they must be the best investments, the large growth stocks tend to get overpriced by the time you buy them. In the past year or two, for example, everyone I know seems to be talking about Facebook. Yes, the company is growing faster than crabgrass. And it probably will continue to grow. But with a price-to-earnings ratio of 75, your stock investment in Facebook is dependent on continued super-sonic growth. Anything less than supersonic growth, and the stock is not going to shine. If people expected the stock to tank (in which case, the P/E would be much lower), value investors might jump in and make a profit even if the company didn't grow at all — but merely didn't tank!

Let history serve as only a rough guide

So given that large value stocks historically have done better than large growth stocks, and given that small caps histori-cally have knocked the socks off large, does it still make sense to sink some of your investment dollars into large growth? Oh yes, it does. The past is only an indication of what the future may bring. No one knows whether value stocks will continue to outshine. In the past 10 years or so, growth stocks have outpaced value stocks, in both the large- and the small-cap arenas. This period has been similar to much of the 1990s when growth trumped value. The next 10 years? Who knows?

 Stocks of large companies — value and growth combined — should make up between 50 and 65 percent of your total domestic stock portfolio. The higher your risk tolerance, the closer you'll want to be to the lower end of that range.

Whatever your allocation to domestic large cap stocks, I rec-ommend that you invest anywhere from 40 to 50 percent of that amount in large growth. Take a tilt toward value, if you wish, but don't tilt so far that you risk tipping over.

Large Cap ETF Options Galore

The roster of ETFs on the market now includes about 160 broad-based domestic large cap funds, of which 30 or so are acceptable large growth options. The remainder of the broad-based (as opposed to industry sector or other specialized) large cap funds are either *blend* (a growth-and-value cocktail) or strictly large value. As I emphasize throughout this book, each and every investment you make should be evaluated in the context of your entire portfolio.

Before you start shopping for a large growth ETF, you need to ask yourself whether one belongs in your portfolio at all. In a nutshell, it does, but only if your portfolio is large enough to be divided into various styles.

Strictly large cap or blend?

All things being equal, I'd like to see you invest in large growth and large value stocks — separately. That approach gives you the opportunity to rebalance once a year and, by so doing, juice out added return while reducing risk. (More on rebalancing in Chapter 11.) But the profit you expect to reap from that tweak must exceed the transaction costs of making two trades (generally selling shares of the outperforming ETF for the year and adding to the underperformer).

If your portfolio isn't big enough for the profit of the tweaking to outweigh the cost of the trading, you're better off with a blend of value and growth. If your portfolio is so small that any tweaking is unlikely to be profitable, I would suggest not only a blend of large value and growth, but a blend of *everything*. Keep these parameters in mind as you read on.

"Everything" investment options

I don't know where you park your money, and I don't know exactly how much you spend per trade, but I would say that if you have a portfolio of $10,000 or less, you should either be thinking mutual funds (not ETFs), or you should seek to invest at a brokerage that will not charge you for trading ETFs. Otherwise, the trading costs could eat you alive. If, however, you are unlikely to do any trading in the next several years, an ETF portfolio may make sense. In that case, consider a simple and all-encompassing "everything" (total ball of wax) ETF for your domestic stock holdings.

Good options in the "everything" domestic stock category include the iShares Dow Jones U.S. Total Market ETF (IYY), the Vanguard Total Stock Market ETF (VTI), and the Schwab U.S. Broad Market ETF (SCHB). Of the three, I have a slight preference for the Schwab and the Vanguard choices because of their ultra-low costs (0.04 and 0.054 percent, respectively, versus 0.20 percent for the iShares offering).

(*Note:* There are several "everything" ETFs where you can tap into even broader investments than the entire U.S. stock market; I discuss a few of these options in Chapter 6.)

Large and small cap blends

If you have more than $10,000 but less than $20,000 or so, and you're able to invest it and keep it put for a good while, consider splitting up your domestic stock portfolio into large and small cap. In this case, I'd recommend a diversified small cap blend and a diversified large cap blend. Good options among the large cap blends would include the Vanguard Large Cap ETF (VV), the Vanguard Mega Cap 300 ETF (MGC), the iShares Russell 1000 ETF (IWB), and the Schwab U.S. Large-Cap ETF (SCHX). I discuss these options in detail in the upcoming section "Blended options for large cap exposure."

Large cap growth and value options

If you have a portfolio of more than $20,000, you should split up the large caps into growth and value. Good large growth options would include the Vanguard Growth ETF (VUG), Vanguard Mega Cap Growth ETF (MGK), iShares Morningstar Large Growth ETF (JKE), and the Schwab U.S. Large-Cap Growth ETF (SCHG). See the upcoming section "Strictly large growth" for details on these ETFs.

Blended options for large cap exposure

Among the *blended* (large cap value and growth) options for smaller portfolios ($10,000 to $20,000), I feel comfortable recommending any of the ETFs discussed in this section.

Please keep in mind that all the expense ratios, average cap sizes, price/earnings ratios, and top five holdings for the ETFs I list here and elsewhere in the book are true as of a certain date and are subject to change. You should verify all key details before making any purchase.

Vanguard Large Cap ETF (VV)

Indexed to: MSCI U.S. Prime Market 750 Index (750 corporate biggies from both the value and growth sides of the grid)

Expense ratio: 0.09 percent
Average cap size: $66.1 billion
P/E ratio: 19.6
Top five holdings: Apple, Exxon Mobil, Microsoft, Johnson & Johnson, Wells Fargo
Russell's review: The low cost, as with nearly all Vanguard offerings, makes me want to stand up and cheer. The MSCI U.S. Prime Market 750, as the name implies, encompasses a larger universe of stocks than the more popular S&P 500, which translates to holdings with a somewhat smaller average cap size than you'll find with some other large cap options. The MSCI index is also more "indexy" than the S&P 500: The choice of companies is purely quantitative, whereas with the S&P, some human judgment is applied. Personally, I like the hands-off approach. This ETF is an excellent choice for people with smaller portfolios trying to limit the number of ETFs they have to manage. Shares trade free of commissions if held at Vanguard.

Vanguard Mega Cap 300 ETF (MGC)

Indexed to: MSCI U.S. Large Cap 300 Index (the biggest 300 U.S. companies, regardless of type)
Expense ratio: 0.11 percent
Average cap size: $95.2 billion (whooeeee!)
P/E ratio: 19.2
Top five holdings: Apple, Exxon Mobil, Microsoft, Johnson & Johnson, Wells Fargo
Russell's review: What the heck? If you're going to go big, why not go all the way? Note that the top five holdings are the very same that you'll find with the other Vanguard blended option, the Vanguard Large Cap ETF (VV). But in the case of this ETF, you won't be getting the lesser sized of the large cap companies. That's less than optimal from a diversification standpoint, and for that reason, I wouldn't recommend MGC over VV as a stand-alone investment. But if you are combining either of these funds with a blended small cap fund, then MGC will give you somewhat lower correlation (in other words, greater simultaneous zig and zag potential), which is a good thing. For most investors' portfolios, either Vanguard option would be an excellent choice. Shares trade free of commissions if held at Vanguard.

Schwab U.S. Large-Cap ETF (SCHX)

Indexed to: Dow Jones U.S. Large-Cap Total Stock Market Index (approximately 750 of America's largest corporations)
Expense ratio: 0.04 percent
Average cap size: $60.5 billion
P/E ratio: 19.3
Top five holdings: Apple, Exxon Mobil, Microsoft, Johnson & Johnson, Bershire Hathaway
Russell's review: For frugality's sake alone, this fund makes a good option. The management fee is one of the lowest in the industry. And, like all Schwab ETFs, you can trade this baby for free if held at Schwab. Most importantly, the index is a good one. I expect Schwab to do a good job of tracking the index.

iShares Russell 1000 ETF (IWB)

Indexed to: Russell 1000 (the largest 1,000 publicly traded companies in the land)
Expense ratio: 0.15 percent
Average cap size: $53.7 billion
P/E ratio: 19.2
Top five holdings: Apple, Exxon Mobil, Microsoft, Johnson & Johnson, Berkshire Hathaway
Russell's review: The cost isn't high, but it is higher than the comparable Vanguard and Schwab funds . On the other hand, this ETF offers somewhat greater diversification — only a potential plus, really, if this is going to be a major part of your portfolio. Given the exposure to smaller companies, which tend to see greater price flux than large companies, this fund may prove over the long run to be slightly more volatile but slightly more rewarding than the comparable Vanguard or Schwab or other iShares options. Like a number of other broad-based iShares ETFs, IWB trades are free if held at Fidelity.

Strictly large growth

For large growth and large growth alone (complemented by large value, of course) — a position I much prefer for people with adequate assets ($20,000+) — the four options I list here all provide good exposure to the asset class at very reasonable cost.

Vanguard Growth ETF (VUG)

Indexed to: MSCI U.S. Prime Market Growth Index (400 or so of the nation's largest growth stocks)
Expense ratio: 0.09 percent
Average cap size: $57.7 billion
P/E ratio: 23.2
Top five holdings: Facebook, Google, Walt Disney, Gilead Sciences, Home Depot
Russell's review: The price is right. The index makes sense. There's good diversification. The companies represented are certainly large, even though they could be a bit more growthy. This ETF is certainly a very good option. Shares trade free of commissions if held at Vanguard.

Vanguard Mega Cap 300 Growth ETF (MGK)

Indexed to: MSCI U.S. Large Cap Growth Index (300 of the largest growth companies in the United States)
Expense ratio: 0.11 percent
Average cap size: $91.3 billion
P/E ratio: 22.4
Top five holdings: Apple, Facebook, Google, Comcast, Walt Disney
Russell's review: Bigger is better . . . sometimes. If you have small caps in your portfolio, this mega cap fund will give you slightly better diversification than the Vanguard Growth ETF (VUG), but this fund is also a tad less growthy than VUG, so you'll get a bit less divergence from your large value holdings. Nothing to sweat. Either fund, given Vanguard's low expenses and reasonable indexes, would make for a fine holding. Shares trade free of commissions if held at Vanguard.

iShares Morningstar Large Growth ETF (JKE)

Indexed to: Morningstar Large Growth Index (90 of the largest and most growthy U.S. companies)
Expense ratio: 0.25 percent
Average cap size: $95.5 billion
P/E ratio: 23.3
Top five holdings: Apple, Facebook, Google, Comcast, Walt Disney
Russell's review: Nothing in life is perfect. This ETF offers the growthiness that the Vanguard ETFs lack, but the flip side is

that the diversification leaves something to be desired. The top five holdings together make up about one-quarter the value of the index; that's a little more than I would like to see for five companies, especially when the first three holdings are more or less in the same industry. And perhaps because Morningstar indexes aren't nearly as popular as S&P indexes, this ETF is thinly traded, which could result in a larger spread when you buy or sell. What tips the scales for me, however, and makes this one a contender, is that Morningstar indexes are crisp and distinct: Any company that appears in the growth index is not going to be popping up in the value index. Even though that crispness could lead to slightly higher turnover, I like it.

Schwab U.S. Large-Cap Growth ETF (SCHG)

Indexed to: Dow Jones U.S. Large-Cap Growth Total Stock Market Index (450 or so of the largest and presumably fastest-growing U.S. firms)
Expense ratio: 0.07 percent
Average cap size: $55.8 billion
P/E ratio: 22.4
Top five holdings: Apple, Facebook, Google, Comcast, Walt Disney
Russell's review: For the sake of economy alone, this fund, like all Schwab ETFs, makes a good option. The management fee is one of the lowest in the industry. And, like all Schwab ETFs, you can trade this fund for free if held at Schwab. Most importantly, the index is a good one. You can expect Schwab to do a reasonable job of tracking the index.

ETFs I wouldn't go out of my way to own

None of the ETFs listed below is horrible — far from it. But given the plethora of choices, barring very special circumstances, I would not recommend these:

✔ **DIAMONDS Trust Series 1 (DIA):** Based on the index on which this ETF is based, I basically don't like it. The Dow Jones Industrial Average is an antiquated and somewhat arbitrary index of 30 large companies that look good to the editors of *The Wall Street Journal.* That isn't enough on which to build a portfolio.

✔ **SPDR S&P 500 (SPY):** It's the oldest and largest and among the cheapest (0.09 percent), but it's not the best thing on the ETF market. The S&P 500, which the fund tracks, isn't the greatest of indexes. The legal structure of SPY — unlike the vast majority of ETFs — does not allow for the immediate reinvestment of dividends, which can create a cash drag. Its popularity alone may also create extra drag, for as new companies are admitted into the 500 club, their stock prices tend to pop a bit, requiring fund managers to pay premium prices.

✔ **PowerShares Dynamic Large Cap Growth (PWB):** This ETF doesn't make me recoil in horror; you could do worse. But the high-by-ETF-standards expense ratio (0.58 percent) is something of a turn-off. And the "dynamic" index reminds me too much of active investing, which has a less than gleaming track record. I may change my mind if this new fund still shines after many more years on the market, but for right now — with a 10-year track record that slightly lags the Russell 1000 Growth Index by more than 1 percent — I'd shy away.

Large Value: Counterintuitive Cash Cows

You often find big value stocks in the companies you've probably heard of, yes, but those that aren't nearly as glamorous as Google or as exciting as Facebook. I'm talking about companies that usually ply their trade in older, slow-growing industries, like insurance, petroleum, pharmaceuticals, underwear, and transportation. I'm talking about companies such as Pfizer, Merck & Co., Wal-Mart Stores, Occidental Petroleum, and MetLife.

Those large value stocks can play an important role in a portfolio, and in fact you may want them to be the largest single asset class in your portfolio. Take a gander at Figure 3-2. This is where large value stocks fit into the investment style grid and the impressive return of large value stocks over the past eight or so decades.

Pass the dandelion fertilizer, will ya?

Bargain-Basement (Value) Stocks	In-Between Priced Stocks	Hot and Pricey (Growth) Stocks	
			Big Companies
			In-Between Sized Companies
			Little Companies

Figure 3-2: Large value stocks occupy the northwest corner of the grid.

Warren Buffett knows a value stock when he sees one. Do you? Different investment pros and different indexes (upon which ETFs are fashioned) may define "value" differently, but here are some of the most common criteria:

- ✔ **P/E ratio:** As early as 1934, Benjamin Graham and David Dodd (in their book with the blockbuster title *Security Analysis*) suggested that investors should pay heavy consideration to the ratio of a stock's market price (P) to its earnings per share (E). Sometimes called the *multiple,* this venerable ratio sheds light on how much the market is willing to cough up for a company's earning power. The lower the ratio, the more "valuey" the stock. (The P/E ratio as it relates to growth stocks is addressed in the previous chapter.)

- ✔ **P/B ratio:** Graham and Dodd also advised that the ratio of market price to book value (B) should be given at least "a fleeting glance." Many of today's investment gurus have awarded the P/B ratio the chief role in defining value versus growth. A ratio well below sea level is what floats a value investor's boat. *Book value* refers to the guesstimated value of a corporation's total assets, both tangible (factories, inventory, and so on) and intangible (goodwill, patents, and so on), minus any liabilities.

✔ **Dividend distributions:** You like dividends? Value stocks are the ones that pay them.

✔ **The cover of *Forbes*:** Magazine covers are rarely adorned with photos of the CEOs of value companies. While growth companies receive broad exposure, value companies tend to wallow in obscurity.

✔ **Earnings growth:** Growth companies' earnings tend to impress, while you can expect value companies to have less than awe-inspiring earnings growth.

✔ **The industry sector:** Growth stocks are typically found in high-flying industries, such as computers, wireless, and biotechnology. Value stocks are more often found in older-than-the-hills sectors, such as energy, banking, transportation, and toiletries.

Looking for the Best Value Buys

Some people say there is hidden risk in value investing that warrants greater returns. They explain that although the standard deviation for the two asset classes is about the same, value stocks tend to plummet at the worst economic times. This argument is not very persuasive. Although value was hit harder than growth in the market plunge of 2008, the reverse held true in the prior market nosedive of 2000–2002. In the late summer of 2011, after S&P decided to downgrade U.S. Treasuries, U.S. value and growth stocks fell at about the same pace.

Others say that value stocks outperform growth stocks because of the greater dividends paid by value companies. Growth companies tend to plow their cash into acquisitions and new product development rather than issuing dividends to those pesky shareholders.

Here's the best explanation for the value premium, if you ask this humble author: Value stocks simply tend to be ignored by the market — or have been in the past — and therefore come relatively cheap. When value stocks do receive attention, it's usually negative. And studies show that investors tend to overreact to bad news. Such overreactions end up being reflected in a discounted price.

Taking the index route

Famous value investors like Warren Buffett make their money finding stocks that come at an especially discounted price. They recognize that companies making lackluster profits, and even sometimes companies bleeding money, can turn around (especially when Mr. Buffett sends in his team of whip-cracking consultants). When a lackluster company turns around, the stock that was formerly seen as a financial turd (that's a technical term) can suddenly turn into 14-karat gold. It's a formula that has worked well for the Oracle of Omaha.

Good luck making it work for you.

 Unlike Warren Buffett, many or most value stock pickers repeatedly take gambles on failing companies that continue to fail. I say the best way to invest in large value is to buy the index. There is no better way of doing that than through ETFs.

Making an ETF selection

Of the 160 or so diversified large cap ETFs on the market, perhaps 30 or so are worth particular attention for tapping into the value market. The following five offer good large value indexes at reasonable prices: the Vanguard Value ETF (VTV), Vanguard Mega Cap 300 Value Index ETF (MGV), iShares Russell 1000 Value ETF (IWD), iShares Morningstar Large Value ETF (JKF), and the Schwab U.S. Large-Cap Value ETF (SCHV).

I suggest that you read through my descriptions that follow and make the choice that you think is best for you. Whatever your allocation to domestic large cap stocks, your allocation to value should be somewhere in the ballpark of 50 to 60 percent of that amount. In other words, I suggest that you tilt toward value, but don't go overboard.

 The criteria you use in picking the best large cap value ETF should include expense ratios, appropriateness of the index, and tax efficiency (if you're investing in a taxable account). If you have a modest portfolio, or if you are making regular contributions, the trading costs need to be factored in as well. Note that the expense ratios, average cap sizes, price/earning ratios, and top five holdings are all subject to change; you should definitely check for updated figures before investing.

Vanguard Value Index ETF (VTV)

Indexed to: MSCI U.S. Prime Market Value Index (400 or so of the nation's largest value stocks)
Expense ratio: 0.09 percent
Average cap size: $74.6 billion
P/E ratio: 17.3
Top five holdings: Exxon Mobil, Microsoft, Johnson & Johnson, Wells Fargo, Berkshire Hathaway
Russell's review: The price is right. The index makes sense. There's good diversification. The companies represented are certainly large. This ETF is a very good option, although I'd like it even more if it were a tad more valuey. (On the other hand, making it more valuey could increase turnover, which might increase costs and taxation.) All told, I like the VTV. I like it a lot. If you already own the Vanguard Value Index mutual fund and you're considering moving to ETFs, this fund would clearly be your choice. If held at Vanguard, this ETF, like all Vanguard ETFs, trades for free.

Vanguard Mega Cap 300 Value Index ETF (MGV)

Indexed to: The MSCI U.S. Large Cap Value Index (150 or so of the largest U.S. stocks with value characteristics)
Expense ratio: 0.11 percent
Average cap size: $98.6 billion
P/E ratio: 17.2
Top five holdings: Exxon Mobil, Microsoft, Johnson & Johnson, Wells Fargo, Berkshire Hathaway
Russell's review: This fund offers exposure to larger companies than does the more popular VTV featured above. Is bigger better? Could be. If you have small caps in your portfolio (which you should!), this mega cap fund will give you slightly less correlation than you'll get with VTV. As a stand-alone investment, however, I would expect that the very long-term returns on this fund will lag VTV, given that giant caps historically have lagged large caps. Given Vanguard's low expenses and reasonable indexes, either fund would make a fine holding. MGV also trades free of commission if held at Vanguard.

iShares Russell 1000 Value ETF (IWD)

Indexed to: The 600 or so more-valuey stocks in the Russell 1000 Index (the largest 1,000 publicly traded companies in the land)
Expense ratio: 0.20 percent
Average cap size: $51.4 billion

P/E ratio: 17.2
Top five holdings: Exxon Mobil, Berkshire Hathaway, Wells Fargo, General Electric, Johnson & Johnson
Russell's review: The cost isn't high, but it is higher than the comparable Vanguard and Schwab funds. On the other hand, this ETF offers a slightly more valuey lean than the others. Like a number of other broad-based iShares ETFs, IWD trades free if held at Fidelity.

iShares Morningstar Large Value ETF (JKF)

Indexed to: Morningstar Large Value Index (76 of the largest U.S. value stocks, "value" being determined by Morningstar's proprietary formula)
Expense ratio: 0.25 percent
Average cap size: $104.6 billion
P/E ratio: 14.7
Top five holdings: Exxon Mobil, Wells Fargo, General Electric, JPMorgan Chase, Chevron
Russell's review: Exxon Mobil alone makes up 8 percent of this ETF, and that, in my mind, is less than ideal. Add the 5.2 percent held in Wells Fargo, and the 5.1 percent in General Electric, and you have nearly one-fifth of the fund in three stocks. (That concentration in the giants explains why the average cap size of this fund is even greater than Vanguard's Mega Cap ETF.) To boot, Morningstar indexes aren't nearly as popular as S&P indexes, so this ETF is thinly traded, which could result in a larger spread when you buy or sell. On the positive side, however, Morningstar indexes are neat boxes: Any company that appears in the value index is not going to pop up in the growth index. I think that's worth something, for sure.

Schwab U.S. Large-Cap Value ETF (SCHV)

Indexed to: Dow Jones U.S. Large-Cap Value Total Stock Market Index (made up of the more valuey half of the 600 or so stocks that comprise the DJ U.S. Large Cap Stock Market Index)
Expense ratio: 0.07 percent
Average cap size: $64.9 billion
P/E ratio: 17.1
Top five holdings: Exxon Mobil, Microsoft, Johnson & Johnson, Wells Fargo, General Electric

Russell's review: For the sake of economy alone, this fund is a good option. The management fee is one of the lowest in the industry. And, like all Schwab ETFs, you can trade this fund for free if held at Schwab. Most importantly, the index is a good one. I expect Schwab to do a reasonable job of tracking the index, even though its ETFs were introduced only in late 2009.

Chapter 4

Small Growth and Small Value

* *

In This Chapter

▶ Factoring small company stocks into your investment pie

▶ Recognizing ETFs that tap into this asset class

▶ Introducing micro caps

▶ Recognizing a small value stock

▶ Earmarking ETFs that track small value indexes

* *

*O*nce upon a time in the kingdom of Redmond, there was a young company called Microsoft. It was a very small company with very big ideas, and it grew and grew and grew. Its founder and its original investors became very, very rich and lived happily ever after.

Oh, you've heard that story? Then you understand the appeal of small growth companies. These are companies that typically have *market capitalization* (the market value of total outstanding stock) of about $300 million to $1 billion. They frequently boast a hot product or patent, often fall into the high tech arena, and always seem to be on their way to stardom. Some of them make it, and along with them, their investors take a joy ride all the way to early retirement.

Unfortunately, for every Microsoft, there are a dozen, or two or three dozen, small companies that go belly up long before their prime. For every investor who gambles on a small company stock and takes early retirement, 100 others still drive their cars to work every Monday morning.

Look at the list of some of the top companies represented in the Vanguard Small Cap Growth ETF: Alkermes PLC, Mednax, Duke Realty, Whitewave Foods, Extra Space Storage . . . . These are not household names. Nor are they industry leaders. If you wanted to pick one of these companies to sink a wad of cash into, I would tell you that you're crazy.

But if you wanted to sink that cash into the entire small growth index, well, that's another matter altogether. Assuming you could handle some risk, I'd tell you by all means to go for it. Your odds of making money are pretty darned good — at least if history is our guide.

This chapter shows you how small growth and small value stocks can fit into your ETF portfolio.

Harnessing Small Growth with Sweet Start-Ups

Take a ride with me through the world of small cap growth stocks to determine what role, if any, they should play in your ETF portfolio. First stop along the ride: Figure 4-1, where you can see how small growth fits into the investment style grid I introduce in Chapter 3.

In the past century, small cap stocks have outperformed large cap stocks just as assuredly as Honduras has produced more Hondurans than the United States. The volatility of small cap stocks has also been greater, just as assuredly as the United States has more roller coasters than Honduras. In terms of return per unit of risk (risk-adjusted rate of return), however, small caps are clearly winners. And so it would seem that investing in small caps is a pretty smart thing to do. But please know that not all small caps are created equal.

The true stars of the small cap world have been small cap *value* stocks rather than small cap *growth* stocks. (Take a look at Chapter 3 if you aren't sure what I mean by these terms.) How slow-growing, often ailing companies have beat out their hot-to-trot cousins remains one of the unresolved mysteries of the investing world. But the numbers don't lie.

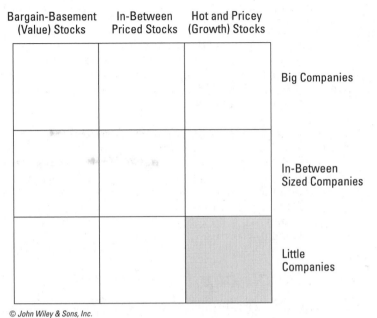

Bargain-Basement   In-Between   Hot and Pricey
(Value) Stocks   Priced Stocks   (Growth) Stocks

Big Companies

In-Between
Sized Companies

Little
Companies

© *John Wiley & Sons, Inc.*

Figure 4-1: The shaded area is the portion of the investment grid
represented by small growth stocks.

In fact, if you look at the numbers — over the past 20 years, small-cap value has returned 15 percent a year, while small-cap growth has returned 11.5 percent a year — you may be inclined to treat small growth stocks as a pariah. Please don't. They belong in a well-diversified portfolio. Some years are clearly small growth years. The best example is rather recent: As I'm writing this chapter, small cap growth stocks have beaten both small value and large caps by a good margin over the past five years. Back in 2003, small growth was the undisputed King of Returns, clocking in at an astounding 50.37 percent. Who is to say that the long-term past wasn't a fluke and that small growth may actually go on to outperform all other asset classes in the next 20 years?

Your Choices for Small Growth

If you have a portfolio of under $20,000 or so, I recommend that you consider a small cap *blend* fund, which combines small value and small growth stocks. Small cap domestic stocks shouldn't occupy more than 20 percent or so of your portfolio (more on that topic in Chapter 9), and if you divide up 20 percent of less than $20,000, the trading costs (some you'll see, and some that may be hidden) could seriously impact your returns. So keep it simple until your portfolio grows to the point that you can start slicing and dicing a bit more economically.

If you have a portfolio of more than $20,000 and you are a buy-and-hold kind of guy or gal, I suggest that you break up your small cap holdings into a growth ETF and a value ETF. Given the dramatic outperformance of value in the past, you might tilt in that direction — more so than you do with large caps. A reasonable tilt may call for somewhere between 60 and 75 of your small cap exposure going to value, and 25 to 40 percent going to growth.

Small cap blend funds

A bit of growth, a bit of value, your choice in small cap blend funds should take into consideration such things as expense ratios, average cap size, and P/E ratio (explained in Chapter 3). Keep in mind that these numbers are subject to change, so I recommend checking them before you act.

Some good ETF options for people with limited-size portfolios include the Vanguard Small Cap (VB), iShares Morningstar Small Core (JKJ), iShares S&P Small Cap 600 (IJR), and Schwab U.S. Small-Cap (SCHA) ETFs.

Vanguard Small Cap ETF (VB)

Indexed to: MSCI U.S. Small Cap 1750 Index (1,750 broadly diversified smaller U.S. companies)
Expense ratio: 0.09 percent
Average cap size: $3.1 billion
P/E ratio: 22.3
Top five holdings: Alkermes, Harman International, Alaska Air, Snap-on Inc, Packaging Corp of America
Russell's review: The expense ratio is quite low, especially when compared to most other offerings in the small cap arena. The diversification is lovely. And Vanguard's ETFs — largely because they are pegged to indexes with little turnover — are arguably the most tax-efficient of all ETFs. Those are the three positives. On the downside, the P/E ratio

is higher than that of some competing ETFs (an indication of a greater orientation toward growth and away from value). And the average cap size is larger than some others. On balance, this is a very good selection, but (as with all blend funds) I'd scrap it for something more refined — a growth and value split — as soon as your portfolio is large enough to allow for such refinement. There are no commissions for trading this ETF if it's held at Vanguard.

iShares Morningstar Small Core ETF (JKJ)

Indexed to: 260 companies from the Morningstar Small Core Index that fall somewhere between extreme growth and value
Expense ratio: 0.25 percent
Average cap size: $2.6 billion
P/E ratio: 22.1
Top five holdings: Alkermes, Harman International, Alaska Air, Snap-on Inc, Packaging Corp of America
Russell's review: The diversification isn't quite what you get with Vanguard, but it's adequate. The somewhat lower P/E could translate into slightly higher returns over the next few years, but that may be offset by the higher expense ratio. If you already own this ETF, that's not reason enough to switch unless you're holding a rather large position and capital gains are not an issue. But if you're starting from scratch, I don't know if paying the higher fee would be warranted. These Morningstar iShares aren't heavily traded, so you could get zonked with a larger spread when you buy and sell.

iShares S&P Small Cap 600 ETF (IJR)

Indexed to: Roughly 600 companies that make up the S&P Small Cap 600 Index
Expense ratio: 0.12
Average cap size: $1.5 billion
P/E ratio: 22.0
Top five holdings: Tiquint Semiconductor, West Pharmaceutical Services Inc, Teledyne Technologies, Maximus Inc, Toro Co.
Russell's review: This is a perfectly acceptable ETF for small cap exposure at a fair price. The average cap size is smaller than most other small cap funds, which could add juice (but also volatility) to this holding. This ETF trades free of commission if held at Fidelity, so it may be an optimal selection in smaller portfolios where trading costs can make a more serious dent.

Schwab U.S. Small-Cap ETF (SCHA)

Indexed to: Dow Jones U.S. Small-Cap Total Stock Market Index (1,750 of America's most modest-sized publicly traded companies)
Expense ratio: 0.08 percent
Average cap size: $2.5 billion
P/E ratio: 20.6
Top five holdings: Tiquint Semiconductor, West Pharmaceutical Services Inc, Teledyne Technologies, Maximus Inc, Toro Co.
Russell's review: The low P/E ratio indicates something of a value lean, which isn't a bad thing to have if this one fund is your only exposure to U.S. small caps. The number of stocks represented is large, and (all other things being equal) a larger number of stocks in an index is better. The expense ratio of this ETF is the lowest in the category, and the fund trades free of commissions if held at Schwab. All in all, it isn't a bad package. In fact, I find it quite attractive.

Strictly small cap growth funds

If you have enough assets to warrant splitting up small value and small growth, go for it, by all means. Following are some good small growth options from iShares and Vanguard. I also review the Guggenheim small cap "pure growth," fund, even though I have some mixed feelings about that one. In the next section, I present small value options to complement the funds presented here.

Vanguard Small Cap Growth ETF (VBK)

Indexed to: MSCI U.S. Small Cap Growth Index (approximately 970 small cap growth companies in the United States)
Expense ratio: 0.09 percent
Average cap size: $3.2 billion
P/E ratio: 27.3
Top five holdings: Alkermes PLC, Harman International, CMT Market Liquidity Rate, ISIS Pharmaceuticals, Cooper Companies
Russell's review: Add economy to wide diversification, tax efficiency beyond compare, and a very definite growth exposure, and I really have no complaints. The Vanguard Small Cap Growth ETF offers an excellent way to tap into this asset class. And that's especially true if you happen to hold your portfolio at Vanguard, where trading Vanguard ETFs incurs no commissions.

iShares Morningstar Small Growth Index ETF (JKK)

Indexed to: Approximately 370 companies from the Morningstar Small Growth Index
Expense ratio: 0.30 percent
Average cap size: $2.5 billion
P/E ratio: 31.5
Top five holdings: NorthStar Asset Management, Kate Spade & Co, DexCom Inc, Zebra Technologies, United Natural Foods
Russell's review: My only beef with the Morningstar indexes is that they tend to be a bit too concentrated, at least in the large cap arena. In their small caps, however, concentration isn't a problem. The largest holding here, NorthStar Asset Management, gets an acceptably small 0.9 percent allocation. The expense ratio, too, is acceptable, although higher than most others in this category. I like that Morningstar promises no crossover between growth and value. If you own this ETF along with the iShares Morningstar Small Value Index, you should get pleasantly limited correlation.

iShares S&P Small Cap 600 Growth ETF (IJT)

Indexed to: Despite the "600" in its name, this ETF tracks the 350 or so holdings that make up the S&P Small Cap 600/Citigroup Growth Index
Expense ratio: 0.25 percent
Average cap size: $1.8 billion
P/E ratio: 25.3
Top five holdings: Triguint Semiconductor, Maximus Inc, Toro Co, Buffalo Wild Wings Inc, Curtiss-Wright Corp.
Russell's review: S&P indexes are a bit too subjective for me to really love them. But this fund's price is reasonable, and there's no reason to snub this iShares offering. Apparently, Fidelity likes it because it allows you to buy and sell this ETF without paying any commission. (Of course, Fidelity gets some remuneration from iShares.)

Guggenheim S&P 600 Small Cap Pure Growth ETF (RZG)

Indexed to: Approximately 150 of the smallest and most growthy of the S&P 600 companies
Expense ratio: 0.35
Average cap size: $1.6 billion
P/E ratio: 23.9

Top five holdings: Lannett Co, Take-Two Interactive Software Inc, Carrizo Oil & Gas, Taser International, Synergy Resources Corp

Russell's review: The price is higher than others in this category, and the promise of "purity" is a bit murky — especially if the quest for purity leads to high turnover, which could reduce tax efficiency. Guggenheim also seems to cater mostly to traders rather than to buy-and-hold investors, and that makes me uncomfortable. Traders usually trade themselves into losses. All that being said, the fund's first five years of existence have seen pretty good performance: about 1 percent a year higher than the Russell 2000 (small cap) Growth Index. That's on a before-tax basis, however.

Opting for Small Value: Diminutive Dazzlers

Don't let "small value" fool you. If you can stomach a bit of risk, these stocks can more than pull their weight. Don't take my word for it; consult history. On the way there, see Figure 4-2, which shows where small value fits into the investment style grid. And then, follow me as I explain the importance of small value stocks in a poised-for-performance ETF portfolio.

Small value stocks collectively have returned more to investors than have large value stocks or any kind of growth stocks. In fact, the difference in returns has been somewhat staggering: I'm talking about an annualized return of about 15 percent over the past 20 years for small value versus 11.6 percent for large value, 11.5 for large growth, and 10.7 for small growth. Compounded over time, the outperformance of small value stocks has been HUGE.

What are small value stocks? Some of the top holdings of the Vanguard Small-Cap Value ETF (VBR) include Snap-on Inc, Alaska Air, Gannett Co, Rite Aid, and Arthur J Gallagher & Co. Face it, there is not much excitement to be seen in companies such as Snap-on Inc. (Snap-on Inc manufactures and markets tools, equipment, diagnostics, and repair information and systems solutions for professional users worldwide.) And most of these companies aren't growing very fast.

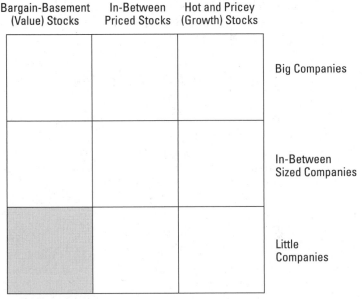

Bargain-Basement | In-Between | Hot and Pricey
(Value) Stocks | Priced Stocks | (Growth) Stocks

Big Companies

In-Between
Sized Companies

Little
Companies

© John Wiley & Sons, Inc.

Figure 4-2: Small value stocks occupy the southwest corner of the investment style grid.

As you go farther down the list of holdings, you'll likely find some companies in financial distress. Others may be facing serious lawsuits, expiration of patents, or labor unrest.

Welcome to the world of small value investing!

Latching on for fun and profit

To be sure, small value stocks are risky little suckers. Even the entire index (available to you in neat ETF form) is more volatile than any conservative investor may feel comfortable with. But as part — a very handsome part — of a diversified portfolio, a small value ETF can be a beautiful thing indeed.

If we knew the past was going to repeat, such as it did in the movie *Groundhog Day,* there'd be no reason to have anything but small value in your portfolio. But, of course, we don't know that the past will repeat. Bill Murray's radio alarm clock may not go off at sunrise. And the small value premium, like Bill Murray's hairline, may start to seriously recede. Still, the outperformance of small value has historically been so much greater than that of small growth that I favor a good tilt in the direction of value.

Keeping your balance

Whatever your total allocation to domestic small cap stocks, I recommend that anywhere from 60 to 75 percent of that amount be allocated to small value. But no more than that, please. If the value premium disappears or becomes a value discount, I don't want you left holding the bag. And even if small value continues to outperform, having both small value and small growth (along with their bigger cousins, all of which tend to rise and fall in different cycles) will help smooth out some of the inevitable volatility of holding stocks.

The best choices among small value ETFs include offerings from Vanguard and iShares. I also review an option from Guggenheim, which isn't terrible.

Vanguard Small Cap Value ETF (VBR)

Indexed to: MSCI U.S. Small Cap Value Index (about 1,000 small value domestic companies)
Expense ratio: 0.09 percent
Average cap size: $2.9 billion
P/E ratio: 16.6
Top five holdings: Snap-on Inc, Alaska Air, Gannett Co, Rite Aid, Arthur J Gallagher & Co
Russell's review: Low cost, wide diversification, tax efficiency beyond compare, and a very definite value lean — what's not to like? The Vanguard Small Cap Value ETF offers an excellent way to tap into this asset class. If you hold this fund at Vanguard, you get a bonus: You can trade with no commission.

iShares Morningstar Small Value Index (JKL)

Indexed to: Morningstar's Small Value Index (about 230 companies of modest size and modest stock price)
Expense ratio: 0.30 percent
Average cap size: $2.5 billion
P/E ratio: 15.0
Top five holdings: Office Depot, Health Net Inc, Retail Properties of America, JetBlue Airways, Validus Holdings
Russell's review: My only complaint with the Morningstar indexes is that they tend to be a bit too concentrated, at least in the large cap arena where a company like Exxon Mobil can

hold too much sway. In the Morningstar small cap indexes, that isn't a problem. The largest holding here, Office Depot, gets only a 0.83 allocation, which is fine and dandy. The expense ratio, too, is acceptable although higher than some others in this category. I like that Morningstar promises no crossover between growth and value. If you own this ETF along with the iShares Morningstar Small Growth Index, you should get pleasantly modest correlation. (In lay terms, if one fund gets slammed, the other may not.)

iShares S&P Small Cap 600 Value Index (IJS)

Indexed to: 457 of the S&P SmallCap 600 Value Index
Expense ratio: 0.25 percent
Average cap size: $1.3 billion
P/E ratio: 19.7
Top five holdings: Casey's General Stores, Stifel Financial Corp, Darling Ingredients Inc, Southwest Gas Corp, EMCOR Group, Inc.
Russell's review: S&P indexes are a bit too subjective for me to want to marry them. Nonetheless, this fund's price is reasonable, and there's no reason to entirely snub this iShares offering. (Marry it, but have a pre-nup. You may later decide that you'll do better elsewhere.) Oh, this fund also trades commission-free on the Fidelity platform.

Guggenheim S&P 600 Small Cap Pure Value (RZV)

Indexed to: S&P SmallCap Pure Value Index (approximately 150 of the most valuey and small of the S&P 600 companies)
Expense ratio: 0.35
Average cap size: $736 million
P/E ratio: 16.3
Top five holdings: Meadowbrook Insurance Group, Universal Corp, TTM Technologies, SkyWest Inc, Cash America International Inc.
Russell's review: The price is higher than others in this category, and the promise of "purity" is a bit murky, especially if that quest for purity leads to high turnover, which blows much of the tax efficiency. Guggenheim also seems to cater mostly to traders rather than buy-and-hold investors, which gives me something of a feeling of discomfort. Traders usually trade themselves into hamburger-eating misery. In addition, although the low P/E ratio is tantalizing, the smaller-than-small cap size makes me concerned. When cap size gets too small (and small caps start looking like micro caps), liquidity becomes an issue, and index funds can sometimes get hurt.

Chapter 5

Going Global: ETFs Without Borders

In This Chapter

▶ Understanding how global diversification lowers risk

▶ Calculating how much of your ETF portfolio to allocate overseas

▶ Deciding upon your investment destinations

▶ Choosing your best ETF options

▶ Knowing what to avoid and when to stay home

*I*f you were standing on a ship in the middle of the ocean (doesn't matter whether it's the Atlantic or Pacific), and you looked up and squinted real hard, you might see investment dollars sailing overhead. For about a decade, U.S. fund investors had been steadily adding money to the international side of their stock portfolios. In the past several years, some of that money has sailed back home.

Just to be clear: The terms *foreign* and *international* are used interchangeably to refer to stocks of companies outside of the United States. The word *global* refers to stocks of companies based anywhere in the world, including the United States.

Many investors have been moving to foreign stocks and back again for the same reason that they move into or out of any other kind of investment: They're lured by high returns and repelled by low returns.

As of the end of 2014, the 5-year annualized return of the U.S. stock market stood at about 15.5 percent. In sharp contrast, stocks of the world's developed-market nations outside of the U.S. clocked in with a rather lackluster 5.3 percent per year for the past half decade. Emerging-market nations showed an average return of about 2.1 percent.

But there have been other 5-year periods, including the one immediately prior, where foreign stocks have far outclocked U.S. stocks.

Most Americans are woefully under-invested abroad, especially after the past couple of years with money coming back from overseas. Industry tallies indicate that less than one-quarter of all the money Americans have invested in stocks is invested outside of the United States. I believe it should be double that. In this chapter, I explain my love for global diversification and reveal how you can accomplish it easily with ETFs.

The Ups and Downs of Different Markets around the World

If you expect U.S. stocks to continue to clock such phenomenal returns in relation to non-U.S. stocks, you are sure to be disappointed. If you expect European stock markets to sorely lag U.S. markets, as they have in the past few years, I think you may be similarly in for a surprise. In fact, there's pretty good reason to expect that foreign stocks overall may do better than U.S. stocks in the coming decade or two. But I certainly wouldn't bet the farm on international stocks outperforming U.S. stocks — or underperforming them, for that matter. The difference in returns in the future, as it has been in the long-term past, is not likely to be all that extreme.

In all likelihood, international stocks as a whole will have their day. U.S. stocks will then come up from behind. Then international stocks will have their day again. And then U.S. stocks will get the jump. This type of horse race has been going on since, oh, long before *Mr. Ed* was on the air.

The reason to invest abroad isn't primarily to try to outperform the Joneses . . . or the LeBlancs, or the Yamashitas. Rather, the purpose is to diversify your portfolio so as to capture overall stock market gains while tempering risk. You reduce risk whenever you own two or more asset classes that move up and down at different times. Stocks of different geographic regions tend to do exactly that.

Low correlation is the name of the game

Why, you may ask, do you need European and Japanese stocks when you already have all the lovely diversification discussed in past chapters: large, small, value, and growth stocks, and a good mix of industries? (See Chapter 3 if you need a reminder of what these terms mean.) The answer, *mon ami, mi amigo,* is quite simple: You get better diversification when you diversify across borders.

I'll use several iShares ETFs to illustrate my point. Suppose you have a wad of money invested in the iShares S&P 500 Growth Index fund (IVW), and you want to diversify:

- ✔ If you combine IVW with its large value counterpart, the iShares S&P 500 Value Index Fund (IVE), you find that your two investments have a five-year correlation of 0.92. In other words, over the past five years, the funds have had a tendency to move in the same direction 92 percent of the time. Only 8 percent of the time have they tended to move in opposite directions.

- ✔ If you combine IVW with the iShares S&P Small Cap 600 Growth Index Fund (IJT), you find that your two investments have tended to move up and down together roughly 91 percent of the time.

- ✔ If you combine IVW with the iShares S&P Small Cap 600 Value Index Fund (IJS), your investments tend to move north or south at the same time 86 percent of time. Not bad. But not great.

Now consider adding some Japanese stock to your original portfolio of large growth stocks. The iShares MSCI Japan Index Fund (EWJ) has tended to move in sync with large U.S. growth stocks only about 76 percent of the time. And the ETF that tracks the FTSE China 25 Index (FXI) has moved in the same direction as large cap U.S. growth stocks only 65 percent of the time. There's clearly more zig and zag when you cross oceans to invest, and that's what makes international investing a must for a well-balanced portfolio.

The increasing inter-dependence of the world's markets wrought by globalization may cause these correlation numbers to rise over time. Indeed, we saw in 2008 that in a global financial crisis, stocks markets around the world will suffer. The trend toward rising correlations has led some pundits to make the claim that diversification is dead. Sorry, those pundits are wrong. In down times, yes, stocks of different colors, here and abroad, tend to turn a depressing shade of gray together. When investors are nervous in New York, they are often nervous in Berlin. And Sydney. And Cape Town. That's been true for years. The great apple-cart-turnover of 2008 was a particular case in point. But even in 2008, it still paid to be diversified, as U.S. and foreign stocks recovered, and have been moving upward, at very different rates.

 Diversification lowers, but does not eliminate, stock-market risk. Never did. Never will. Your portfolio, in addition to being well-diversified, should also have some components, such as cash and bonds, that are less volatile than stocks.

Remember what happened to Japan

To just "stay home" on the stock side of your portfolio would be to exhibit the very same conceit seen among Japanese investors in 1990. If you recall, that's when the dynamic and seemingly all-powerful rising sun slipped and then sank. Japanese investors, holding domestically stuffed portfolios, bid *sayonara* to two-thirds of their wealth, which, more than two decades later, they have yet to fully recapture. (By year-end 2010, a basket of large-company Japanese stocks purchased in 1989 would have returned a very sad –1.3 percent a year over two full decades. Ouch.) It could happen here. Or worse.

Finding Your Best Mix of Domestic and International

 About 65 percent of the entire world stock market is now outside of the United States. Should you invest that much of your stock portfolio in foreign ETFs? No, I think that may be overdoing it. Many financial experts say 20 to 25 percent of your stock holdings should be international, but that was also their recommendation back when the United States represented more than half of the world's stock value. I think that percentage may be under-doing it today. I say that 40 to 50 percent of your stock portfolio should be international, and this section explains why.

Not too high

I see five distinct reasons to avoid overloading your portfolio to the tune of 65 percent foreign stocks:

✔ **Currency volatility:** When you invest abroad, you are usually investing in stocks that are denominated in other currencies. Because your foreign ETFs are denominated in Euros, Yen, or Pounds, they tend to be more volatile than the markets they represent. In other words, if European stock markets fall and the dollar rises (*vis-à-vis* the Euro) on the same day, your European ETF will fall doubly hard. If, however, the dollar falls on a day when the sun is shining on European stocks, your European ETF will soar.

Over the long run, individual currencies tend to go up and down. Although it could happen, it is unlikely that the dollar (or Euro) would rise or fall to such a degree — and stay there — that it would seriously affect your nest egg. Still, if this is a concern — and if you decide to invest very heavily in overseas stocks it might be — you can invest in dollar-hedged ETFs that eliminate currency volatility. I discuss these later in this chapter.

✔ **Inflation issues:** Another risk with going whole hog for foreign stock ETFs is that to a certain extent, your fortunes are tied to those of your home economy. Stocks tend to do best in a heated economy. But in a heated economy, we also tend to see inflation. Because of that correlation between general price inflation and stock inflation, stock investors are generally able to stay ahead of the inflation game. If you were to invest all your money in, say, England, and should the economy here take off while the economy there sits idly on the launch pad, you could be rocketed into Dickensian poverty.

✔ **Higher fees for foreign ETFs:** In the world of ETFs, the really good buys are to be had on the domestic side of the offerings. For whatever reason, global and international ETFs are about 50 percent more the price of broadly diversified U.S. ETFs. For example, while many Vanguard, Schwab, and Fidelity domestic ETFs carry management expenses of 0.10 percent or less, few foreign funds go that low.

✓ **Lower correlation with homegrown options:** Certain kinds of stock funds in the United States offer even lower correlation to the rest of the U.S. market than do many international stock funds, and I suggest leaving room in your portfolio for some of those. I discuss some of these industry-sector funds in Chapter 6. You may also want to make room for *market-neutral* funds.

✓ **A double tax hit:** Foreign governments almost always hit you up for taxes on any dividends paid by stocks of companies in their countries. You don't pay this tax directly, but it is taken from your fund holdings. If your funds are held in certain accounts, Uncle Sam may want your money too, and you wind up taking a double tax hit. This is a relatively minor reason not to go overboard. (Specifics on this tax, and how to avoid getting double-whammied, are in the sidebar at the end of this chapter.)

Not too low

Some well-publicized research indicates that an 80-percent-or-so domestic stock/20-percent-or-so foreign stock portfolio is optimal for maximizing return and minimizing risk. But almost all that research defines *domestic stock* as the S&P 500 and *foreign stock* as the MSCI EAFE. The MSCI EAFE is an index of mostly large companies in the developed world. (*MSCI* stands for Morgan Stanley Capital International, and *EAFE* stands for Europe, Australasia, and Far East.) This analysis takes little account of the fact that you are not limiting yourself to the S&P 500 or to the MSCI EAFE. In the real world, you have the option of adding many asset classes to your portfolio of U.S. stocks. And among your international holdings, you can include developed world stocks in Europe, Australia, and Japan; emerging market stocks in China, India, and elsewhere; and foreign stocks in any and all flavors of large, small, value, and growth.

Many investment pros know well — and several have even told me — that they favor a much larger international position than they publicly advocate. Some may be afraid of seeming unpatriotic. Much more prevalent is a certain lemming-over-the-cliff cover-my-ass mentality. If I, as your financial advisor, suggest a portfolio that resembles the S&P 500 and your portfolio tanks, you'll feel a bit peeved but you won't hate me. That's because all your friends' and neighbors' portfolios will have sunk as well. Should I give you a portfolio that's 50 percent foreign, and should foreign stocks have a bad year, you'll compare your portfolio to your friends' and neighbors' portfolios, and you may hate me. You may even sue me.

I wouldn't want that. Neither would most investment professionals. So most err on the side of caution and give you a portfolio that's more S&P 500 and less foreign — for their own protection, and not in the pursuit of your best interests.

Just right

By mixing and matching your domestic stock funds with 40 to 50 percent international, you will find your investment sweet spot. In Chapter 9, I pull together sample portfolios that use this methodology. Time and time again, I've run the numbers through the most sophisticated (and perhaps most expensive) professional portfolio analysis software available, and time and time again, 40-to-50-percent foreign is where I find the highest returns per unit of risk. And yes, this range has worked very well in the real world, too.

Although I try not to make forecasts because the markets are so incredibly unpredictable, I will say that if you had to err on the side of either U.S. or foreign stock investment, I would err on the side of too much foreign. The world economic and political climate is telling me that the U.S. stock market may be on relatively shakier ground. I could give you a long list of reasons (higher valuations on U.S. stocks [due to recent run-up of stock prices beyond corporate earnings growth], serious infrastructure issues [10 percent of our bridges are in need of repair], a big trade deficit, an aging population, a huge healthcare crisis), but what's most troubling about the United States is the extent to which it is becoming a nation of haves and have-nots. If history tells us anything, it is that great inequality leads eventually to dissension and upheaval.

As for me, personally, I eat my own international cooking: I have fully half of my own stock portfolio in foreign stocks — the vast majority of it held in ETFs.

Not All Foreign Nations — or Stocks — Are Created Equal

At present, you have more than 350 global and international ETFs from which to choose. (Once again, *global* ETFs hold U.S. as well as international stocks; *international* or *foreign* ETFs hold purely non-U.S. stocks.) I'd like you to consider the following half dozen factors when deciding which ones to invest in:

✔ **What's the correlation?** Certain economies are more closely linked to the U.S. economy than others, and the behavior of their stock markets reflects that. Canada, for example, offers limited diversification. Western Europe offers a bit more. For the least amount of correlation among developed nations, you want Japan (the world's second-largest stock market) or emerging market nations like Russia, Brazil, India, and China.

✔ **How large is the home market?** Although you can invest in individual countries, I generally wouldn't recommend it. Oh, I suppose you could slice and dice your portfolio to include 50 or so ETFs that represent individual countries (from Belgium to Austria and Singapore to Spain and, more recently, Vietnam to Poland), but that is going to be an awfully hard portfolio to manage. So why do it? Choose large regions in which to invest. (The only exceptions might be Japan and the United Kingdom, which have such large stock markets that they each qualify, in my mind, as a region.)

✔ **Think style.** If you have a large enough portfolio, consider dividing your international holdings into value and growth, large and small, just as you do with your domestic holdings. You can also divvy up your portfolio into global industry groupings. I discuss this strategy in Chapter 6. I generally prefer style diversification to sector diversification, but using both together can be truly powerful. You'll note that I take the combined approach in my sample portfolios in Part III of this book.

✔ **Consider your risk tolerance.** Developed countries (United Kingdom, France, Japan) tend to have less volatile stock markets than do emerging market nations (such as those of Latin America, the Middle East, China,

Russia, or India). You want both types of investments in your portfolio, but if you are inclined to invest in one much more than the other, know what you're getting into.

✔ **What's the bounce factor?** As with any other kind of investment, you can pretty safely assume that risk and return will have a close relationship over many years. Emerging market ETFs will likely be more volatile but, over the long run, more rewarding than ETFs that track the stock markets of developed nations. *One caveat:* Don't assume that countries with fast-growing economies will necessarily be the most profitable investments.

✔ **Look to P/E ratios.** How expensive is the stock compared to the earnings you're buying? You may ask yourself this question when buying a company stock, and it's just as valid a question when buying a nation's or a region's stocks. In general, a lower P/E ratio is more indicative of promising returns than is a high P/E ratio. (See Chapter 3 for a reminder of how to calculate a P/E ratio.)

Using ETFs as our proxies for world markets, we find that the Vanguard Total (U.S.) Stock Market ETF (VTI) currently has a P/E of about 19.7; the Vanguard European ETF (VGK) has a P/E of about 19; the Vanguard Pacific ETF (VPL) has a P/E of approximately 15.7; and the Vanguard Emerging Market ETF (VWO) also has a P/E of roughly 14. So it seems as if foreign stocks are currently the "value stocks" of the world.

You want your portfolio to include U.S., European, Pacific, and emerging market stocks, but if you are going to overweight any particular area, you may want to consider the relative P/E ratios, among other factors.

Choosing the Best International ETFs for Your Portfolio

Although I'm (obviously) a huge fan of international investing, and I believe that ETFs are the best way to achieve that end, there are only a dozen or so foreign ETFs that I think really fit the bill for most portfolios. This section introduces my favorites, complete with explanations of why I like them.

Note that I've split them up into three major categories: European, Pacific region, and emerging markets. For most portfolios, a reasonable split of foreign stock holdings would be something in the neighborhood of 40/40/20, with 40 percent going to Europe (England, France, Germany, Switzerland), 40 percent to the developed Pacific region (mostly Japan, with a smattering of Australia, New Zealand, and Singapore), and 20 percent to the emerging market nations (Brazil, Russia, Turkey, South Africa, Mexico, and a host of countries where the entire value of all outstanding stock may be far less than, say, Apple or Microsoft).

Four brands to choose from

The ETFs I discuss here by and large belong to four ETF families: Vanguard, BlackRock (iShares); Schwab; and BLDRS (pronounced "builders"), a small product line issued by Invesco PowerShares. Yes, there are other global and international ETFs from which to choose. I discuss some of your other options in the next chapter, where I turn to global stocks divvied up by industry sector. As for global stocks that fit into a regional- or style-based portfolio, those mentioned in this section are among your best bets.

BLDRS stands for "Baskets of Listed Depositary Receipts," which is a very fancy way of saying "foreign stocks that trade on American stock exchanges." Vanguard and iShares foreign ETFs also include some Depositary Receipts (often referred to as *ADRs* — the *A* is for "American") but are made up more of true foreign stocks. That is to say that they own mostly foreign stocks only traded on foreign exchanges. For you, the investor, these nuances don't matter much, if at all, if you are holding your stock ETFs for the long haul (which, of course, you are!). In the short run, however, "true" foreign stocks and ADRs may diverge somewhat in performance.

For more information on any of the international ETFs I discuss next, keep the following contact information handy:

✔ **Vanguard:** www.vanguard.com; 1-877-662-7447

✔ **BlackRock iShares:** www.ishares.com; 1-800-474-2737

✔ **BLDRS:** www.invescopowershares.com;
1-800-983-0903

✔ **Schwab:** www.schwab.com; 1-866-232-9890

✔ **WisdomTree:** www.wisdomtree; 1-866-909-9473

All the world's your apple: ETFs that cover the planet

If you have a portfolio of under $10,000, or if you have a strong desire to keep your investment management simple, you may be best off combining one of the total-market U.S. funds I discuss in Chapter 3 with a total international fund, the best of which are the Vanguard FTSE All-World ex-US ETF (VEU) and the Schwab International Equity ETF (SCHF). Both of these funds give you instant exposure to everything in the world of stocks, minus U.S. investments. Both ETFs are ultra low-cost (0.08 percent for Schwab, and 0.14 percent for Vanguard), well-diversified, and tax-efficient. The iShares MSCI ACWI (All Country World Index) ex US Index (ACWX) is also a perfectly acceptable option, although it will cost you 0.33 percent a year.

If you *really* want to keep things simple, you can buy a single ETF that tracks an index of all stocks everywhere, U.S. and foreign. That one fund would be the Vanguard Total World Stock ETF (VT), with an expense ratio of 0.17 percent, or the iShares MSCI ACWI Index Fund ETF (ACWI), with an expense ratio of 0.33 percent. Both are perfectly fine options. These indexed ETFs, like practically all others, are self-adjusting. That is, if your goal is to own a single global fund that reflects each country's percentage of the global economy, as that percentage grows or shrinks, so will its representation in these ETFs. Easy!

And if you *really, really* want simplicity — stocks and bonds and the kitchen sink, all in one package — see the end of Chapter 6 for suggestions.

If you have a portfolio larger than $10,000 and you are okay with adjusting its alignment (via rebalancing) once a year or so, I suggest that you keep your stocks and bonds in separate funds and that you furthermore break down your stock holdings into U.S. and non-U.S. Then, just as I have advised for your domestic stocks, assign your foreign holdings to each of at least three categories.

If you've read Chapters 3 and 4, you know that my preferred way to split up your U.S. stock holdings is by style: large growth, large value, small growth, and small value. On the international side, alas, such a breakdown is difficult to achieve. I'm not sure why the ETF purveyors have not given us international stocks in four neat styles, but they haven't. That's okay. You can slice the pie into regions: European, Pacific, and emerging markets. Or slice it into large value, large growth, and small cap.

I help you weigh the options in the pages that follow. In Part III, you'll see how both means of diversification can be used to build sample portfolios.

European stock ETFs

Europe boasts the oldest, most established stock markets in the world: the Netherlands, 1611; Germany, 1685; and the United Kingdom, 1698. Relative to the stocks of the United States, European stocks, as a whole, are seemingly low-priced (going by their P/E ratios, anyway).

Europe's strengths include political stability (for the most part), an educated workforce, and a confederation of national economies, making for the world's largest single market. Germany, the largest economy in Europe, has been growing its export industry faster than any nation on the planet.

Europe's great weaknesses include a persistently high rate of unemployment (outside of Germany); a rapidly aging population; and a few member nations, most notably Greece and Portugal (and to a lesser extent Spain, Italy, and Ireland), whose governments have racked up some very serious debt. These nations are collectively — and none too flat-teringly — known as the "PIGS" (**P**ortugal, **I**reland, **G**reece, **S**pain) or sometimes "PIIGS" (with **I**taly thrown in).

Even with its weaknesses on full display, the European market definitely deserves a piece of your portfolio. The ETFs I present here are good options to consider when you make that investment.

Vanguard MSCI Europe ETF (VGK)

Indexed to: MSCI Europe Index, which tracks approximately 465 companies in 16 European nations
Expense ratio: 0.12 percent
Top five country holdings: United Kingdom, France, Germany, Switzerland, Spain
Russell's review: This ETF has everything going for it: low cost, good diversification, and tax efficiency. You can't go wrong (unless the European stock market falters, which, of course, could happen). The mix of many nations and currencies (Euro, British Pound, Swiss Franc, Swedish Krona) gives this fund an especially good balance and an especially good way to help protect your portfolio from any single-country (or currency) collapse. Like all Vanguard ETFs, VGK trades free of commission if held at Vanguard.

BLDRS Europe 100 ADR (ADRU)

Indexed to: The Bank of New York Mellon Europe 100 ADR Index, a market-weighted basket of 100 European market-based ADRs (American Depositary Receipts) representing the United Kingdom (about half the money pot) and major nations of the European continent, in addition to, for some unknown reason, Israel
Expense ratio: 0.30 percent
Top five country holdings: United Kingdom, Switzerland, France, Spain, Germany
Russell's review: Not as diverse as the Vanguard European ETF, but with 100 stocks, it's plenty diverse enough. The yearly expense ratio is about midway between the Vanguard European offering and the iShares Europe offering. All told, the BLDRS Europe is a good choice, although it may not be the best. (That, as is so typically the case, would be Vanguard.)

iShares S&P Europe 350 (IEV)

Indexed to: Standard & Poor's Europe 350 Index, a collection of 350 large cap companies in 16 European countries
Expense ratio: 0.60 percent
Top five country holdings: United Kingdom, France, Germany, Switzerland, Spain

Russell's review: I really like iShares domestic offerings, and their foreign ETFs aren't bad products — not at all. The diversification is excellent. The indexes make sense. The tax efficiency is top notch. I only wish the darned things didn't cost so much. At five times the cost of the Vanguard European offering, IEV just isn't anything to write home about.

Pacific region stock ETFs

The nations of the Pacific have evidenced a good comeback in recent years. With the rapid growth of China as the world's apparent soon-to-be largest consumer, surrounding nations may bask in economic glory. Australia, in particular, has benefited greatly from the recent run-up in prices for natural resources caused in part by Chinese demand. And Japan still leads the world in labor productivity, despite some obvious economic challenges (such as a serious real-estate collapse and a level of debt greater than that of any other major nation). On the other hand, the threat posed by North Korea, the tensions between China and Taiwan, and the presence of nuclear weapons in unfriendly neighbors India and Pakistan loom like black clouds over the region.

But black clouds and all, the Pacific region merits a chunk of any balanced portfolio. Investing that chunk can be fairly easy; start by considering the ETF options laid out here.

Vanguard Pacific ETF (VPL)

Indexed to: MSCI Pacific Index, which follows roughly 500 companies in five Pacific region nations
Expense ratio: 0.12 percent
Top five country holdings: Japan, Australia, Hong Kong, Singapore, New Zealand
Russell's review: The cost can't be beat. And 500 companies certainly allows for good diversification. As with all Vanguard funds, tax efficiency is tops. Japan — the world's second-largest stock market — makes up two-thirds of this fund, considerably more than the BLDRS Asia 50. I have a preference for VPL over all other Pacific options. If you hold this ETF at Vanguard, you'll pay no commission to buy or sell.

BLDRS Asia 50 ADR (ADRA)

Indexed to: The Bank of New York Mellon Asia 50 ADR Index, a market-weighted basket of 50 Asian market-based ADRs representing a total of 8 countries. (Japan accounts for 44 percent of the pie.)

Expense ratio: 0.30 percent

Top five country holdings: Japan, Australia, China, Taiwan, India

Russell's review: The cost is higher than Vanguard's Pacific ETF, and you're tapping into fewer companies. Still, 50 companies isn't bad diversification. This fund also gives a bit more weight to non-Japan stock markets, which may be a good thing — although note that some of the countries represented are clearly emerging market nations. If you use ADRA, you'll want to factor that fact into your overall portfolio analysis. All in all, ADRA is a good investment, although if you bent my arm to choose between it and VPL, I'd probably choose the Vanguard ETF.

iShares MSCI Japan (EWJ)

Indexed to: MSCI Japan Index, representing approximately 340 of Japan's largest companies

Expense ratio: 0.48 percent

Top five country holdings: Just Japan here

Russell's review: For the life of me, I can't understand why iShares doesn't offer a Pacific region ETF. If you want the equivalent of either the BLDRS or Vanguard Pacific ETFs, you need to buy at least two iShares ETFs: the MSCI Japan and the MSCI Pacific ex-Japan (EPP). That's a doable option for larger portfolios, but with a cost ratio several times greater than Vanguard's, I'm not sure I see the point.

Emerging-market stock ETFs

Called "emerging market" nations when economists are feeling optimistic, these same countries are also sometimes referred to as the Third World or, even more to the point, "poor countries." As I write these words, the recent lackluster returns of emerging market stocks are due in good part to sharp falls in the prices of commodities, such as oil, which come largely from these nations. But commodity prices fluctuate greatly. And political unrest, corruption, and overpopulation, as well as serious environmental challenges, plague many of these countries.

On the other hand, emerging market stocks are perhaps underpriced. Many emerging economies seem especially strong. Ironically, a good number have considerably less debt than Western nations. And — perhaps most importantly — these countries have young populations. Children tend to grow up to be workers, consumers, and perhaps even investors. Future growth seems very likely.

Vanguard MSCI Emerging Market ETF (VWO)

Indexed to: The MSCI Emerging Markets Index, which tracks roughly 1,000 companies in 23 emerging market nations
Expense ratio: 0.15 percent
Top five country holdings: China, Brazil, Korea, Taiwan, South Africa
Russell's review: There's no better way that I know to capture the potential growth of emerging market stocks than through VWO. The cost is the lowest in the pack, and the diversity of investments is more than adequate.

BLDRS Emerging Markets 50 ADR (ADRE)

Indexed to: The Bank of New York Mellon Emerging Markets 50 ADR Index, a market-weighted basket of 50 emerging market–based ADRs
Expense ratio: 0.30 percent
Top five country holdings: Brazil, China, Taiwan, South Korea, India
Russell's review: Yeah, 50 companies falls way short of Vanguard's 1,000, but 50 companies is still enough to give you pretty good diversification. I have no problem whatsoever recommending this ETF as a way to tap into emerging markets, although I do have a wee preference, once again, for Vanguard. Note that there is some overlap in the countries represented by this fund and the BLDRS Asia fund.

iShares MSCI Emerging Markets (EEM)

Indexed to: MSCI Emerging Markets Index, a basket of approximately 860 companies in 20 emerging market nations
Expense ratio: 0.68 percent

Top five country holdings: China, Brazil, South Korea, Taiwan, South Africa
Russell's review: Good fund. Good company. Good index. If it weren't more than four times the price of some of the other options in this area, I'd jump to recommend it.

iShares value and growth

Studies show that the same *value premium* — the tendency for value stocks to outperform growth stocks — that seemingly exists here in the United States can be found around the world. Therefore, I suggest a mild tilt toward value in your international stock portfolio, just as I recommend for your domestic portfolio.

You can accomplish this tilt easily by using the iShares MSCI EAFE Value Index (EFV) along with the iShares MSCI EAFE Growth Index (EFG).

Using these two funds together — allotting perhaps 55 to 60 percent to the value fund and 40 to 45 percent to growth — will give you full exposure to large cap, developed nation stocks. You still want to allocate some of your portfolio to emerging markets and to small cap international stocks.

Or, if you've already decided to split your international stocks up by regions — Europe, Pacific, emerging market — then adding a bit of EFV can give you the value lean you seek.

iShares MSCI EAFE Value Index (EFV)

Indexed to: MSCI EAFE Value Index, which is made up of approximately 500 large value companies of developed world nations, with about 40 percent of the fund's net assets in either Japan or the United Kingdom, the second and third largest equity markets on the planet
Expense ratio: 0.40 percent
Top five country holdings: Japan, United Kingdom, Switzerland, Germany, France
Russell's review: It's the only fund of its kind, and I'm greatly appreciative that it exists. It's a bit costly when compared to the Vanguard funds but still considerably less than most of the other international iShares options.

iShares MSCI EAFE Growth Index (EFG)

Indexed to: MSCI EAFE Growth Index, which is made up of approximately 560 large growth companies of the developed world nations, with about 44 percent of the fund's money invested in the United Kingdom and Japan, the second and third largest stock markets
Expense ratio: 0.40 percent
Top five country holdings: United Kingdom, Japan, Switzerland, Australia, Germany
Russell's review: Like EFV, this international growth fund is the only one of its kind. I'm grateful for its existence, and I'm grateful that iShares has kept the expense ratio lower than what it charges for most of its other international funds.

WisdomTree currency hedged funds

If you wish to dampen the volatility of your foreign stock holdings, you can opt to own funds that specifically eliminate or "hedge" against currently flux.

This may not be a bad idea if you are especially risk-averse and if you are heavily invested overseas.

But know that hedging will cost you.

WisdomTree Investments currently has a lineup of 14 currency-hedging ETFs, such as the WisdomTree Europe Hedged Equity ETF (HEDJ) and the WisdomTree Europe Small-Cap Hedged Equity ETF (EUSC). Both of these charge 0.58 percent a year in management fees.

Other WisdomTree offerings allow you to invest in the United Kingdom, Japan and Germany, eliminating any risk that the British Pound, Japanese Yen, or the Euro will fall in relation to the dollar, resulting in depressed returns.

But know, in addition to the cost of these funds, that you will also be lowering your take-home should these currencies rise against the dollar. If that's the case, you'll be wishing you were invested in non-hedged funds.

Small cap international

Small cap international stocks have even less correlation to the U.S. stock market than larger foreign stocks. The reason is simple: If the U.S. economy takes a swan dive, it will seriously hurt conglomerates — Nestle, Toyota, and British Petroleum, for example — that serve the U.S. market, regardless of where their corporate headquarters are located. A fall in the U.S. economy and U.S. stock market is less likely to affect smaller foreign corporations that sell mostly within their national borders.

Regardless of the investment vehicle you choose, I suggest that a good chunk of your international stock holdings — perhaps as much as 50 percent, if you can stomach the volatility — go to small cap holdings. The two ETFs I'd like you to consider are from Vanguard and iShares. Note that there are considerable differences between the two.

Vanguard FTSE All-World ex-US Small Cap Index (VSS)

Indexed to: The FTSE Global Small Cap ex-US Index, which tracks more than 3,000 small cap company stocks in both developed nations (76 percent of the stocks) and emerging markets (24 percent)
Expense ratio: 0.19percent
Top five country holdings: Canada, United Kingdom, Japan, Taiwan, Australia
Russell's review: For exposure to small cap international, you aren't going to find a less expensive or more diversified avenue. This fund trades commission-free if held at Vanguard.

iShares MSCI EAFE Small Cap Index (SCZ)

Indexed to: The MSCI EAFE Small Cap Index, which tracks more than 2,300 stocks from developed market nations other than the United States
Expense ratio: 0.40 percent
Top five country holdings: Japan, United Kingdom, Australia, Germany, Switzerland

Russell's review: Although more expensive than the Vanguard offering, this fund is still a good choice for international small cap exposure. Note, however, that unlike the Vanguard ETF, SCZ does not allocate any portion of its portfolio to emerging markets. If you own SCZ and you want that exposure, you might consider a modest position in one of a handful of small cap emerging market ETFs, such as the SPDR S&P Emerging Markets Small Cap (EWX) or the WisdomTree Emerging Markets SmallCap Dividend ETF (DGS).

A word on foreign taxes

If you are buying both a foreign and a domestic ETF, with one going into a taxable account and the other into your IRA, Roth IRA, or other tax-deferred retirement plan, choose the foreign fund for the taxable account and plug the domestic fund into your tax-deferred account. That's because many foreign countries will slap you with a withholding tax on your dividends, which you can write off only in a taxable account.

Typically, such a tax may be 15 percent. (If you invest, say, $30,000 in a foreign fund with a dividend yield of 3 percent, you'll be losing $135 a year to foreign taxes.) If the foreign ETF is in a non-retirement account, your brokerage house will likely supply you with a year-end statement noting the foreign tax paid. You can then write that amount off in full against your U.S. taxes. (See line 43 of your friendly IRS Form 1040.) If the foreign fund is held in your retirement account, however, no year-end statement, no write-off; you eat the loss.

Chapter 6

Sector Investing and Specialized Stocks

In This Chapter

▶ Weighing the pros and cons of sector and style investing

▶ Listing the ETFs that work best for sector investing

▶ Choosing the best options for your portfolio

▶ Unearthing some facts about socially responsible investing

▶ Determining the potential payoff of dividend and other funds

Despite the firm convictions of zealots on both sides, style investing (large/small/growth/value) and sector investing (technology/utilities/healthcare/energy) can, and sometimes do, exist very peacefully side-by-side.

In this chapter, I present the nuts and bolts of sector investing: how it can function alone, or in conjunction with style investing, to provide diversity both on the domestic and international sides of your portfolio (or overlapping the two). However you decide to slice the pie (whether by style and/or sector), using ETFs as building blocks makes for an excellent strategy. (Hmm, am I starting to sound like a zealot myself?)

I also introduce a few stock ETFs that don't fit into any of the categories I discuss in previous chapters. They are neither growth nor value, large nor small. They are not industry sector funds, nor are they international. If ETFs were ice cream, the funds presented here would not represent chocolate and vanilla, but rather, the outliers on the Baskin Robbins menu: Turtle Cheesecake, Tiramisu, No Sugar Added Chocolate Chip, Pink Bubblegum, and Wild 'N Reckless (a swirl of green apple, blue raspberry, and fruit punch sherbets).

Selecting Stocks by Sector, Not Style

As of this writing, there are about 250 U.S. industry-sector ETFs. You can find a fund to mirror each of the major industry sectors in the U.S. economy: energy, basic materials, financial services, consumer goods, and so on.

No standard methodology exists for breaking up the U.S. industry into sectors; MSCI does it one way, and S&P does it a slightly different way. Some ETFs mirror subsections of the economy, such as semiconductors (a subset of information technology) and biotechnology (a subset of healthcare). In some cases, subsectors of the economy you may not even know exist — such as nanotech, cloud computing, and water resources — are represented with ETFs!

A good number of newer ETFs allow you to invest in industry sectors in foreign countries or in *global* industries (which is to say U.S. and foreign countries together). About 200 international and global sector ETFs are available.

Certain ETFs — such as the PowerShares S&P SmallCap Industrials Portfolio ETF (PSCI) or the PowerShares S&P SmallCap Health Care Portfolio ETF (PSCH) — allow you to invest in industry sectors *and* styles at the same time.

And finally, the living proof that you can, if you so wish, slice and dice a portfolio to ultimate death: You can even find some ETFs that allow you to buy into a particular industry within a particular country. Examples include the Global X Brazil Financials ETF (BRAF) and Global X China Materials ETF (CHIM). WisdomTree goes even a step further! You can purchase an ETF that allows you to buy into an industry within a country, and then you can pay to have the company eliminate ("hedge") currency risk. One example would be the WisdomTree Japan Hedged Real Estate ETF (DXJR). Unless you have a really compelling reason to purchase such a specialized fund (and pay the hefty expenses and subject your portfolio to excess concentration), I suggest you don't.

Calculating your optimal mix

If you are going to go the sector route and build your entire stock portfolio, or a good part of it, out of industry-sector ETFs, I suggest that you make sure you can have allocations to all or most major sectors of the economy.

Some advisors would tell you to keep your allocations roughly proportionate to each sector's share of the broad market. I think that's decent advice, with just a bit of caution: Had you taken that approach in 1999, your portfolio would have been chocked to the top with technology, given the gross overpricing of the sector at that point. (And you would have taken a bath the following year.) I'd suggest that no matter what sectors are hot at the moment, no single sector should ever make up more than 20 percent of your stock portfolio.

 Start perhaps with roughly allocating your sector-based portfolio according to the market cap of each sector, and then tweak from there — based not on crystal ball predictions of the future but on the unique characteristics of each sector. What do I mean? Read on.

Seeking risk adjustment with high and low volatility sectors

Some industry sectors have historically evidenced greater return and greater risk. (Return and risk tend to go hand-in-hand, as I discuss in Chapter 10.) The same rules that apply to style investing apply to sector investing. Know how much volatility you can stomach, and then, and only then, build your portfolio in tune with your risk tolerance.

As for historical risk and return, keep in mind that *any* single sector — even utilities, the least volatile of all — will tend to be more volatile than the entire market because there is little diversification. Don't overindulge!

Finally, know that your allocation between bonds and stocks will almost certainly have much more bearing on your overall level of risk and return than will your mix of stocks. In Chapter 7, I introduce bonds and discuss how an ETF investor should hold them.

Knowing where the style grid comes through

There is nothing wrong with dividing up a stock portfolio into industry sectors, but please don't be hasty in scrapping style investing. I really believe that if you're going to pick one strategy over the other, the edge goes to style investing. For one thing, we know that it works. Style investing helps to diffuse (but not eliminate) risk. Scads of data show that.

In addition, style investing allows you to take advantage of years of other data that indicate you can goose returns without raising your risk, or raising it by much, by leaning your portfolio toward value and small cap (see Chapters 3 and 4). When you invest in industry sectors through ETFs, you are most often investing the vast majority of your funds in large caps, and you're usually splitting growth and value evenly. That approach may limit your investment success.

Another reason ETF investors shouldn't scrap style investing: Style ETFs are the cheaper choice. For whatever reason (yes, another one of those eternal mysteries that keeps me awake at night), style ETFs tend to cost much less than industry-sector ETFs. On average, they're about half the cost.

And one final reason to prefer style to sector for the core of your portfolio: You will require fewer funds. With large growth, large value, small growth, and small value, you pretty much can capture the entire stock market. With sector funds, you need a dozen or so funds to achieve the same effect. Each sector fund offers minimal diversification because the price movements of companies in the same industry sector tend to be closely correlated.

Seeking low correlations for added diversification

Some sectors, or industry subsectors, even though they are part of the stock market, tend to move out of lockstep with the rest of the market. By way of example, consider REITs: real estate investment trusts. I tell you about REITS and REIT ETFs in Chapter 8.

Another sector that fits the bill, at least of late, is energy. Yes, Exxon Mobil and Chevron are part of the entire market, but they tend to zig when everything else zags (in part because when the price of oil rises, these companies profit more, while the rest of the economy, at least outside of Texas, suffers).

For example, consider that in 2002, when the total U.S. stock market tanked by almost 11 percent, REITs were up 31 percent. The year 2005 was pretty lackluster for the total stock market, yet energy stocks were up 31 percent.

Of course, there are years when it works the other way, and these sectors may fall way short of the overall market. In Chapter 9, where I draw up some sample portfolios, you see more of REITs, energy, and basic materials.

 If you decide to build your portfolio around industry sector funds, I urge you at the very least to dip into the style funds to give yourself the value/small cap tilt that I discuss in Chapters 3 and 4. That's especially true if you use SPDRs to build your sector portfolio. This fund group is especially weighted toward large cap. Again, in Chapter 9, I offer a few sample portfolios to illustrate workable allocations.

Sector Choices by the Dozen

After you decide which industry sectors you wish to invest in, you need to pick and choose among ETFs. Blackrock's iShares offers about 40 U.S. selections and 40 global or international selections. PowerShares has about 50 domestic and a dozen international sector funds. State Street Global Advisors offers about two dozen SPDRs that cover U.S. industry sectors and nearly as many that cover international and global markets. Vanguard has 11 U.S. sector funds and one international. And there are other players, too.

Begin your sector selection here:

> ✔ **Do you want representation in large industry sectors (healthcare, technology, utilities)?** Your options include Vanguard ETFs, Blackrock's iShares, State Street Global Advisors Select Sector SPDRs, as well as funds from Fidelity, First Trust, Global X, Jefferies, Market Vectors, PowerShares, and WisdomTree.

> ✔ **Do you want to zero in on narrow industry niches (insurance, oil service, nanotech)?** Consider PowerShares, First Trust, or Market Vectors ETFs.
>
> ✔ **Are you looking for sometimes ridiculously narrow industry niches (aluminum) or sectors within sectors within small countries?** You should look at EGShares, Global X, and Guggenheim ETFs.
>
> ✔ **Do you want to keep your expense ratios to a minimum?** Vanguard's ETFs, the State Street Global Advisors Select Sector SPDRs, and FocusShares from Scottrade tend to cost the least.

Specialized Stock ETFs: Investing for a Better World

Increasingly, individuals and institutions are investing using some kind of moral compass. The investments are screened not only for potential profitability but for social, environmental, and even biblical factors as well. Some screens, for example, attempt to eliminate all companies that profit from tobacco or weapons of mass destruction. Others try to block out the worst-polluting companies, or companies that use child labor in countries that have no effective child labor laws.

The total amount of money invested in socially screened portfolios (which include more than 100 mutual funds, certain state and city pension funds, union and church monies, some university endowments, and, as of recently, two dozen or so ETFs) has grown from about $1 trillion in 1997 to an estimated $4 trillion or so today.

Many of the funds that call themselves socially responsible (otherwise known as *SRI funds* – the *I* stands for "investment") not only invest with a purpose but also use their financial muscle to lobby companies to become better world citizens. The movement's greatest victory to date may have been the role it played in ending apartheid in South Africa. SRI seems to have had some impact on corporate America as well, most notably by pushing certain auto, oil, and utility companies to research ways to reduce emissions of greenhouse gasses. Other victories include a nationwide ban on mercury thermometers and commitments from various corporations to start recycling programs, reduce toxic waste emissions, and end discrimination against employees based on their sexual orientation.

Tracking the history of SRI performance

Over the past decade or so, the collective performance of socially responsible mutual funds has been very similar to that of all other mutual funds. It could be argued that a tie should be resolved in favor of socially responsible investing. If one can achieve market returns while at the same time prodding companies to improve their behavior, why not do that?

What about the specific performance of the socially responsible ETFs? To be blunt, they haven't been around long enough for their collective performance record to count for much. And, of course, performance is only one factor I look at when deciding whether to recommend an ETF.

Your growing number of choices for social investing

The growing number of ETFs designed to appeal to your conscience spans the spectrum from U.S. to foreign to *global* (foreign and U.S. combined). There are ETFs that emphasize environmental awareness, social responsibility, clean energy, and more. Here are just a handful of examples:

> ✔ **ETFs focused on social issues:** Among domestic ETFs aiming to show commitment to broad social issues are these:
>
>> • iShares KLD 400 Social Index ETF (DSI)
>>
>> • iShares MSCI USA ESG Select (KLD)
>>
>> • Workplace Equality ETF (EQLT)

Funds that invest in global stocks focused on clean energy include:

- Market Vectors Global Alternative Energy ETF (GEX)
- Market Vectors Solar Energy ETF (KWT)
- PowerShares Global Clean Energy ETF (PBD)
- Guggenheim Solar ETF (TAN)

 If you want to invest for a better world and a better portfolio, I suggest you do additional research. One person's idea of socially responsible may be very different from another's. What works for one portfolio may not work for another. There's a ton of information on the website of the Forum for Sustainable and Responsible Investment: `www.ussif.org`.

 If you decide to invest in an SRI fund, I urge you to review a fund's statement of values before investing. Otherwise, you could end up investing at cross purposes with your own values.

Dividend Funds: The Search for Steady Money

To many investors, the thought of regular cash payments is a definite turn-on. Always willing to oblige, the financial industry of late has been churning out "high dividend" funds — both mutual funds and ETFs — like there's no tomorrow. These funds attempt to cobble together the stocks of companies that are issuing high dividends, have high dividend growth rates, or promise future high dividends. In this section, I spell out some of the high dividend ETF options and then debate the value of investing in them.

Your high dividend ETF options

The oldest and largest of the ETF dividend funds is the iShares Dow Jones Select Dividend Index Fund (DVY). For U.S. domestic investments, here are some other options:

- SPDR Dividend ETF (SDY)
- Vanguard Dividend Appreciation ETF (VIG)

✔ First Trust Morningstar Dividend Leaders Index Fund (FDL)

✔ PowerShares Dividend Achievers Portfolio (PFM)

✔ PowerShares High Yield Equity Dividend Achievers Portfolio (PEY)

Why *two* PowerShares domestic dividend ETFs? The first one (PFM) "seeks to identify a diversified group of dividend paying companies." The second one (PEY) "seeks to deliver high current dividend income and capital appreciation." (A third, the PowerShares High Growth Rate Dividend Achievers Portfolios [PHJ], sought "to identify companies with the highest ten-year annual dividend growth rate," but that ETF has been closed.) If you're having a hard time telling these dividend funds apart based on their descriptions, you aren't alone. I'm confused as heck!

And if your choices on the U.S. front aren't enough — or aren't confusing enough — you could also go with the PowerShares International Dividend Achievers Portfolio (PID), which "seeks international companies that have increased their annual dividend for five or more consecutive fiscal years."

And if *that* weren't enough choice (or confusion), the newest among the dividend-crazed pack, WisdomTree, offers a broad array of high dividend funds . . . with every wrinkle or sub-wrinkle imaginable.

In a way, seeking dividends makes sense. In another, larger way, the logic is a bit loopy, just as the marketing (sort of like toilet paper and breakfast cereal marketing) is a bit intense and sometimes silly. I explain in the next section.

Promise of riches or smoke and mirrors?

Dividends! Dividends! On the face of it, they look like free money. But nothing in life is quite so simple. Here are the typical arguments for buying a high dividend fund, along with my retort to each:

Argument for dividends #1: Steady money is just like honey.

Huh? Are you crazy, Russell? Who in his right mind wouldn't want dividends? A stock that pays dividends is *obviously* more valuable than a stock that doesn't pay dividends. If I buy a high dividend ETF, my account balance will grow every month.

Retort: Suppose you own an individual share of stock in the McDummy Corporation (ticker MCDM), and MCDM issues a dividend of $1. The market price of your one share of MCDM, as a rule, will fall by $1 as soon as the McDummy Corporation sends out the dividend. That's because the dividend comes from the company's cash reserves, and as those cash reserves diminish, the value of the McDummy Corporation diminishes (just as it would if it gave away, say, 100 plastic pink flamingoes from the front lawn of its corporate headquarters, or any other asset for that matter). As the value of the company diminishes, so too does the value of its shares. And the very same holds true for every stock held in an ETF.

Argument for dividends #2: They lower my tax hit.

Suppose I need a steady stream of income? Isn't it better that I rely on dividends, which are generally taxed at 15, maybe 20 percent, instead of interest from bonds or CDs, which is taxed at my higher income tax rate?

First retort: First, if you need a steady stream of income, nothing is stopping you from creating *artificial dividends* by selling off any security you like. You may pay capital gains tax, but that will be no higher than the tax on dividends. In the end, whether you pull $1,000 from your account in the form of recently issued dividends or $1,000 from the sale of a security, you are withdrawing the same amount. And what if one month you find you don't need the income? You can sell nothing and pay no tax, whereas with a high dividend ETF, you'll pay the tax regardless.

Second retort: If you're really concerned about taxes, maybe you should be investing in tax-free municipal bonds.

Argument for dividends #3: Taxes, what taxes?

Russell, what gives? If I invest in an ETF, I won't have to worry about taxes because, as you've told us all along, ETFs are incredibly tax efficient.

Retort: ETFs are head-and-shoulders above most mutual funds when it comes to tax efficiency, but that tax efficiency is aimed at reducing taxable capital gains, not dividends. An ETF can't do a whole lot to lessen the tax hit from dividends. ETF or mutual fund, you'll pay.

Argument for dividends #4: It's a new world!

Russell, you sound like a stick in the mud. This is an exciting new development in the world of investments.

Retort: New development? Really? Equity income funds have been around for years and years, and they haven't exactly set the world on fire. And consider the age-old *Dogs of the Dow* strategy. Many people have believed that if every year you purchase the ten highest-paying dividend stocks in the Dow (the so-called *Dogs*), you can rack up serious returns. The strategy has been well studied, and it clearly isn't as powerful as the hype. The Dogs do seem to have some bark, but no more so than any other similarly sized and similarly volatile stocks. In other words, put a value lean on your portfolio, as I suggest in numerous places throughout this book (see especially Chapters 3 and 4), and you'll be getting plenty of dividends and much of the edge that high dividend investors seek.

Argument for dividends #5: Don't you read history?

Over the course of history, Russell, much of the stock market's returns have come from dividends.

Retort: Yeah, so? During the longest bull market in history — the 1990s — stock market returns were running double digits a year, and very little was being shelled out in dividends. A company that isn't paying dividends is either investing its cash in operations or buying back its own stock. Either way, shareholders stand to gain. Just because much of the stock market's past returns have come from dividends doesn't mean that future returns must or will come from the same source.

Argument for dividends #6: Dividends offer protection.

Stocks that pay high dividends are going to be less risky than stocks that don't. Those dividends create a floor, even if only psychologically. High-dividend-paying stocks cannot become worthless.

Retort: Studies of high-dividend-paying stocks reveal that they actually tend to be somewhat *more* volatile than the broad market. Go figure. Besides, if your main goal is to temper risk, you have other, more effective, ways of doing that. (See Chapter 7 on bonds.)

Argument for dividends #7: But still, it can't hurt.

All right, I concede, maybe these funds aren't the greatest thing since sliced bread. Still, can it hurt to buy one?

Retort: Look, I don't *despise* these funds. Far from it. If you want to buy one, buy one. Buy two. Put them into your retirement account, if there's room in there, and you won't even have to worry about any tax on the dividends. But don't assume that you're going to beat the broad market over the long haul. And know that you are buying funds that are mostly large value stocks, typically within just a handful of industries (notably pharmaceuticals, banks, utilities, and consumer staples). Your risk may be greater than you think. And if dividend-paying stocks are incredibly hot at the moment (as they are while I write these words), be aware that their prices may be inflated.

Investing in Initial Public Offerings

Want to take a real joyride? In April 2006, First Trust Advisors introduced the First Trust IPOX-100 Index Fund (FPX). You can invest in an ETF that, according to the prospectus, tracks the 100 "largest, typically best performing, and most liquid initial public offerings" in the United States.

Just prior to the introduction of the fund, the index on which it is based clocked a three-year annualized return of 33.74 percent. Needless to say, with that kind of return, this new ETF got the attention of a good number of investors. Those who jumped on board didn't exactly have a smooth ride. When the market tanked in 2008, FPX lost 43.79 percent — almost 7 percentage points more than the S&P 500 lost. Ooooh, the pain. But in 2009, this fund gained 44.56 percent, and as of this writing, it has continued to outperform the broad market.

Thinking about plunking some cash into FPX or IPO? I may not have a crystal ball, but I do have an inkling of what the future will bring for this fund: more extreme volatility. Keep reading to find out why.

The roller coaster of recent IPO performance

When times are good for small and mid cap stocks, as they were in the three years prior to the launch of FPX, times are typically very good for IPOs. But when times are bad, you can guess what happens. The index on which this ETF is based suffered terribly during the bear market of 2000, 2001, and 2002, with respective annual dips of –24.55 percent, –22.77 percent, and –21.64 percent. (If you started with $10,000 in 2000, you would have been left at the end of 2002 with a rather pathetic $4,566.04.) And I've already addressed the more recent recession of 2008.

Taking a broader look at IPOs

But what about the very long-term performance of IPOs? Jay Ritter, a professor of Finance at the University of Florida, keeps copious records on the returns of IPOs. Dr. Ritter asserts that, collectively, they haven't done all that well in relation to the broad market. But he hastens to add that long-term performance is dragged down by the smaller IPOs, and that larger IPOs — the ones included in the IPOX ETF — as a group have modestly outperformed the market, albeit with greater volatility.

Indeed. As the IPOX Index now stands, tech stocks, volatile as heck in their own right, make up slightly more than 25 percent of the roster. The top three companies together represent nearly one-third of the index's value. Do you really want that kind of swing in your portfolio, on top of an expense ratio of 0.60 percent?

Maybe you do. But if you are inclined to take such a gamble, please don't do it with any more money than you can afford to lose. Of course, that's true of all stocks, but especially of these youngsters.

If FPX doesn't offer enough volatility for you, consider the Renaissance IPO ETF (IPO), which seeks to profit from both U.S. and non-U.S. initial public offerings. This fund, since its inception in 2013, has slightly trailed the S&P 500, which is understandable, as the U.S. stock market has been the world rocker in the past few years.

Funds That (Supposedly) Thrive When the Market Takes a Dive

In June 2006, an outfit called ProShares introduced the first ETFs designed to *short* the market. That means these *inverse* ETFs are designed to go up as their market benchmark goes down, and vice versa. The four original ProShares ETFs are the Short QQQ fund (PSQ), which is betting against the NASDAQ-100; the Short S&P500 (SH); the Short MidCap400 (MYY); and the Short Dow30 (DOG).

DOG, indeed. If I were to devise a ticker for the entire lot, it would be "HUH?"

As it happens, this HUH? category of ETFs and exchange-traded notes (ETNs) has proliferated like no other. You can now find well over 200 exchange-traded products, from Direxion, ProShares, PowerShares, Direxion, iPath, and VelocityShares, allowing you to short anything and every-thing, including the kitchen sink (see the ProShares UltraShort Consumer Goods ETF [SZK]). From the U.S. stock market, to various industry sectors, to the stock markets of other coun-tries, to Treasury bonds, to gold and oil, it is now easy to bet that prices are heading south.

And for the truly pessimistic investor, many of these short ETFs now allow you to bet in *multiples*. In other words, if the market falls, these funds promise to rise on a leveraged basis. For example, the Direxion Daily Technology Bear 3x (TECS) is designed to rise 30 percent if tech stocks fall 10 percent.

From where I sit, these funds look an awful lot like legalized gambling.

Funds That Double the Thrill of Investing (for Better or Worse)

ProShares introduced four other ETFs in 2006, targeting investors at the other end of the sentiment spectrum: extreme optimists. These are leveraged funds that include the Ultra QQQ (QLD), which "seeks daily investment results, before fees and expenses, that correspond to twice (200%) the daily performance of the NASDAQ-100 Index," and the similarly designed Ultra S&P500 (SSO), Ultra MidCap400 (MVV), and Ultra Dow30 (DDM).

You think the market is going to rock? These funds, which use futures and other derivatives to magnify market returns, promise to make you twice the money you would make by simply investing in the NASDAQ-100, the S&P 500, the S&P MidCap 400, or the Dow. Of course, you'll have to accept twice the volatility. It seems like it might be a fair bet. But it really isn't.

Suppose you invest in the Ultra S&P500 (SSO), as opposed to, say, the SPDR S&P 500 (SPY). On a daily basis, if the underlying index goes up, your investment will go up twice as much. If the underlying index goes down, your investment will go down twice as much. Clearly the volatility is double. But let's look at the potential returns, as well.

The SPY is going to cost you 0.09 percent in operating expenses. The SSO is going to cost you 0.89 percent. That's a difference of 0.80 percent a year, or $400 on a $50,000 investment. You can expect about 2 percent in annualized dividends on SPY. Because SSO invests largely in futures, you aren't going to get much in dividends — probably less than half. On a $50,000 investment, that's a difference of an additional $500 or so. Already you've lost $900 ($400 + $5,000), regardless of which way the market goes.

But it isn't actually the loss of dividends or the high operating expenses that will hurt you the most with leveraged funds. It's more the added volatility — daily volatility — that will eat up and spit out your principal regardless of which way the market goes.

Follow closely:

Suppose you invest $1,000 in the ProShares Ultra QQQ ETF (QLD), which seeks a return of 200 percent of the return of the NASDAQ-100 index (the 100 largest over-the-counter stocks in the land). Now suppose that the index goes up 10 percent tomorrow but then drops 10 percent the day after tomorrow. You think you're back to $1,000? Guess again. The math of compounding is such that, even if you had invested in the index itself — unleveraged — you'd be in the hole after Day Two. Run the numbers: Your 10 percent gain on Day One would take you up to $1,100, but your loss of 10 percent of $1,100 the next day equals $110. Subtract that amount from $1,100, and you're left with $990 on Day Two, or an overall loss of 1 percent.

With QLD, you're going to get double socked. On Day One, you'll happily be up 20 percent to $1,200. But on Day Two, you'll lose 20 percent of that amount and find yourself with $960. You didn't lose the promised *double* (2 percent); you just lost *quadruple* (4 percent). Pull out your calculator if you don't believe me.

In a classic illustration of the principle that life is not fair, you are not helped if the market goes down and then up, instead of the other way around. Lose 10 percent of $1,000 and you've got $900. Gain 10 percent the next day, and what do you have? $990 ($900 + $90). The situation is magnified with QLD: You would lose 20 percent on Day One for a balance of $800 and gain 20 percent on Day Two to bring you right back to the same $960 you were left with in the first example.

And that, dear reader, is how these funds eat up your hard-earned savings, and why I strongly suggest that you do not use them.

All-in-One ETFs: For the Ultimate Lazy Portfolio

In this section, I introduce you to funds that cast a wide net, allowing you to invest in enormous pools of stocks and bonds without having to focus at all. First I present a handful of ETF options that fit the bill, and then I explain why you probably don't want them.

Getting worldwide exposure to stocks and bonds

Even the laziest investor has to make choices: Do you want worldwide exposure to stocks only? Or to stocks and bonds? Do you want the allocation between stocks and bonds to remain the same for the life of your investment? Or do you want that allocation to adjust as you get closer to retirement? In this section, I lay out your options.

Buying into the world's stock markets

If you want instant exposure to the broadest possible index of stocks, including U.S. and all sorts of foreign stocks (from both developed and emerging market countries), here are your options as of this writing:

- ✔ iShares MSCI ACWI Index Fund (ACWI), with 1,280 stock holdings and management fees of 0.33 percent

- ✔ Vanguard Total World Stock ETF (VT), with 6,955 holdings and management fees that are slightly lower at 0.17 percent

Adding bonds to the mix

Not enough diversity for you? Never fear: You can go even broader than the worldwide stock funds, buying one ETF that will give you exposure not only to the entire world of stocks but to bonds as well. (I discuss bond ETFs in Chapter 7.)

These all-in-one ETFs are referred to as *asset allocation funds* when they are *static,* meaning the division between stocks and bonds stays more or less the same for the life of the fund (for example, 50 percent stock and 50 percent bonds). The folks from iShares offer a dozen of these babies, including these:

- ✔ iShares S&P Aggressive Allocation Fund (AOA)

- ✔ iShares S&P Moderate Allocation Fund (AOM)

- ✔ iShares S&P Conservative Allocation Fund (AOK)

These three funds, which carry total net management expenses of about 0.25 percent, offer varying exposure to stocks and bonds depending on how aggressive a portfolio you want.

Russell's average review for the average reader on an average day

"For every complex problem," said H. L. Mencken, "there is an answer that is clear, simple — and wrong." Certainly, finding the optimal portfolio is a complex problem. The all-in-one ETFs I introduce in this section provide an answer that is clear, simple — and usually wrong. What's wrong is that there is no one-size-fits-all portfolio that makes sense for most people. Oh, I suppose if you were the average 50-year-old, with the average amount of money, looking to work an average number of years, expecting to die at the average age, and you were willing to take on an average amount of risk. . . . Well, if you were all those things and planned on remaining forever average, these funds might make sense for you.

But if you are anything other than perfectly average, I urge you to move on to Part III of this book whenever you feel ready. Take a look at my model portfolios and craft an ETF portfolio that makes sense for *you*.

Chapter 7

For Your Interest: The World of Bond ETFs

* *

In This Chapter

▶ Examining the rationale behind bond investing

▶ Recognizing different kinds of bonds

▶ Appreciating the risk that bond investing entails

▶ Selecting the best bond ETFs for your portfolio

▶ Knowing how much to allocate

* *

I love inline skating. Sometimes, I admit, I take to the Pennsylvania hills a bit too fast. There's just something about the trees racing by and the wind in my face that I can't resist. Whoosh!

On occasion, I hit a bump, or some tiny woman in a monster SUV who can barely see over the steering wheel (they're all over my neighborhood) cuts me off and I crash to the pavement. But thanks to the heavy black plastic armor that covers my knees, elbows, wrists, and head (just call me the Black Knight of Wealth Management), I've never been seriously injured.

Bonds are your portfolio's knee and elbow pads. When the going gets rough, and you hit the big bump (by any chance, do you remember 2008?), you'll be very, very glad to have bonds in your portfolio.

Plain and simple, there is no time-honored diversification tool for your portfolio that even comes close to bonds. They are as good as gold . . . even better than gold when you look at the long-term returns. Bonds are what may have saved your grandparents from selling apples on the street following the stock market crash of 1929.

The one thing that grandpa and grandma never had — but you do — is the ability to invest in bond ETFs. Like stock ETFs, most bond ETFs (at least the ones I'm going to suggest) are inexpensive, transparent (you know exactly what you're investing in), and highly liquid (you can sell them in a flash). Like individual bonds or bond mutual funds, bond ETFs can also be used to produce a reliable flow of cash in the form of interest payments, making them especially popular among grandparent types of any generation.

Throughout this chapter, I discuss a few things about bond investing in general. Then, without knowing the intimate particulars of your individual economics, I try my best to help you decide if bond ETFs belong in your portfolio, and if so, which ones. I also address that all-important and highly controversial question of how to achieve an optimal mix of stocks and bonds.

 The single most important investment decision you ever make may occur when you determine the split between stocks and bonds in your portfolio. No pressure.

Tracing the Track Record of Bonds

Bonds, more or less in their present form, have been used as financial instruments since the Middle Ages. Then, as now, bonds of varying risk existed. Then, as now, risks and returns were highly correlated.

For the most part, bonds are less volatile than stocks, and their returns over time tend to be less. Over the past 80 years, the average annualized nominal return of the S&P 500 has been around 10 percent, while the return of long-term U.S. government bonds has been approximately 5.7 percent.

Comparing the *real* returns of stocks versus bonds (the return *after* inflation, which happens to be the return that really counts), stocks over the past 80 years clock in at about 7.0 percent and bonds at 2.7percent — a huge difference. A dollar invested in the stock market in 1926 (ignoring all taxes, investment fees, and so on) would today be worth $400.00. That same dollar invested in bonds would be worth about $10.

These numbers may lead you to look at bonds and say to yourself, "Why bother?" Well, in fact, there's good reason to bother. Please read on before you decide to forsake this all-important asset class.

Portfolio protection when you need it most

When determining the attractiveness of bonds, you need to look not only at historical return but also at volatility: Long-term U.S. government bonds (which tend, like all long-term bonds, to be rather volatile) in their worst year *ever* (2009) returned –17.2 percent. In their second worst year ever (1980) they returned –14.6 percent. Those are big moves but still a walk in the park compared to the worst stock market years of 1931 (–43.3 percent), 1937 (–35 percent), 1974 (–26.5 percent), and 2008 (–36.7 percent).

As I note in the introduction to this chapter, during the Great Depression years, bonds may have saved your grandma and grandpa from destitution. The annualized real return of the S&P 500 from 1930–1932 was –20 percent. The annualized real return of long-term U.S. government bonds during the same three years was 14.9 percent.

There are two reasons that U.S. government bonds (and other high-quality bonds) often do well in the roughest economic times:

✔ People flock to them for safety, raising demand.

✔ Interest rates often (not always, but often) drop during tough economic times. Interest rates and bond prices have an inverse relationship. When interest rates fall, already-issued bonds (carrying older, relatively high coupon rates) shoot up in price.

As in the past, bonds may similarly spare your hide should the upcoming years prove disastrous for Wall Street. (You never know.) Whereas international stocks and certain industry sectors, like energy and real estate, have limited correlation to the broad U.S. stock market, bonds (not U.S. junk bonds, but most others) actually have a slight *negative* correlation to stocks. In other words, when the bear market is at its growliest, the complicated labyrinth of economic factors that typically coincide with that situation — lower inflation (possible deflation), lower interest rates — can bode quite well for fixed income. They certainly have done so in the past.

History may or may not repeat

Of course, as investment experts say again and again (although few people listen), historical returns are only mildly indicative of what will happen in the future; they are merely reference points. Despite all the crystal balls, tea leaves, and CNBC commentators in the world, we simply don't know what the future will bring.

Although the vast majority of financial professionals use the past century as pretty much their sole reference point, some point out that in the 19th century, stocks and bonds actually had more similar — nearly equal, in fact — rates of return. And perhaps that may be true for the 21st century as well. Time will tell. In the meantime, given all this uncertainty, it would be most prudent to have both stocks and bonds represented in your portfolio.

Tapping into Bonds in Various Ways

Like stocks, bonds can be bought individually, or you can invest in any of hundreds of bond mutual funds or about 300 bond ETFs. The primary reason for picking a bond fund over individual bonds is the same reason you might pick a stock fund over individual stocks: diversification.

Sure, you have to pay to get your bonds in fund form, but the management fees on bond ETFs tend to be very low, as you'll see later in this chapter. Conversely, the cost to trade individual bonds can be quite high. That's especially true of corporate and municipal bonds.

I'm not saying that you should not consider ever buying individual bonds. Doing so may make sense, provided that you know how to get a good price on an individual bond (if not, please read my book on that topic, *Bond Investing For Dummies*, published by Wiley) and provided that you are buying a bond with little default risk (such as a Treasury bond). That's especially true when you know that you will be needing x amount of money on y date. But for the most part, investors do better with low-cost, indexed bond funds.

Like stocks, bonds can (and should, if your portfolio is large enough) be broken up into different categories. Instead of U.S. and international, large, small, value, and growth (the way stocks are often broken up), bond categories may include U.S. government (both conventional and inflation-adjusted), corporate, international, and municipal bonds — all of varying maturity dates and credit ratings. Unless you're a billionaire, you simply can't effectively own enough individual bonds to tap into each and every fixed income class.

Finding strength in numbers

Diversification in bonds, while important, isn't quite as crucial as diversification in stocks. If you own high-quality U.S. government bonds (as long as they aren't terribly long-term) and you own a bevy of bonds from the most financially secure corporations, you're very unlikely to lose a lot of your principal, as you can with any stock. But the benefits of diversification exceed protecting principal. There's also much to be said for smoothing out returns and moderating risk.

Bond returns from one category of bonds to another can vary greatly, especially in the short run. In 2008, for example, high-yield corporate bonds, as represented by the SPDR Barclays Capital High Yield Bond ETF (JNK), saw a return of –24.68 percent. That same year, U.S. Treasury bonds, as represented by the iShares Barclays 7–10 Year Treasury Bond ETF (IEF), returned 17.9 percent. But the very next year, 2009, was a terrible year for Treasurys; IEF sagged –6.56 percent and JNK shot up 37.65 percent.

By owning a handful of bond funds, you can effectively diversify across the map. You can have Treasurys of varying maturities, corporate bonds of varying credit worthiness, international bonds of varying continents and currencies, and municipal bonds from across the nation. As you see throughout the rest of this chapter, I urge investors primarily to seek safety in bonds. If you're looking for high returns, go to stocks. The purpose of bonds, as far as I'm concerned, is to provide ballast to a portfolio.

The purposes served by bond funds are to make your bond investing easy, help you to diversify, and keep your costs low. Just as in the world of stock funds, all bond funds are not created equal. Some Treasury funds are better than others. Some corporate bond funds are better than others. Ditto for funds holding municipal bonds and foreign bonds.

Considering bond fund costs

Low costs are even more essential in picking a bond fund than they are in picking a stock fund. When (historically, at least over the past century) you're looking at maybe earning 2.7 percent above inflation, paying a manager even 1.2 percent a year is going to cut your profits almost in half . . . probably more than half if you are paying taxes on the bond dividends. Do you really care to do that?

As I write these words, interest rates are very low, which means that real interest rates (factoring in inflation) for most bonds are considerably less than 2.7 percent. That fact means paying attention to the cost of your bond funds is more essential than ever.

The most economical bond funds are index funds, and you have a number of excellent index bond mutual funds to choose from. The index bond ETFs I highlight in this chapter include some of the cheapest funds on the planet, which is a reason to like them.

 Although I'm a big proponent of ETFs, I must tell you that the ETF edge in the fixed income arena isn't nearly as sharp as it is in stocks. The tax efficiency of a bond index mutual fund and a bond ETF are just about the same. The wonderful structure of ETFs that I discuss in Chapter 1 simply doesn't matter much when it comes to bonds. Bonds pay interest — that's how you make money with bonds — and they rarely see any substantial capital gains. To the extent that they do have capital gains, however, ETFs may have an edge over mutual funds. But that's generally not going to be any big deal.

Sampling a Basic Bond-ETF Menu

At the time of this writing, there are about 300 bond ETFs, most of them introduced in the past five years. They are issued by iShares, PIMCO, PowerShares, State Street SPDRs, Vanguard, iPath, Guggenheim, and WisdomTree.

The U.S. Securities and Exchange Commission is sitting on applications for many other fixed-income ETFs. So not only do you have many choices today, but also many more choices are coming. In this section, I present some of my favorites.

Please note that with the discussion of each bond ETF, I include the *current yield:* how much each share is paying as a percentage of your investment on the day I'm writing this chapter. I do so only to give you a flavor of how the yields differ among the funds. Current yields on a bond or bond fund, especially a long-term bond or bond fund, can change dramatically from week to week. So, too, can the difference in yields between short- and long-term bonds (known as the yield *curve*). You can check the current yield of any bond fund, as well as the yield curve, on the sites of the ETF providers themselves or on general investing sites such as www. morningstar.com. One great site for all sorts of information on bonds, including yields for all bond categories, is www. investinginbonds.com.

 Note that several different kinds of bond yield exist. (For detailed information, I refer you to my book *Bond Investing For Dummies.*) For the sake of consistency, the bond yield I refer to throughout the rest of this chapter is the "SEC 30-Day Yield." (Here's the formula for you techno-heads: $2[\{(a-b)/cd+1\}^6-1]!]$.)

For you non-techno-heads, here's what this yield essentially means: If you (or the fund manager) were to hold to maturity each and every one of the bonds in a fund's portfolio, as it

stood over the past 30 days, and reinvest all interest payments (that is, you plow those interest payments right back
into your bond portfolio), your SEC yield is what you'd get
over the course of a year. It takes into account all fund fees
and expenses. The formula was created, and the methodology
is enforced, by the U.S. Securities and Exchange Commission,
which is where the "SEC" in the formula's name comes from.

Tapping the Treasurys: Uncle Sam's IOUs

If the creator/issuer of a bond is a national government, the
issue is called a *sovereign* bond. The vast majority of sovereign bonds sold in the United States are Uncle Sam's own
Treasurys. (Yeah, that's how they're typically spelled. I don't
know why.) Treasury bonds' claim to fame is the allegedly
absolute assuredness that you'll get your principal back if you
hold a bond to maturity. The United States government guarantees it. For that reason, Treasurys are sometimes called
"risk-free."

Treasury bond ETFs come in short-term, intermediate-term,
and long-term varieties, depending on the average maturity
date of the bonds in the ETF's portfolio. In general, the longer
the term, the higher the interest rate but the greater the
volatility. Note that interest paid on Treasurys — including
Treasury ETFs — is federally taxable but not taxed by the
states. As it happens, bonds issued by state and local governments in the United States, known as *municipal bonds,* are not
taxed by the federal government. This reciprocal deal was
orchestrated by the Supremes (those judges in Washington,
not the singing group) back in 1895.

Following are detailed descriptions of three popular iShares
Treasury ETFs, along with my reviews. I also identify some
other options, although I don't think you're going to do much
better than iShares in this particular category.

iShares Barclays 1–3 Year Treasury Bond Fund (SHY)

Indexed to: The Barclays Capital U.S. 1–3 Year Treasury
Bond Index, an index tracking the short-term sector of the
U.S. Treasury Bond Index. The fund uses a representative
sampling — typically around 35 individual bond issues.

Expense ratio: 0.15 percent
Current yield: 0.5 percent
Average weighted maturity: 1.9 years
Russell's review: This ETF and others of its ilk (such as the Vanguard Short-Term Government Bond ETF [VGSH]) are fine for what they are, but the asset class they represent is not among my favorite asset classes. Sure, very short-term Treasurys are ultra-safe investments with little — almost no — volatility. And the yield may be better than you can get in your local savings bank. Maybe. As I write this, with yields on short-term Treasurys so low, that may not be the case. But even if the yield were a wee bit higher than a savings account, is this really where you want to stash your cash? Keep in mind that every time you make a deposit or withdrawal, unless you hold VGSH at Vanguard, you'll very likely pay a commission. You may do better keeping your short-term money in a three- to six-month CD or in an Internet bank like EmigrantDirect or Ally Bank. The latter two options generally pay just as much as SHY; they are FDIC insured (making them just as safe); and you won't pay for each and every transaction.

iShares Barclays 7–10 Year Treasury Bond Fund (IEF)

Indexed to: The Barclays Capital U.S. 7–10 Year Treasury Bond Index, an index tracking the intermediate-term sector of the U.S. Treasury market. The fund uses a representative sampling — typically around 15 individual bond issues.
Expense ratio: 0.15 percent
Current yield: 1.8 percent
Average weighted maturity: 7.6 years
Russell's review: Expect modest returns and modest volatility. Of the three kinds of Treasurys, the intermediate-term bonds make the most sense for most people's portfolios, and IEF is an excellent way to invest in them. Vanguard's Intermediate-Term Government Bond Index ETF (VGIT) would be another good option; it is a very similar fund with just about the same components and costs. Whatever your total allocation to fixed income, IEF (or VGIT) deserves an allotment of perhaps one-fifth to one-third of that amount. See how I work these ETFs into model portfolios in Chapter 9.

iShares Barclays 20+ Year Treasury Bond Fund (TLT)

Indexed to: The Barclays Capital U.S. 20+ Year Treasury Bond Index, an index tracking the long-term sector of the U.S. Treasury market. The fund uses a representative sampling — typically around 30 individual bond issues.

Expense ratio: 0.15 percent
Current yield: 2.5 percent
Average weighted maturity: 17 years
Russell's review: Hmmm. I believe that Treasurys are perhaps the safest investment in the land, but not *entirely* risk-free. I don't mean to sound unpatriotic. I don't mean to sound alarmist. But the size of our nation's debt and deficit makes the hills of Pennsylvania look flat by comparison. Honestly, this issue scares me, and only recently has the U.S. electorate (thanks to a debt stalemate in Congress in 2011) seemed to take notice. I may consider a short-term Treasury bill to be risk-free, but a 20+ year Treasury? Wave your flag all you like, but you take on *some* risk of principal loss here. And given the maturity of the bond, you're certainly going to encounter a heck of a lot of volatility.

Bread at $10 a loaf? Getting inflation protection in a flash

Technically, U.S. Treasury Inflation-Protected Securities are Treasurys, but they are usually referred to as *TIPS*. I discuss them separately from the other Treasury obligations here because they play a distinctly different role in your portfolio.

The gig with TIPS is this: They pay you only a nominal amount of interest (currently long-term TIPS are paying about 1.6 percent), but they also kick in an adjustment for inflation. So, for example, if inflation is running at 3 percent, all things being equal, your long-term TIPs will yield 4.6 percent.

 If you want to know what the rate of inflation is going to be over the next few years, I can't tell you, but I can tell you what rate of inflation the bond market expects. That would be the difference between conventional Treasury bonds and TIPS. If, for example, a 10-year conventional Treasury bond were paying 5 percent and the 10-year TIP security were paying 2 percent, the difference (3 percent) would be the rate of inflation that bond buyers collectively expect to see.

Either the iShares Barclays TIPS Bond Fund ETF (TIP) or the very similar SPDR Barclays Capital TIPS ETF (IPE) is a fabulous way to tap into this almost essential ingredient in a well-balanced portfolio.

iShares Barclays TIPS Bond Fund (TIP)

Indexed to: The Barclays Capital U.S. Treasury Inflation-Protected Securities Index. The fund uses a representative sampling of roughly 30 bond issues.
Expense ratio: 0.20 percent
Current yield: 1.6 percent + adjustment for inflation
Average weighted maturity: 7.6 years
Russell's review: TIPS belong in your portfolio, and this fund may be the best way to hold them. You won't get rich off this fund, and the volatility may be more than you like. But if inflation goes on a tear, you are protected. Not so with other bonds. Of course, if inflation doesn't go on a tear, your money will earn sub-par returns. But that's okay — you can think of any lost interest as the premium on an insurance policy that you know you should have.

Note that TIPS are notoriously tax inefficient, even when held in an ETF. Ideally, you would hold your shares of TIP in a tax-advantaged retirement account. In general, whatever your overall allocation is to fixed income (excluding short-term cash needs), perhaps one-quarter to one-third of that amount could be put into a fund such as TIP or IPE. Err more toward one-quarter if you have a fairly aggressive portfolio. Err more toward one-third if you have a more conservative portfolio. Rationale: Your stocks are also, historically speaking at least, a good hedge against inflation. The more stocks you own, the less important the role of TIPS.

Banking on business: Corporate bond ETFs

Logically enough, corporations issue bonds called *corporate* bonds, and you can buy a dizzying array of them with varying maturities, yields, and ratings. Or you can buy a representative sampling through the iShares iBoxx $ Investment Grade Corporate Bond Fund (LQD). Corporate bonds typically pay higher rates than government bonds (historically about 1 percent a year higher), so you would expect the long-term payout from this ETF to be higher than any government bond ETF, except perhaps for the longest of the long-term government bond ETFs.

In the area of corporate bonds, credit ratings are essential. Know that the average bond rating of the iShares iBoxx $ Investment Grade Corporate Bond Fund is A, which means, more or less, that the bonds are issued by companies that are fairly solvent (although certainly not on a par with the U.S. government — yet, anyway).

iBoxx $ Investment Grade Corporate Bond Fund (LQD)

Indexed to: The iBoxx $ Liquid Investment Grade Index — an index of bond issues sponsored by a chorus line of companies rated "investment grade" (which means highly unlikely to go bankrupt any time soon) or above. Technically, we're speaking of bonds rated BBB or better by S&P. About 600 bonds are typically used to create a representative sampling of this universe.
Expense ratio: 0.15 percent
Current yield: 3.0 percent
Average credit quality: A
Average weighted maturity: 7.8 years
Russell's review: Investment-grade corporate bonds have done a pretty good job of holding their own in bad times. You get more return than you do with Treasurys of equal maturity, although unlike Treasurys, with corporate bonds you pay state taxes on the dividends. If your portfolio is large enough, you want LQD, as well as one of the conventional Treasury and inflation-adjusted Treasury ETFs. See how I include all three of these winners in the sample portfolios presented in Chapter 9.

Vanguard Short-Term Corporate Bond Index (VCSH)

Indexed to: The Barclays U.S. 1–5 Year Corporate Index, a pot of about 1,800 bonds from corporations that the raters think have little chance of going belly up
Expense ratio: 0.12 percent
Current yield: 1.7 percent
Average credit quality: A
Average weighted maturity: 3.0 years
Russell's review: In normal times, I would encourage most investors to stick with intermediate-term bonds and forget about short-term bonds that typically yield considerably less. However, when interest rates are as low as they have been in decades (as they are while I'm writing this chapter), I tend to lean my client portfolios more to the short-term. Reason:

When interest rates rise, as eventually they will, longer-term bonds are going to get hit. During times of very low interest rates, more conservative investors, especially those who may need to tap their bond money within the next five years, may want half their allocation to corporate bonds in a short-term fund such as VCSH. When interest rates start to climb back up to more normal historical levels, it might then make sense to shift most of the bond money back to more intermediate-term bonds, such as those offered by LQD.

The whole shebang: Investing in the entire U.S. bond market

The broadest fixed income ETFs are all-around good bets, especially for more modest sized portfolios. Note that these bonds use a total (taxable) bond market approach, which means about two-thirds government bonds and one-third corporate (no municipal). These funds also make the most sense for investors with lots of room in their tax-advantaged retirement accounts. If you have to stick your bonds in a taxable account, you're probably better off separating your Treasury bonds and your corporate bonds. Reason: You get a tax break on Treasury bond interest, in that you do not have to pay state income tax. If, however, your Treasury bonds are buried in an aggregate fund, such as these, you have to pay state income tax on the interest.

Vanguard Total Bond Market (BND)

Indexed to: The Barclays Capital U.S. Aggregate Float Adjusted Index, which is made up of about 8,000 bonds, two-thirds of which are U.S. government bonds and one-third of which are higher quality corporate bonds. The average credit quality indicates that there is very little chance any of the bonds in the index will default. (Even if a few did, with about 8,000 holdings, the entire apple cart wouldn't turn over.)
Expense ratio: 0.08 percent
Current yield: 2.0 percent
Average credit quality: AA
Average weighted maturity: 7.7 years
Russell's review: How can you go wrong with the world's largest provider of index funds tracking the entire bond market for you and charging you only 0.08 percent (that's 8 percent of

1 percent)? BND makes an excellent building block in smaller portfolios or for any investor seeking the ultimate in simplicity, especially where there's lots of room in tax-advantaged accounts. For larger portfolios, however, where you can afford to mix and match other bond funds of different flavors, the need for BND becomes less clear.

iShares Barclays Aggregate Bond Fund (AGG)

Indexed to: The Barclays Capital U.S. Aggregate Bond Index, which tracks the performance of the total U.S. investment grade bond market, including both government bonds and the highest quality corporate bonds
Expense ratio: 0.08 percent
Current yield: 1.9 percent
Average credit quality: AA
Average weighted maturity: 7.6 years
Russell's review: AGG is a good fund, without any great differences from BND, although it uses a smaller sampling of bonds. I'd rather have a larger sampling than a smaller sampling, but even so, 3,600 bonds (versus BND's 16,400) still offer darned good diversification.

Vanguard Short-Term Bond (BSV)

Indexed to: The Barclays Capital U.S.1–5 Year Government/ Credit Float Adjusted Index, which is about 2,300 bonds, two-thirds of which are short-term U.S. government and one-third of which are higher quality corporate bonds, also of short-term maturity
Expense ratio: 0.10 percent
Current yield: 1.1 percent
Average credit quality: AA
Average weighted maturity: 2.8 years
Russell's review: In normal times, I encourage most investors to stick with intermediate-term bonds and forget about short-term bonds that typically yield considerably less. Recently, however, with interest rates so low, low, low, I've been leaning my client portfolios more to the short-term. Reason: When interest rates pop, as eventually they will, longer-term bonds are going to suffer. For more conservative investors especially, BSV may warrant half of your allocation to U.S. bonds. When interest rates start to climb back up to historical norms, you may then want to move some or all of your BSV assets to BND.

Moving Beyond Basics into Municipal and Foreign Bonds

Every investor needs bonds. Not every investor needs municipal bonds or foreign bonds. But for higher-income investors who find themselves in the northern tax zones, municipal bonds, which pay interest exempt from federal income tax (and possibly state income tax as well) can make enormous sense. For those with larger bond portfolios, the added diversification of foreign bonds is something to consider very seriously.

Municipals for mostly tax-free income

Historically, municipal bonds have yielded about 80 percent of what Treasury bonds of similar maturity yield. As I write these words, the two kinds of bonds have yielded about the same recently — mostly due to Treasurys paying less and less. But that's on a before-tax basis. After taxes, you do better with munis, even if you're in a low tax bracket. In a higher tax bracket, you do *much* better with munis . . . assuming the munis you buy don't default.

In fact, munis rarely do default. The largest default in history occurred only recently, when Detroit stopped paying its creditors. It was a wake-up call to remind us all that diversification is crucial. The diversification offered by many municipal ETFs lessens your risk considerably. Still, muni ETFs are more risky than Treasurys. You don't want your entire portfolio in munis.

To figure out the tax-equivalent yield on a muni or muni fund, you may want to visit one of the gazillion tax-equivalent yield calculators on the Internet. One of my faves is to be found on www.dinkytown.com. Click *Investments* in the column on the far left of your screen. Then click on *Municipal Bond Tax Equivalent Yield*. You'll figure it out from there.

Note that I'm about to highlight a few *national* muni ETFs — that is, funds that offer munis from across the land. If you live in a state with high income taxes, such as New York or California, and you're in a high tax bracket, you may want to investigate state-specific muni mutual funds; plenty of them are out there (try Vanguard, T. Rowe Price, and Fidelity). ETF purveyors PowerShares and SPDRs also offer a handful of state-specific ETFs.

When you buy muni funds that are specific to your home state, you exempt yourself from having to pay state or federal income tax on the interest.

iShares S&P National Municipal Bond Fund (MUB)

Indexed to: The S&P National AMT-Free Municipal Bond Index, which includes investment-grade municipal bonds from all 50 states, as well as Puerto Rico and U.S territories such as Guam and the U.S. Virgin Islands. There are 8,500 constituent bonds in the index.
Expense ratio: 0.25 percent
Current yield: 1.6 percent
Average credit quality: AA
Average weighted maturity: 8.0 years
Russell's review: This fund offers a reasonable expense ratio and excellent diversification. It is also free of the AMT (alternative minimum tax), which is a decidedly good thing if you derive a lot of income from tax-free sources.

SPDR Nuveen Barclays Capital Municipal Bond (TFI)

Indexed to: The Barclays Capital Municipal Managed Money Index, which features about 18,000 bonds from the Atlantic to the Pacific states and everything in between
Expense ratio: 0.30 percent
Current yield: 1.9
Average credit quality: AA
Average weighted maturity: 9.0
Russell's review: This fund is slightly more expensive than MUB, with a bit more volatility given the longer average maturity of the bonds. For example, in 2013 (a fairly bad year for municipal bonds, given the upset over what was going on in Detroit), this fund saw a return of -3.9 percent versus -3.4 percent for MUB.

Foreign bonds for fixed-income diversification

Over the long haul, bonds of similar default risk and maturity will likely yield about the same percentage. But in the short run, substantial differences can exist in the yields and total returns of U.S. versus foreign bonds. The big difference is often due to currency exchange rates. If you are holding foreign bonds and the dollar drops *vis-à-vis* your foreign currencies, your foreign bond funds tend to do better. If the dollar rises, you'll likely be disappointed in your foreign bond fund returns.

Some foreign bond funds, such as Vanguard's BNDX, are dollar-hedged, removing the currency flux. Here, the difference in returns between U.S. bonds and similarly rated non-U.S. bonds is not likely to be very large. If you follow my advice on the stock side of the portfolio and allocate roughly half your equities to overseas positions, you'll have plenty of exposure to foreign currencies. If that is the case, I would recommend a dollar-hedged bond fund, such as BNDX. But regardless of whether you go with dollar-hedged or no, I see little advantage in allocating more than perhaps 20 to 25 percent of your bonds to overseas ETFs.

iShares S&P/Citigroup International Treasury Bond Fund (IGOV)

Indexed to: The S&P/Citigroup International Treasury Bond Index Ex-US, which holds about 600 bonds that, collectively, track the sovereign debt of developed foreign nations, mostly in Western Europe and Japan
Expense ratio: 0.35
Current yield: .30 percent
Average credit quality: AA
Average weighted maturity: 8.5 years
Top five countries: Japan, Italy, France, Germany, the Netherlands
Russell's review: Be aware that about half of the fund's holdings are denominated in Euros. Your returns will therefore be very dependent on the Euro-Greenback exchange rate. (You want the Euro to fly.) This fund is very, very similar to the SPDR Barclays Capital International Treasury Bond (BWX), but BWX carries an expense ratio of 0.50 percent. Go with the iShares fund.

Vanguard Total International Bond ETF (BNDX)

Indexed to: The Barclays Global Aggregate ex-USD Float Adjusted RIC Capped Index (USD Hedged).
Expense ratio: 0.19 percent
Current yield: 0.8
Average credit quality: AA

Average weighted maturity: 8.4 years
Top five countries: Japan, France, Germany, Italy, United Kingdom
Russell's review: It you're going to own one international bond fund, this is probably the fund for you. Low-cost, with the diversification of 3,500 bonds from around the world (96 percent from developed nations; 4 percent from emerging markets). Best of all, this fund is dollar-hedged, which is the way to go, if you have plenty of foreign-currency exposure already on the stock side of your portfolio.

Emerging-market bonds: High risk, high return

I don't like U.S. high-yield ("junk") bonds. They tend to be highly volatile, and they tend to move up and down with the stock market. In other words, they don't provide much of the diversification power or soft cushion that bonds are famous for. Foreign junk bonds are different. These bonds, issued by the governments of countries that may not be entirely stable, can be just as volatile as bonds issued by unstable U.S. corporations, but they do not tend to go up and down with the U.S. stock market (although they certainly may at times . . . and did so in 2008).

For reasons of diversification, investors with fairly good sized portfolios may want to consider allocating a modest part of their portfolios to emerging-market debt. In my personal portfolio, I have allocated 5 percent of the total to this asset class. Note that I'm not referring to "my bond portfolio" but to my "portfolio." I actually think of my holdings in emerging-market debt as more of a stock-like investment than a true bond investment. After all, you're likely to see stock-like volatility and long-term stock-like returns with these investments.

Although these ETFs have been around for only a few years, emerging-market bond mutual funds have been in existence for much longer. The T. Rowe Price Emerging Markets Bond Fund (PREMX), for example, has a 15-year average annual return of 9.4 percent. But there has been volatility, for sure: In 2008, the fund lost nearly 18 percent of its value.

iShares JP Morgan USD Emerging Markets Bond Fund (EMB)

Indexed to: The JPMorgan EMBI Global Core Index, which is made up of all U.S. dollar denominated bonds, from various emerging-market nations
Expense ratio: 0.40
Current yield: 5.0 percent
Average credit quality: BB
Average weighted maturity: 10.5 years
Top five countries: Turkey, Philippines, Indonesia, Mexico, Brazil
Russell's review: The iShares fund is a perfectly good way to tap into this asset class.

Vanguard Emerging Markets Governement Bond (VWOB)

Indexed to: Barclays USD Emerging Markets Government RIC Capped Index.
Expense ratio: 0.34
Current yield: 4.8 percent
Average credit quality: BB
Average weighted maturity: 10.6 years
Top five countries: China, Brazil, Mexico, Russia, Indonesia
Russell's review: This fund is slightly cheaper and a bit more diversified than the iShares emerging-market fund, and I like both of those facts. But the two funds are really quite similar.

Chapter 8

REITs, Commodities, and Active ETFs

● ●

In This Chapter

▶ Understanding what makes a REIT a REIT

▶ Knowing how much to invest

▶ Weighing commodities as investments

▶ Digging for gold and silver, drilling for oil

▶ Taking a chance with active ETFs

● ●

*W*hen I wrote the first edition of this book in 2006, building an entire, optimally diversified portfolio out of ETFs was just about impossible — sort of like trying to paint a landscape with no blues or yellows. There were holes, and many of them. You could not, for example, buy an ETF that gave you exposure to tax-free municipal bonds. Or international bonds. Only one ETF at that time allowed you to tap into international small cap stocks. And none allowed for investing in international REITs.

Back then, when there were but 300 ETFs from which to choose, and many of those tracked the same kinds of investments (such as large cap U.S. stocks), you had to look elsewhere if you wished to invest in certain asset classes. Today, the landscape is quite different. Among the 2,300 or so available ETFs, you have blues, yellows, greens . . . an entire palette from which to compose a very well-diversified portfolio. In fact, you have more than enough. Now, not only can you track just about any conceivable stock, bond, or commodity index with passive ETFs, but also you have actively managed ETFs to consider.

Here, I run you through some of those options and the ways they can help you pretty up your portfolio (or not).

Real Estate Investment Trusts (REITs)

At the onset of the 21st century, the value of commercial real estate — just about anywhere in the nation — softened right along with the housing market. But again, unless you bought just prior to the decline that began its serious fall in 2006, any investment in commercial property has probably done well. In fact, if you happen to own some commercial property, perhaps through a real estate investment trust (REIT), you likely made out very well in more recent years after the dust from the crash had at least partially settled.

In a nutshell, *real estate investment trusts,* popularly known as *REITs* (rhymes with "beets"), are companies that hold portfolios of properties, such as shopping malls, office buildings, hotels, amusement parks, or timberland. Or they may hold certain real estate–related assets, such as commercial mortgages. More than 150 REITs in the United States are publicly held, and their stock trades on the open market just like any other stock.

Via dozens of mutual funds, you can buy into a collection of REITs at one time. Via about 30 or so ETFs, you can similarly buy a bevy of REITs. And that may not be a bad idea. For the 10 years that ended December 2014, the U.S. REIT market has enjoyed an average annual return of 10.2 percent. That outshines by 2.2 percentage points per year the S&P 500's 8.0 percent return during the same period.

Why REITs should be in your portfolio

Some holders of REITs and REIT funds believe (and fervently hope) that such performance will continue. Others argue that the glory of REITs may already be gone with the wind. In the following sections, I provide you with several reasons why REITs deserve a permanent allocation in most portfolios.

Limited correlation to the broad markets

An index of U.S. REITs has evidenced a correlation of 0.4 with the S&P 500 over the past 20 years. That means the price of an S&P 500 index fund and the share price of a REIT index fund have tended to move in the same direction considerably less than half the time. The REIT index has practically no correlation to bonds.

Holding 20 percent REITs in your portfolio over the past 20 years — regardless of whether your portfolio was made up of mostly stocks or bonds — would have both raised your returns and lowered your volatility. It's the Efficient Frontier (as I discuss in Chapter 10) in action.

Unusually high dividends

REITs typically deliver annual dividend yields significantly higher than even the highest dividend-paying non-REIT stocks, and twice that of the average stock. (Many stocks, of course, pay no dividends.) At the time of this writing, the Vanguard Total Stock Market Index ETF (VTI) is producing a yield of 1.8 percent, versus 3.5 percent for the Vanguard REIT Index ETF (VNQ).

So the cash usually keeps flowing regardless of whether a particular REIT's share price rises or falls, just as long as the REIT is pulling in some money. That's because REITs, which get special tax status, are required by law to pay out 90 percent of their income as dividends to shareholders. Cool, huh?

Different taxation of dividends

Because REITs are blessed in that they don't have to pay income taxes, their dividends are usually fully taxable to shareholders as ordinary income. In other words, whatever dividends you get will be taxed at year-end according to your income tax bracket. Few, if any, REIT dividends you receive will qualify for the special 15 or 20 percent dividend tax rate. For that reason, your accountant will undoubtedly urge you to handle your REITs a bit carefully. I urge you to do so, as well.

Special status among financial pros

The vast majority of wealth advisors — whether they primarily use style investing, sector investing, or astrology charts and tea leaves — recognize REITs as a separate asset class and tend to include it in most people's portfolios. Is that distinction logical and just? Yes, but . . . I've asked myself this question: If REITs deserve that distinction of honor, what about some other industry sectors, such as utilities and energy? After all, both utilities and energy have lately shown less correlation to the S&P 500 than have REITs. Don't they deserve their own slice of the portfolio pie?

I don't mean to slam REITs; I like REITs. But one possible reason they are seen as a separate asset class (in addition to the three reasons I explain in the previous sections) may be that the REIT marketers are savvier than the marketers of utility stocks (which, in addition to having low correlation to the broad market, *also* pay exceptionally high dividends).

Connection to tangible property

Some people argue that REITs are different than other stocks because they represent tangible property. Well yeah, REITs do represent stores filled with useless junk and condos filled with single people desperately looking for dates, and I suppose that makes them different from, say, stock in Microsoft or Procter & Gamble. (Isn't toothpaste tangible?) But the reality is that REITs are stocks. And to a great degree, they behave like stocks. If REITs are different than other stocks, dividends and lack of market correlation are the likely distinctions — not their tangibility.

Calculating a proper REIT allocation

You don't really need REITs for the income they provide. Some people have this notion that withdrawing dividends from savings is somehow okay but withdrawing principal is not. Don't make that mistake. The reality is that if you withdraw $100 from your account, it doesn't matter whether it came from cash dividends or the sale of stock.

If you need cash, you can always create your own "artificial dividend" by selling any security you like (preferably one that has appreciated). Not that I have anything against dividends — they're fine — but they shouldn't be your primary reason for purchasing REITs.

Your primary motivations for buying REITs should be diversification and potential growth. In the past, the diversification afforded by REITs has been significant, as has the growth. In this section, I help you consider how much of your portfolio you may want to allot to REITs.

Putting all the factors together, I suggest that most investors devote 15 to 20 percent of the equity side of their portfolios to REITs. If your portfolio is 50 percent stock and 50 percent bonds, I might suggest that 7.5 to 10 percent of your entire portfolio be devoted to REITs.

What if, like many people, you're a homeowner whose home represents most of your net worth? You may want to play it a little light on the REITs, but don't let the value of your home affect your portfolio decisions to any great degree.

International REITs are worth breaking out of your international stock holdings for all the same reasons that U.S. REITs are worth having tucked into a larger portfolio of U.S. stocks. The REIT allotment you give to your portfolio might be evenly split between U.S. and international REITs, in keeping with the 50/50 split between U.S. and non-U.S. stocks that I suggest for your overall portfolio.

Picking REIT ETFs for your portfolio

If you want REITs in your portfolio, you won't get a whole lot of them unless you purchase a REIT fund. For all the room they take up, REITs simply don't make up that large a segment of the economy.

If, for example, you were to buy an S&P 500 index fund, only about 1 percent of that fund would be made up of stock from REITs. If you were to buy an S&P mid cap index fund (most REITs would probably qualify as mid caps), you would still be holding an investment that's only about 4 percent REITs.

So if you want the diversification power of this special asset class, you need to go out of your way to get it. But thanks to ETFs, doing so shouldn't be much of a hassle, and you get many of ETFs' other benefits in the bargain, including rock-bottom expenses.

The tax efficiency of ETFs will help cap any capital gains you enjoy on your REIT fund, but it can't do anything to diminish the taxes you'll owe on the dividends. For that reason, all REIT funds — ETFs or otherwise — are best kept in tax-advantaged retirement accounts, such as your IRA or Roth IRA.

If you're curious to see the whole buffet of REIT ETFs available, visit www.reit.com; click on "Investing," then "List of REIT Funds," and finally "Exchange-Traded Funds." I would ask that you remember that REITs are a small part of the economy. I see no need to invest in any particular sliver of the REIT market, nor any individual country REIT funds.

All That Glitters: Gold, Silver, and Other Commodities

Historically, gold has been seen as the ultimate hedge against both inflation and market turmoil. Most people through the ages have bought gold as coins, or sometimes in bricks. Alternatively, in more recent decades, they may have invested in shares of gold-mining companies.

Whether people invested in the physical metal or the stock of companies that mined it, the traditional ways of investing in gold have always been a pain in the neck. With shares of gold-mining companies, factors other than the price of gold come into play. For example, political turbulence in South Africa, or a fall in the value of the Rand, might send your stock down the mines. Buying gold coins entails hefty commissions. Likewise for gold bricks, with possible added expenses for assaying. And both bricks and coins have to be stored and should be insured.

All these hassles became optional for gold investors with the introduction of the first gold ETF in November 2004. Suddenly it became possible to buy gold at its spot price — in an instant — with very little commission and no need to fret about storage or insurance. Thanks to ETFs, you can now also buy silver in the same way. Or platinum.

In fact, you can invest in just about any commodity you please. You can invest in just about any precious or industrial metal: tin, nickel, you name it. Even natural gas, or crude oil, if that's your cup of Texas tea, can be purchased (sort of) with an ETF, as can coffee futures and contracts on wheat, sugar, or corn. Indeed, it seems the only commodity that's not available for purchase by the retail investor is weapons-grade plutonium.

Gold, gold, gold!

Stocks and bonds rise and fall. Currencies ebb and flow. Economies go boom and then bust. Inflation tears nest eggs apart. And through it all, gold retains its value. Or so we're told.

Table 8-1 shows the price of gold in a sampling of years between 1980 and 2015; the average price of a basic Hershey chocolate bar in those years (which I found on a website called www.foodtimeline.org); and how many Hershey bars you could buy with an ounce of gold. Note that one ounce of gold in 1980 bought 2,460 Hershey bars, while 20 years later, in 2000, it bought a mere 558 bars. At mid-2015 prices — about $1,175 for an ounce of gold and about $1.05 cents for a Hershey bar — you'd get 1,119 chocolate bars for the same nugget.

Table 8-1	Trading Gold for Hershey Bars		
Year	Average price of a Hershey bar	Average price of an ounce of gold	Hershey bars per ounce of gold
1980	$0.25	$615	2,460
2000	$0.50	$279	558
2013	$1.05	$1,175	1,119

If you type "gold" into your favorite search engine, you'll find 10,000 vendors selling it and 10,000 reasons, according to those vendors, why *now* is the time to buy. (Um, excuse me, sirs, but if the price of gold "can only go up," why are you trying so hard to sell it?) Every day I hear one explanation or another as to why gold "must" go up from here on (India's demand for gold . . . dentists' demand for gold . . . the mines are drying up . . . gold demand in the tech industry . . . and so on and so on). These are the very same arguments I've been hearing for years. Only now there's one more: All these ETF investors are demanding gold!

I believe that the best you can expect from gold over the very long term, is that it will maintain its purchasing power. In the final analysis, it probably wouldn't hurt you to hold gold in your portfolio. But please don't buy the nonsense that gold "must go up." It will go up. It will go down. It will go up again. Have a ball. Just don't bank your retirement on it, okay? (Personally, I only recently bought a modest position in gold, given how it has taken such a clobbering of late.)

If you allot a small percentage of your portfolio to gold — no more than, say, 5 percent please (actually make that 5 percent *total* precious metals) — and keep that percentage constant, you'll likely eke out a few dollars over time. Every year, if the price of gold falls, you might buy a bit; if the price rises, perhaps you sell. That strategy is called *rebalancing,* and I recommend it for all your portfolio allocations. (See my discussion of yearly portfolio rebalancing in Chapter 11.)

And if all goes to hell in a hand basket, your gold may offer you some protection.

A vastly improved way to buy the precious metal

When, in November 2004, State Street Global Advisors introduced the first gold ETF, it was a truly revolutionary moment. You buy a share just as you would buy a share of any other security, and each share gives you an ownership interest in one-tenth of an ounce of gold held by the fund. Yes, the gold is actually held in various bank vaults.

If you are going to buy gold, this is the easiest and most sensible way to do it.

You currently have several ETF options for buying gold. Two that would work just fine include the original from State Street — the **SPDR Gold Shares (GLD)** — and a second from iShares introduced months later — the **iShares Gold Trust (IAU).** Both funds are essentially the same. Flip a coin (gold or other), but then go with the iShares fund, simply because it costs less: 0.25 percent versus 0.40 percent.

The tax man cometh

Strange as it seems, the Internal Revenue Service considers gold to be a collectible for tax purposes. A share of a gold ETF is considered the same as, say, a gold Turkish coin from 1923 (don't ask). So what, you ask? As it happens, the long-term capital gains tax rate on collectibles is 28 percent and not the more favorable 15 to 20 percent afforded to capital gains on stocks.

Holding the ETF should be no problem from a tax standpoint (gold certainly won't pay dividends), but when you sell, you could get hit hard on any gains. Gold ETFs, therefore, are best kept in tax-advantaged accounts, such as your IRA. (Note that this advice won't serve you well if gold prices tumble and you sell. In that event, you'd rather have held the ETF in a taxable account so that you could write off the capital loss. Life is complicated, isn't it?)

Silver: The second metal

Talk about a silver bullet. In early 2006, after years of lackluster performance, the price of silver suddenly, within three short months, shot up 67 percent. Why? Largely, the move served as testimony to the growing power of ETFs!

The price jump anticipated the introduction of the **iShares Silver Trust (SLV)** ETF in April 2006. SLV operates much the same as the iShares COMEX Gold Trust (IAU). When you buy a share of SLV, you obtain virtual ownership of 10 ounces of silver.

To be able to convey that ownership interest, iShares had to buy many ounces of silver (initially 1.5 million), and that pending demand caused the silver market to bubble and fizz. Within several weeks after the introduction of the ETF, the price of silver continued to rise, reaching a 23-year high in May 2006 before tumbling in the following weeks. . . and months . . . and years. . . .

Quick silver on the move

To say that silver is volatile is a gross understatement. In 1979, the price of an ounce of silver was about $5. It then rose tenfold in less than a year — to as high as $54 an ounce in

1980 — after the infamous Hunt brothers had cornered the silver market (until they were caught, because, y'know, it's illegal to corner the market in just about anything). The price then fell again. Hard.

Fast forward to April 2011. The price of silver, having risen steadily and sharply since the introduction of the first silver ETF, had topped $48 an ounce and seemed headed back to the highs of 1980. And then . . . pop! Within a mere several days, the price fell about 30 percent to slightly under $34. Then it rose back up in the following months to $42, and then, in September 2011 . . . pop! In a mere two days, it fell back down to $30.

As I am writing this, in mid-2015, silver is selling for about $16 an ounce.

If there is any reason to stomach such volatility, it stems from the fact that silver has a very low correlation to other investments. For the three years prior to my writing these words, the price of silver has had very, very little correlation to stocks (except for some modest correlation to the stocks of silver-producing countries, such as Chile); almost no correlation to bonds; and even a decidedly limited correlation (0.75) to the price of gold.

If you must . . .

If you're going to take a position in silver, the iShares ETF is an option to consider. The expense ratio of 0.50 percent will eat into your profits or magnify your losses, but it will still likely be cheaper than paying a commission to buy silver bars or coins and then paying for a good-sized lockbox.

Oil and gas: Truly volatile commodities

The **United States Oil Fund (USO)** opened on the American Stock Exchange on April 10, 2006. Even though the fund is technically not an ETF but a very close cousin called a *commodity pool,* in my mind that date marks a sort of end to the Age of Innocence for ETFs. The United States Oil Fund, as official as that sounds, is run by a group called Victoria Bay Asset Management, which I will discuss in just a moment.

Don't mistake this fund for something like the Vanguard Energy ETF (VDE) or the Energy Select Sector SPDR (XLE) funds, both of which invest in oil companies like Exxon Mobil Corp. and Chevron. Don't mistake this fund for something like the precious metal commodity funds discussed in the preceding sections. Victoria Bay, wherever that is, is not filled with oil. Whereas Barclays and State Street maintain vaults filled with gold and silver, Victoria Bay deals in paper: futures contracts, to be exact.

In other words, this company uses your money to speculate on tomorrow's price of oil. If the price of oil rises in the next several weeks, you should, theoretically, earn a profit commensurate with that rise, minus the fund's costs of trading and its expense ratio of 0.61 percent. When the price of oil and gas go on a tear, this fund promises to give you a piece of that action, perhaps offering warm comfort every time you pull up to the pump and have to yank out your credit card. So should you pump your money into USO? Keep reading for my opinion about this slick investment.

Oily business

If you buy into USO and the price of oil escalates, you stand to make money. But is there reason to believe that the price of oil will always (or even usually) escalate? It has certainly gone up and down over the years, as have oil futures.

The issuer of the USO fund is not a major investment bank. Victoria Bay Asset Management, LLC is "a wholly-owned subsidiary of Wainwright Holdings, Inc., a Delaware Corporation . . . that also owns an insurance company organized under Bermuda law." The fund's prospectus, especially the part about the management of Victoria Bay, makes for *very* interesting reading. I would not invest in this fund, and neither should you.

The sad saga of contango

As fate would have it, the promise of the United States Oil Fund has turned out to be nothing like the reality. Consider this: The price of an actual barrel of oil rose from about $40 in January 2009 to nearly $100 in June 2011. In the same time period, USO's share price went from about $35 to $38 — not much of an increase. Since then, of course, oil prices have tumbled, and USO is now selling at about $19.70 a share.

That horrid loss for investors, however, might be considered pure gravy compared to the return suffered by investors in Victoria Bay's United States Natural Gas Fund (UNG) introduced on April 18, 2007. Through mid-2011, this fund's share price, which started at about $90 a share, had fallen to — are you ready? — roughly $11 a share. Investors in UNG have had anything but a gas. Today, in mid-2015, the fund is selling shares at about $12.50.

The explanation for USO's plummeting share price and UNG's sink-like-a-rock share price can be found not only in the lackluster résumés of their managers and the dynamics of supply and demand for natural gas but also in something called *contango*. That's a word that nearly all investors in commodity ETFs, at least those that rely on futures contracts, wish to heck they never heard.

Contango refers to a situation where distant futures prices for a particular commodity start to run well ahead of near futures prices. In other words, if you want to maintain a futures position that looks one month out, you buy futures contracts for the next month that expire in 30 days. Then one month later you replace them with contracts that contango has made more expensive. The effect is sort of like holding a fistful of sand and watching the sand sift through your fingers until you are left with nothing but an empty hand.

As a result of contango, many commodity investors have lost money, and some have lost lots of money, in recent years — even in cases where, as with oil, the price of the commodity itself rose. The illustrious managers at Victoria Bay led their investors to slaughter. But more experienced managers were also caught with their trousers down.

For you, the ETF investor, I would advise much caution before investing in commodities, especially in funds that use futures and other derivatives.

Taxing your tax advisor

ETFs that use futures typically generate special tax forms called *K-1 forms*. If you ask anyone who has ever filed a tax return and needed to account for earnings from K-1 investments, he'll tell you that these forms are a pain in the butt. Not only have investors in UNG been stung by falling share prices, but also they often have found that they were paying their tax advisors considerably more than in previous years, simply to file the dastardly K-1s.

As if that weren't bad enough, any gains on the sale of funds that use futures are taxed largely at short-term capital gains rates, even if the funds were held for more than a year — just another one of those IRS quirks. (Granted, not many people have had this problem recently because gains are hard to come by with these funds.)

Playing the commodity market indirectly: A (somewhat) safer approach

Just as diversification works to dampen the risks of stock investing, it can similarly smooth out — to a degree — the ups and downs of investing in commodities. If you're willing to accept contango, the K-1 forms, and the natural volatility of most commodities (other than perhaps clay or granite), I urge you at least to diversify.

In a recent interview with the *Journal of Indexes,* famed investment guru Burton G. Malkiel, professor of economics at Princeton and author of *A Random Walk Down Wall Street,* had this to say about commodity investing: "I think [commodities] should be in every portfolio, but for individuals, my sense is that the way they should get them is through ensuring that they have in their portfolios companies that mine or manufacture the commodities."

He is not alone. Frustrated with the problems of commodity investing I've outlined in this chapter, and doubtful that commodity investing in the very long run will provide returns commensurate with the risk, many investment advisors of late have turned to Malkiel's solution. The drawback is that stocks in commodity-producing companies are not going to show the same lack of correlation, or offer the same diversification power, as pure commodities do. Investing in commodities this way is a trade-off.

Lately, I have been splitting the difference: Putting perhaps 3 to 4 percent of a portfolio in pure commodities and perhaps another 3 to 4 percent in one of the funds I outline next.

Oil and gas ETFs

More than two dozen ETFs allow you to invest in the stocks of oil and gas companies. Among them are these options:

- ✔ Vanguard Energy ETF (VDE)
- ✔ Energy Select Sector SPDR (XLE)
- ✔ iShares Dow Jones U.S. Energy Index (IYE)
- ✔ PowerShares Dynamic Energy Exploration & Production (PXE)
- ✔ iShares Dow Jones U.S. Oil Equipment & Services Index Fund (IEZ)
- ✔ iShares S&P Global Energy Index Fund (IXC)

The funds all sound different from each other, but when you look at each of their rosters, they are actually quite similar, and I feel equally lukewarm about all of them.

Keep in mind that the energy sector represents a large segment of the U.S. economy. Energy companies make up about 10 percent of the capitalization of the U.S. stock market. So just being invested in the market gives you decent exposure to energy.

Mining ETFs

Several ETFs allow you to invest in mining companies. These include:

- ✔ Market Vectors Gold Miners ETF (GDX)
- ✔ SPDR S&P Metals and Mining ETF (XME)
- ✔ Global X Silver Miners ETF (SIL)

To me, these funds may make more sense in a portfolio than the energy ETFs, but they aren't my preferred way of tapping into commodity-producing companies. For my preference, keep reading.

Materials or natural resources ETFs

To give me extra exposure to companies that mine for gold and silver, produce oil and gas, and either produce or distribute other commodities, I prefer broader natural resource funds. (I say "extra" because I already get exposure in my other stock funds.) If commodity prices pop, the broader natural resource funds generally do well, and I'm not taking on too much risk by banking on any one commodity or commodity group. A natural resources fund may also be called a *materials* fund.

Options in this category include these ETFs:

✔ Materials Select Sector SPDR (XLB)

✔ iShares Dow Jones U.S. Basic Materials (IYM)

✔ Vanguard Materials ETF (VAW)

✔ iShares S&P North American Natural Resources (IGE)

 One of my favorites in this category is the **SPDR S&P Global Natural Resources ETF (GNR)**. This fund has an expense ratio of 0.40 percent. About 48 percent of its holdings are in the United States or Canada, and the remaining 52 percent are spread out through both the developed world and emerging markets. It offers exposure to a good variety of commodity firms: oil and gas, fertilizers and agricultural chemicals, diversified metals and mining, and so on.

Tapping into commodity-rich countries

As commodity prices go, so (often) go the stock markets of countries that supply the world with much of its commodities. By and large, these are the emerging market nations. (Yes, developed nations, such as Canada, Australia, and the United States, also bring the world many commodities. But because their economies are larger and more diverse, commodity prices have a much lesser effect on their stock markets.)

Although country funds can be just as volatile as commodities themselves, you can invest, through Barclays iShares, in the stock markets of nations. For example, you can invest in:

✔ Gold-rich South Africa via **iShares MSCI South Africa (EZA)**

✔ Timber giant Brazil through **iShares MSCI Brazil (EWZ)**

✔ Multi-mineral-laden Malaysia with **iShares MSCI Malaysia (EWM)**

> ✔ Top silver producers Chile and Peru through **iShares MSCI Chile Investable Market (ECH)** and **iShares MSCI All Peru Capped (EPU)**

I would suggest that, instead of needlessly taking on the risks associated with any single country, you diversify any investment in emerging markets through one of several ETFs that allow you to invest in a broad array of emerging market nations. These funds include the **iShares MSCI Emerging Markets Index (EEM)**, the **BLDRS Emerging Markets 50 ADR (ADRE)**, and the **Vanguard Emerging Market ETF (VWO)**. I discuss these funds in some depth in Chapter 5.

Going Active with ETFs

It was perhaps foreshadowing, and somewhat ironic, that the very first actively managed ETF was issued by Bear Stearns. That was in March 2008. Within several months, the financial collapse of the investment banking industry, led by Bear Stearns, was well on its way to creating the worst bear market (more irony) of our lifetimes. That first ETF died, folding (with money returned to investors) in October 2008, as Bear Stearns, after 85 years in business, collapsed and itself folded.

Since that time, we've seen the arrival of about 130 actively managed ETFs and ETNs, most having appeared in only the past year or two. These active funds have thus far failed to accumulate a whole lot in assets. Here's why:

> ✔ **Most ETF buyers are indexers by nature.** They know that index funds, as a group, do much, much better over time than actively managed funds. (Read about this topic in Chapter 1, or for much more detail, see my book *Index Investing For Dummies,* also published by Wiley.)

> ✔ **Most ETF buyers want transparency.** Active managers, reluctant to reveal their "secret sauce," have not been too keen to comply with the transparency rules of ETFs, and they've been lobbying the authorities to do away with those transparency rules.

> ✔ **Many of the active funds are just plain goofy.**

> ✔ **Some of the active funds have been issued by relatively unknown and not terribly well-funded companies.**

As I write this chapter, a good number of ETFs in registration with the SEC are going to be hitting the market shortly (presuming they get the approval they seek). Of these, some will likely be issued by long-standing and respected companies, such as PIMCO (which has already entered the fray with a handful of both passive and actively managed bond ETFs) and T. Rowe Price.

You may be inclined to choose one of these actively managed funds. Heck, I may do so myself someday (maybe, possibly . . . but not likely). After all, if you're going to go active, there's no reason not to do it with an ETF. The active ETFs will probably wind up being less expensive and more tax efficient than their corresponding mutual funds.

But keep in mind that historically, actively managed funds as a group have not done nearly as well as index funds. That being said, active management may sometimes have an edge, especially in some areas of the investment world (such as commodities and non-Treasury bonds). And much of the advantage of index investing has been in its ultra-low costs — something that actively managed ETFs could possibly emulate. We will see.

 If you want to go with an actively managed fund, I would ask you at least to keep in mind the lessons learned from indexing and what has made indexing so effective over time. Basically, you want certain index-like qualities in any actively managed fund you pick:

- ✔ **Choose a fund with low costs.** With so many ETFs allowing you to tap into stocks or bonds for less than one-quarter of a percentage point a year, you do not need or want any fund that charges much more. Any U.S. stock or bond fund that charges more than a percentage point, or any foreign fund or commodity fund that charges more than 1.5 percent, is asking too much, and the odds that such a fund will outperform are very, very slim. Go elsewhere.

- ✔ **Watch your style.** Make sure that any fund you choose fits into your overall portfolio. Studies show that index funds tend to do better than active funds in both large caps and small caps, but you have a better chance in small caps that your active fund will beat the indexes.

✔ **Check the manager's track record — carefully.** Make sure that the track record you're buying is long-term. (Any fool can beat the S&P 500 in a year. Doing so for ten years is immensely more difficult.) I'd look at performance in both bull and bear markets, but your emphasis should be on average annual returns over time compared with the performance of the fund's most representative market index over the same period.

✔ **Don't go overboard with active management.** Studies show *so* conclusively that index investing kicks butt that I would be very hesitant to build anything but a largely indexed portfolio, using the low-cost indexed ETFs that I suggest throughout this book.

Part III
Customizing and Optimizing Your ETF Portfolio

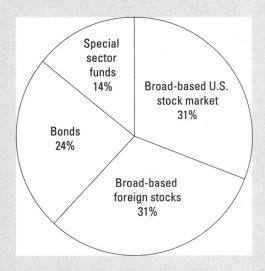

Special sector funds 14%

Broad-based U.S. stock market 31%

Bonds 24%

Broad-based foreign stocks 31%

In this part . . .

🖉 Sift through samples of investment situations and strategies to help visualize the portfolio that will best serve yours.

🖉 Give retirement account options a good look-see.

🖉 Get a firm handle on risk and return so that you can best balance your portfolio.

🖉 Learn when to sit back and wait — and when the time is right to rebalance your portfolio.

🖉 Sample ETF options for a different take on investing.

Chapter 9

Sample ETF Portfolio Menus

● ●

In This Chapter

▶ Revisiting risk and return

▶ Introducing Modern Portfolio Theory (MPT)

▶ Visualizing different portfolio options

▶ Comparing various retirement account options

▶ Taking action if your employer's 401(k) plan stinks

● ●

*T*he ideal portfolio (if such a thing exists) for a 30-year-old who makes $75,000 a year is very different from the portfolio of a 75-year-old whose income is $30,000 a year. The optimal portfolio for a 40-year-old worrywart differs from the optimal portfolio for a 40-year-old devil-may-care type. The portfolio of dreams following a three-year bear market when interest rates are low may look a wee bit different from a prime portfolio following a ten-year bull run when interest rates are high.

Every financial professional I know goes about portfolio construction in a somewhat different way. In this chapter, I walk you through the steps that I take and that have worked well for me.

Needless to say (since this is, after all, a book about exchange-traded funds), my primary materials are ETFs, as I believe they should be for most, but not all, investors. My portfolio-building tools involve some sophisticated Morningstar software, my HP 12C financial calculator, a premise called *Modern Portfolio Theory,* a statistical phenomenon called *reversion to the mean,* and various measures of risk and return. But rest assured that this isn't brain surgery, or even elbow surgery. You can be a pretty good portfolio builder yourself by the time you finish this chapter.

So, How Much Risk Can You Handle and Still Sleep at Night?

The first questions I ask myself — and the first questions anyone building a portfolio should ask — are these: *How much return does the portfolio-holder need to see? And how much volatility can the portfolio-holder stomach?* So few things in the world of investments are sure bets, but this one is: The amount of risk you take or don't take will have a great bearing on your long-term return. You simply are not going to get rich investing in bank CDs. On the other hand, you aren't going to lose your nest egg in a single week, either. The same cannot be said of a tech stock — or even a bevy of tech stocks wrapped up in an ETF.

A well-built ETF portfolio can help to mitigate risks but not eliminate them. Before you build your portfolio, ask yourself how much risk you need to take to get your desired return . . . and take no more risk than that.

 Please forget the dumb old rules about portfolio building and risk. How much risk you can or should take on depends on your wealth, your age, your income, your health, your financial responsibilities, your potential inheritances, and whether you're the kind of person who tosses and turns over life's upsets. If anyone gives you a pat formula — "Take your age, subtract it from 100, and that, dear friend, is how much you should have in stocks" — please take it with a grain of salt. Things just aren't nearly that simple.

A few things that just don't matter

Before I lay out what matters most in determining appropriate risk and appropriate allocations to stocks, bonds, and cash (or stock ETFs and bond ETFs), I want to throw out just a few things that really *shouldn't* enter into your thinking, even though they play into many people's portfolio decisions:

- ✔ The portfolio of your best friend, which has done well.

- ✔ Your personal feelings on the current administration, where the Fed stands on the prime interest rate, and which way hemlines on women's dresses are moving this fall.

- ✔ The article you clipped out of *Lotsa Dough* magazine that tells you that you can earn 50 percent a year by investing in . . . whatever.

Listen: Your best friend may be in a completely different economic place than you are. His well-polished ETF portfolio, laid out by a first-rate financial planner, may be just perfect for him and all wrong for you.

As far as the state of the nation and where the Dow is headed, you simply don't know. Neither do I. (It was once argued that the stock market moves up and down with the hemlines on women's dresses . . . or whether an NFC or AFC team wins the Super Bowl this year.) The talking heads on TV pretend to know, but they don't know squat. Nor does the author of that article in the glossy magazine (filled with ads from mutual fund companies) that tells you how you can get rich quickly in the markets. The secrets to financial success cannot be had by forking over $5.00 for a magazine.

(Whenever I read about some prognosticator suggesting a handful of stocks or mutual funds for the coming year, I Google him to see what projections he made a year prior. Then I check to see how his picks have done. You should do the same! Invariably, my dog Norman, the killer poodle, could do a better job picking stocks.)

The stock market over the course of the past century has returned an average of about 10 percent annually (7 percent or so after inflation). Bonds have returned about half as much. A well-diversified portfolio, by historical standards, has returned something in between stocks and bonds — maybe 7 to 8 percent (4 to 5 percent after inflation). With some of the advice in this book, even though market performance in the future may fall a bit shy of the past, you could see personal returns roughly approximating these numbers. But don't take inordinate risk with any sizeable chunk of your portfolio in the hope that you are going to earn 50 percent a year after inflation — or even before inflation. It won't happen.

On the other hand, don't pooh-pooh a 7 to 8 percent return. Compound interest is a truly miraculous thing. Invest $20,000 today, add $2,000 each year, and within 20 years, with "only" a 7.5 percent return, you'll have $171,566. (If inflation is running in the 3 percent ballpark, that $171,566 will be worth about $110,000 in today's dollars.)

The irony of risk and return

In a few pages, I provide you with some sample portfolios appropriate for someone who should be taking minimal risk as opposed to someone who should be taking more risk. At this point, I want to digress for a moment to say that in a perfect world, those who need to take the most risk would be the most able to take it on. In the real world, sometimes sadly ironic, those who need to take the most risk really can't afford to.

Specifically, a poor person needs whatever financial cushion he has. He can't afford to risk the farm (not that he has a farm) on a portfolio of mostly stocks. A rich person, in contrast, can easily invest a chunk of discretionary money in the stock market, but he really doesn't need to because he's living comfortably without the potential high return. It just isn't fair. Yet no one is to blame, and nothing can be done about it. It is what it is.

The 20x rule

Whatever your age, whatever your station in life, you probably wouldn't mind if your investments could support you. But how much do you need in order for your investments to support you? That's actually not very complicated and has been well studied: You need at least 20 times whatever amount you expect to withdraw each year from your portfolio, assuming you want that portfolio to have a good chance of surviving at least 20 to 25 years.

That is, if you need $30,000 a year — in addition to Social Security and any other income — to live on, you should ideally have $600,000 in your portfolio when you retire, assuming you retire in your mid-60s. You can have less, but you may wind up eating into principal if the market tumbles — in which case you should be prepared to live on less, or get a part-time job.

(Factor in the value or partial value of your home only if it is paid up and if you foresee a day when you can downsize.)

The rationale behind the 20x Rule is this: It allows you to withdraw 5 percent from your portfolio the first year, and then adjust that amount upward each year to keep up with inflation. The studies show that a well-diversified portfolio from which you take such withdrawals has a good chance of lasting at least 20 years, which is how long you may need the cash flow if you retire in your 60s and live to your mid-80s.

If you think you might live beyond your mid-80s, or if you want to retire prior to your mid-60s, then having more than 20 times your anticipated expenses would be an excellent idea. It would also be an excellent idea to limit your initial withdrawal, if you can, to 4 percent a year, just in case you live a long life.

In truth, I'd much rather see you have 25 times your anticipated expenses in your portfolio before you retire at any age. But for many Americans who haven't seen a real pay increase in years, this is indeed a lofty goal. For that reason, I say go with 20 times but be prepared to tighten your belt if you need to.

If you are still far away from that 20 times mark, and you are not in debt, and your income is secure, and you are not burning out at work, and you have enough cash to live on for six months, then with the rest of your loot, you might tilt toward a riskier ETF portfolio (mostly stock ETFs). You need the return.

If you have your 20 times (or better yet, 25 times) annual cash needs already locked up or close to it, and you're thinking of giving up your day job soon, you should probably tilt toward a less risky ETF portfolio (more bond ETFs). After all, you have more to lose than you have to gain. You do need to be careful, however, that your investments keep up with inflation. Savings accounts are unlikely to do that.

If you have way more than 25 times annual expenses, con-
gratulations! You have many options, and how much risk you
take will be a decision that's unrelated to your material needs.
You may, for example, want to leave behind a grand legacy,
in which case you might shoot for higher returns. Or you may
not care what you leave behind, in which case leaving your
money in a tired savings account, or "investing" in a high-
performance but low-yielding Ferrari, wouldn't make much
difference.

Other risk/return considerations

I doubt I can list everything you should consider when determining the proper amount of risk to take with your investments, but here are a few additional things to keep in mind:

- ✔ **What is your safety net?** If worse came to worst, do you
  have family or friends who would help you if you got in
  a real financial bind? If the answer is yes, you can add a
  tablespoon of risk.

- ✔ **What is your family health history? Do you lead a
  healthy lifestyle?** These are the two greatest predictors
  of your longevity. If Mom and Dad lived to 100, and you
  don't smoke and you do eat your vegetables, you may be
  looking at a long retirement. Add a dollop of risk — you'll
  need the return.

- ✔ **How secure is your job?** The less secure your employment, the more you should keep in nonvolatile investments (like short-term bonds or bond funds); you may
  need to draw from them if you get the pink slip next
  Friday afternoon.

- ✔ **Can you downsize?** Say you are close to retirement, and
  you live in a McMansion. If you think that sooner or later
  you will sell it and buy a smaller place, you have some
  financial cushion. You can afford to take a bit more risk.

The limitations of risk questionnaires

Yes, I give my clients a risk questionnaire. And then I go
through it with them to help them interpret their answers.

Lots of websites offer investment risk questionnaires, but instead of having anyone interpret the answers, a computer just spits out a few numbers: You should invest x in stocks and y in bonds. Yikes!

Please, please, don't allow a computer-generated question-naire to determine your financial future! I've tried many of them, and the answers can be wacky.

For example: One question that appears on many web ques-tionnaires is this: *Please rate your previous investment experience and level of satisfaction with the following six asset classes.* And then they list money market funds, bonds, stocks, and so on.

I had a client named Jason who was a 38-year-old with a solid job and no kids. After taking an online questionnaire, he was told he should be invested almost entirely in money market funds and bonds based on his previous "very low" satisfaction with stocks and stock mutual funds. This young man definitely should not invest in any stocks or stock funds, the computer-generated program told him, because of his "very low" satis-faction with the funds he had invested in previously.

Oh, jeesh. The reason Jason had "very low" satisfaction with stocks and stock funds is that he got snookered by some stock broker (posing as a "financial planner") into buying a handful of full-load, high-expense ratio, actively managed mutual funds that (predictably) lost him money. That expe-rience should have *no* bearing on the development of this young man's portfolio, which should have the lion's share invested in stock ETFs or mutual funds.

What I'm saying is that after reading this book, if you aren't too certain where you belong on the risk/return continuum, perhaps you should hire an experienced and impartial finan-cial advisor — if only for a couple of hours — to review your portfolio with you.

Keys to Optimal Investing

When you have a rough idea of where you should be risk-wise, your attention should turn next to fun matters such as Modern Portfolio Theory, reversion to the mean, cost minimization, and tax efficiency, all of which are covered in the sections that follow.

Incorporating Modern Portfolio Theory

The subject I'm about to discuss is a theory much in the same way evolution is a theory: The people who don't believe it — and, yes, there are some — are those who decide to disregard all the science. Modern Portfolio Theory (MPT) says that if you diversify your portfolio — putting all kinds of eggs into all kinds of baskets — you reduce risk and optimize return.

You get the most bang for your buck, according to MPT, when you mix and match investments that have little *correlation*. In other words, if you build your portfolio with different ETFs that tend to do well (and not so well) in different kinds of markets, you'll have a lean and mean portfolio.

Lately, MPT has been the source of a lot of controversy. It hasn't been working as well as it did in the past. At times in the past few years, there have been stretches of days, even weeks and months, when different asset classes — U.S. stocks, foreign stocks, bonds, commodities, and real estate — have all moved up and down nearly in lockstep. This was the case, unfortunately, in 2008. Like a flock of geese, just about every investment you could imagine headed south at the same time.

While correlations can change over time — and lately the major asset classes have shown alarmingly high rates of correlation — you shouldn't simply scrap the idea that diversification and the quest for noncorrelation are crucial. However, you may want to be cautious of too much reliance on diversification. Yes, you can diversify away much risk. But you should also have certain low-risk investments in your portfolio, investments that hold their own in any kind of market. Low-risk investments include FDIC-insured savings accounts; money market funds; short-term, high-credit-quality bonds; and bank CDs.

Minimizing your costs

Most ETFs are cheap, which is one of the things I love about them. The difference between a mutual fund that charges 1.4

percent and a typical ETF that charges 0.2 percent adds up to a *lot* of money over time. One of my favorite financial websites, www.moneychimp.com, offers a fund-cost calculator. Invest $100,000 for 20 years at 8 percent and deduct 0.2 for expenses; you're left with $449,133. Deduct 1.4 percent, and you're left with $359,041. That's a difference of about $90,000. The after-tax difference, given that most ETFs (or at least the ones I tend to recommend) are highly tax-efficient index funds, would likely be much greater.

Because the vast majority of ETFs fall into the super-cheap to cheap range (generally 0.1 to 0.5 percent), the differences among ETFs won't be quite so huge. Still, in picking and choosing ETFs, cost should always be a factor.

Of course, with ETFs, you often pay a small trading fee every time you buy and sell. That too should be examined and minimized. Do all your trading online, and choose a brokerage house that gives you the best deal. If you're going to make frequent buys and sells, either choose ETFs that you can trade commission-free, or opt instead to build your portfolio with mostly low cost, no-load index mutual funds. See my book *Index Investing For Dummies* (Wiley) for more on index mutual funds.

Striving for tax efficiency

Keeping your investment dollars in your pocket and not lining Uncle Sam's is one big reason to choose ETFs over mutual funds. ETFs are, by and large, much more tax efficient than active mutual funds. But some ETFs are going to be more tax efficient than others. I cover this issue later in the chapter.

For now, let me say that you must choose wisely which ETFs get put into which baskets. In general, high dividend and interest-paying ETFs (REIT ETFs, bond ETFs) are best kept in tax-advantaged accounts.

Timing your investments (just a touch)

If you've read much of this book already, by now you realize that I'm largely an *efficient market* kind of guy. I believe that the ups and downs of the stock and bond market — and of any individual security — are, in the absence of true inside information, unpredictable. (And trading on true inside information is illegal.) For that reason, among others, I prefer indexed ETFs and mutual funds over actively managed funds.

However, that being said, I also believe in something called *reversion to the mean.* This is a statistical phenomenon that colloquially translates to the following: What goes up must come down; what goes waaaay up, you need to be careful about investing too much money in.

At the time I'm writing this, for example, commodities (especially gold and silver) and natural resource stocks have been flying high for years. Emerging market stocks and bonds have also been outperforming big time. These are good reasons that you may want to be just a wee bit cautious about overstocking your portfolio in these particular asset classes.

I'm *not* suggesting that you go out and buy any ETF that has underperformed the market for years, or sell any ETF that has outperformed. But to a small degree, you should factor in reversion to the mean when constructing a portfolio.

For example, say you decide that your $100,000 portfolio should include a 15 percent allocation in the Vanguard Mega Cap 300 ETF (MGC) and an equal allocation in the Vanguard Small Cap ETF (VB), and you happen to be entering the market after an incredible several-year bull market in large cap stocks, with small caps falling far behind. If anything, I'd be inclined to slightly overweight small cap stocks, putting perhaps 16 or 17 percent in VB and maybe 13 to 14 percent in MCG.

Please don't go overboard. I'm suggesting that you use reversion to the mean to very gently tweak your portfolio percentages — not ignore them! This "going-against-the-crowd" investment style is popularly known as *contrarian investing.*

Finding the Perfect Portfolio Fit

Time now to peek into my private world, as I reveal some of the ETF-based portfolios I've worked out for clients over the years (and updated, of course, as some newer ETFs proved to be superior to the old). You should look for the client that you most resemble, and that example will give you some *rough* idea of the kind of advice I would give you if you were a client. All names, of course, have been changed to protect privacy. For the sake of brevity, I provide you with only a thumbnail sketch of each client's financial situations.

Considering the simplest of the simple

Before I get into anything complicated or present any actual client portfolios, I want to introduce an easier-than-easy ETF portfolio, which you can see in Table 9-1. What I've constructed is a perfectly fine, workable investment model with decent (although not great) diversification. It may be enough for anyone without a great amount in savings (say less than $50,000), or someone who has more but wants to keep things as simple as simple can be.

Table 9-1	The Simplest ETF Portfolio Model		
	Aggressive	*Middle-of-the-Road*	*Conservative*
Vanguard Mega Cap 300 ETF (MGC)	20 percent	16 percent	12 percent
Vanguard Small Cap ETF (VB)	20 percent	14 percent	8 percent
Vanguard FTSE All-World ex-US ETF (VEU)	20 percent	16 percent	12 percent
Vanguard FTSE All-World ex-US Small Cap Index ETF (VSS)	20 percent	14 percent	8 percent
Vanguard Total Bond Market ETF (BND)	15 percent	30 percent	45 percent
iShares Barclays TIPS Bond Fund (TIP)	5 percent	10 percent	15 percent

I include (in order of appearance) large cap stocks, small cap stocks, international stocks (large and small), and bonds (both conventional and inflation-adjusted).

This portfolio can be tailored to suit the aggressive investor who can deal with some serious ups and downs in the hopes of achieving high long-term returns; the conservative investor who can't stand to lose too much money; or the middle-of-the-road investor. Keep in mind that you should always have three to six months in living expenses sitting in cash or near-cash (money markets, short-term CDs, Internet checking account, or very short-term high-quality bond fund). You should also have all your credit card and other high interest debt paid up. The rest of your money is what you may invest.

Racing toward riches

High-risk/high-return ETF portfolios are made up mostly of stock ETFs. After all, stocks have a very long history of clobbering most other investments — *if* you give them enough time. Any portfolio that is mostly stocks should have both U.S. and international stocks, large cap and small cap, and value and growth, for starters. If the portfolio is diversified into industry sectors, a high-risk/high-return strategy would emphasize fast-growing sectors such as technology.

Let's consider the case of Jason, a single, 38-year-old pharmaceuticals salesman. You met him earlier in the chapter. Jason came to me after getting burned badly by several high cost, load mutual funds that performed miserably over the years. Still, given his steady income of $120,000 and his minimal living expenses (he rents a one-bedroom apartment in Allentown, Pennsylvania), Jason has managed to sock away $220,000. His job is secure. He has good disability insurance. He anticipates saving $20,000 to $30,000 a year over the next several years. He enjoys his work and intends to work till normal retirement age. He plans to buy a new car (ballpark $30,000) in the next few months but otherwise has no major expenditures earmarked.

Jason can clearly take some risk. Following is the ETF-based portfolio that I designed for him, which is represented in Figure 9-1. Note that I had Jason put four to six months of emergency money, plus the $30,000 for the car, into a money market account, and that amount is not factored into this portfolio.

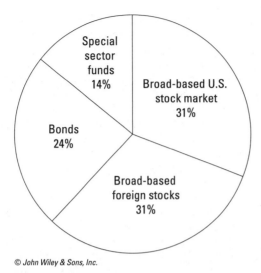

© *John Wiley & Sons, Inc.*

Figure 9-1: A portfolio that assumes some risk.

Also note that although this portfolio is made up almost entirely of ETFs, I do include one Pennsylvania municipal bond mutual fund to gain access to this asset class that's not yet represented by ETFs. Municipal bonds issued in Jason's home state are exempt from both federal and state taxes, which makes particular sense for Jason because he earns a high income and has no appreciable write-offs. At the time of this writing, New York and California were the only two states with their own municipal bond ETFs. In time, and probably sooner rather than later, I'm quite sure there will be others.

Finally, although this portfolio is technically 76 percent stocks and 24 percent bonds, I include a 4 percent position in emerging market bonds, which can be considerably more volatile than your everyday bond. As such, I don't really think of this as a "76/24" portfolio, but more like an "80/20" portfolio, which is just about as volatile a portfolio as I like to see.

Sticking to the middle of the road

Next, I present Jay and Racquel, who are ages 63 and 59, married, and have successful careers. Even though they are old enough to be Jason's parents, their economic situation actually warrants a quite similar high-risk/high-return portfolio. Both husband and wife, however, are risk-averse.

Jay is an independent businessman with several retail properties (valued at roughly $1.6 million); Racquel is a vice presi-
dent at a major publishing house. Their portfolio: $800,000
and growing. Within several years, the couple will qualify for
combined Social Security benefits of roughly $42,000. Racquel
also will receive a fixed pension annuity of about $30,000.
The couple's goal is to retire within five to seven years, and
they have no dreams of living too lavishly; they should have
more than enough money. The fruits of their investments, by
and large, should pass to their three grown children and any
charities named in their wills.

Being risk-averse, Jay and Racquel keep 30 percent of their
portfolio in high quality municipal bonds. They handed me the
other 70 percent ($560,000) and told me to invest it as I saw fit.
My feeling was that 30 percent high quality bonds was quite
enough ballast, so I didn't need to add to their bond position
by very much. I therefore constructed a portfolio of largely
domestic and foreign stock ETFs. The size of their portfolio
(versus Jason's) warranted the addition of a few more asset
classes, such as a couple of market-neutral mutual funds and
holdings in two large timber REITs. At the couple's request,
I also invested a small amount in two commodity ETFs.

I did not include any U.S. REITs other than the timber REITs,
given that so much of the couple's wealth is already tied up
in commercial real estate. Figure 9-2 presents the portfolio
breakdown.

Taking the safer road

We financial professional types hate to admit it, but no matter
how much we tinker with our investment strategies, no matter
how fancy our portfolio software, we can't entirely remove the
luck factor. When you invest in anything, there's always a bit
of a gamble involved. (Even when you decide *not* to invest, by,
say, keeping all your money in cash, stuffed under the proverbial mattress, you're gambling that inflation won't eat it away
or a house fire won't consume it.) Thus, the best investment
advice ever given probably comes from Kenny Rogers:

> *You got to know when to hold 'em, know when to fold 'em*
>
> *Know when to walk away and know when to run.*

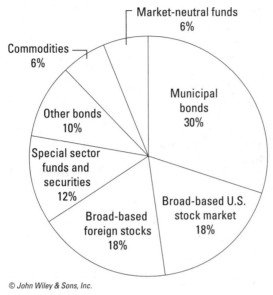

Market-neutral funds
6%

Commodities
6%

Municipal
bonds
30%

Other bonds
10%

Special sector
funds and
securities
12%

Broad-based U.S.
stock market
18%

Broad-based
foreign stocks
18%

Figure 9-2: A middle-of-the-road portfolio.

The time to hold 'em is when you have just enough — when you've pretty much met, or have come close to meeting, your financial goals.

I now present Richard and Maria, who are just about the same age as Jay and Racquel. They are 65 and 58, married, and nearing retirement. Richard, who sank in his chair when I asked about his employment, told me that he was in a job he detests in the ever-changing (and not necessarily changing for the better) newspaper business. Maria was doing part-time public relations work. I added up Richard's Social Security, a small pension from the newspaper, Maria's part-time income, and income from their investments, and I told Richard that he didn't have to stay at a job he hates. There was enough money for him to retire, provided the couple agreed to live somewhat frugally, and provided the investments — $700,000 — could keep up with inflation and not sag too badly in the next bear market.

I should add that the couple owned a home, completely paid for, worth approximately $350,000. They both agreed that they could downsize, if necessary.

For a couple like Richard and Maria, portfolio construction is a tricky matter. Go too conservative, and the couple may run out of money before they die. Go too aggressive, and the couple may run out of money tomorrow. It's a delicate balancing act. In this case, I took Richard and Maria's $700,000 and allocated 25 percent — $175,500 — to a Vanguard immediate fixed annuity. (The annuity was put in Richard's name, with 50 percent survivorship benefit for Maria. It was agreed that should Richard die before Maria, she would sell the home, and buy or rent something more economical.) The rest of the money — $525,000 — I allocated to a broadly diversified portfolio largely constructed using ETFs. Figure 9-3 shows the portfolio breakdown.

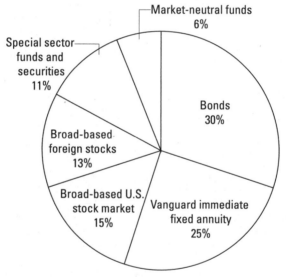

Figure 9-3: A portfolio aimed at safety.

Aiming for Economic Self-Sufficiency in Your Golden Years

I've got all the money I'll ever need — if I die by four o'clock this afternoon.

—Henny Youngman

How much you need in your portfolio to call yourself economically self-sufficient ("retired," if you prefer) starts off with a very simple formula: $A \times B = \$\$\$\$$. A is the amount of money you need to live on for one year. B is the number of years you plan to live without a paycheck. $\$\$\$\$$ is the amount you should have before bidding the boss adieu. There you have it.

Of course, that formula is waaay oversimplified. You also need to factor in such things as return on your future portfolio, inflation, Social Security, and (for the very lucky) potential inheritances.

Taking the basic steps

Whatever amount you set as your goal, you need to do three basic things to achieve it:

- ✔ Perhaps obvious, although most people prefer to ignore it: You have to *save*. A retirement portfolio doesn't just pop up from out of nowhere and grow like Jack's beanstalk. You need to feed it. Regularly.

- ✔ You need to invest your money wisely. That's where a well-diversified portfolio of ETFs comes in.

- ✔ It behooves you to take maximum advantage of retirement plans such as your company 401(k) plan — even if it's sub-par — IRAs, and (my favorite) Roth IRAs. If your 401(k) plan offers only pitiful options, you still need to do the best you can with what you've got. I provide some specific advice on that situation later in this chapter.

Choosing the right vessels

If you will, try to think of your retirement plans — your 401(k), your IRA — as separate vessels of money. How much your nest egg grows depends not just on how much you put into it and which investments you choose, but also which vessels you have. Three basic kinds of vessels exist. (I'm big into threes all of a sudden.)

- ✔ First are your basic vanilla retirement plans, such as the company 401(k), the traditional IRA, or, for the self-employed, the SEP-IRA or Individual 401(k). These are all *tax-deferred* vessels: You don't pay taxes on the money in the year you earn it; rather, you pay taxes at whatever point you withdraw money from your account, typically only after you retire.

✔ Next are the Roth IRA and the 529 college plans. Those are *tax-free* vessels: As long as you play by certain rules (discuss them with your accountant), anything you plunk into these two vessels (money on which you've generally already paid taxes) can double, triple, or (oh please!) quadruple, and you'll never owe the IRS a cent.

✔ Third is your non-retirement brokerage or savings bank account. Except for certain select investments, such as municipal bonds ("munis"), all earnings on your holdings in these vessels are taxable.

Why your choice of vessels matters — a whole lot

How much can your choice of vessels affect the ultimate condition of your nest egg? *Lots.* Even in a portfolio of all ETFs.

True, ETFs are marvelously tax-efficient instruments. Often, in the case of stock ETFs, they eliminate the need to pay any capital gains tax (as you would with most mutual funds) for as long as you hold the ETF. Still, there may be taxes to pay at the end of the game when you finally cash out. And in the case of certain ETFs (such as any of the bond ETFs) that pay either interest or high dividends, you will certainly pay taxes along the way.

Suppose you're an average middle-class guy or gal with a marginal income tax rate of 30 percent (federal + state + local). Next, suppose that you have $50,000 on which you've already paid taxes, and you're ready to squirrel it away for the future. You invest this money in the iShares GS $ InvesTop Corporate Bond Fund (LQD), which yields (hypothetically) 6 percent over the life of the investment, and you keep it for the next 15 years. Now, if that ETF were held in your regular brokerage account, and you had to pay taxes on the interest every year, at the end of 15 years you'd have a pot worth $92,680. Not too shabby. But if you held that very same $50,000 bond ETF in your Roth IRA and let it compound tax free, after 15 years you'd have $119,828 — an extra *$27,148. And* you would pay no income tax on this cash hoard when you eventually draw from it.

Unfortunately, the amount of money that you can put into retirement accounts is limited, although the law has allowed the sum to grow in recent years. For example, as I write this book, the maximum annual contribution to the most commonly used retirement accounts, the IRA and the Roth IRA, is $5,500 if you're younger than 50 and $6,500 if you're 50 or older. (The amount is subject to change each year.) Other retirement plans, such as the 401(k) or SIMPLE plan, have higher limits, but there is always a cap. (Ask your accountant about these plan limits; the formulas can get terribly complicated.)

What should go where?

Given these limitations, which ETFs (and other investments) should get dibs on becoming retirement assets, and which are best deployed elsewhere? Follow these four primary principles (I've given up on threes), and you can't go too wrong:

✔ **Any investment that generates a lot of (otherwise taxable) income belongs in your retirement account.** Any of the bond ETFs, REIT ETFs, or high-dividend ETFs are probably best held in your retirement account. *Note:* Value stocks generally yield more in dividends than growth stocks.

✔ **Keep your emergency funds out of your IRA.** Any money that you think you may need to withdraw in a hurry should be kept out of your retirement accounts. Withdrawing money from a retirement account can often be tricky, possibly involving penalties if done before age 59½, and usually triggering taxation. You don't want to have to worry about such things when you need money by noon tomorrow because your teenage son just totaled the family car.

✔ **House investments with the greatest potential for growth in your tax-free Roth IRA.** This may include your small cap value ETF, your technology stock fund, or your emerging markets ETF. Roth IRA money won't ever be taxed (presuming no change in the law), so why not try to get the most bang for your ETF buck?

✔ **Foreign-stock ETFs are perhaps best kept in your taxable account.** That's because the U.S. government will reimburse you for any taxes your fund paid out to foreign governments, but only if you have that fund in a taxable account. Over the long run, this "rebate" can add about half a percentage point a year to the returns you get on these funds; it doesn't sound like a lot, but it can add up over time.

Before you decide where to plunk your investments, refer to the following two sections for the basic rules.

Caveat: Tax laws change all the time. For example, the current low rates on capital gains and dividends of 15 to 20 percent, is a fairly constant source of Congressional debate. Because of the constant changes in tax laws, I advise you (and your accountant) to review your portfolio every year or two to make sure that you have your assets in the right "vessels." Of course, there are other good reasons to review your portfolio, as well.

Curing the 401(k) Blues

Got one of those plans at work that's certain to eat you up alive in fees, about as well-diversified as a lunar landscape? Don't despair. All is not lost. Here's what I suggest:

- ✔ **Take the boss's money with a smile.** Make a big effort to shovel in at least the minimum required to get your full company match (which will differ from company to company). If you do not contribute enough to receive your employer's full matching contribution, you are, in essence, leaving free money on the table. Even if the investment options are horrible, you'll still end up well ahead of the game if your employer is kicking in an extra 25 or 50 percent.

- ✔ **Invest to the best of your ability, however poor the menu.** Among the horrible choices, pick the least horrible. Choose those that will give you exposure to different asset classes. Choose index funds if available. Strongly favor whichever funds are least expensive.

If you need help understanding the different offerings in your 401(k) plan, ask someone in the human resources department, or the plan administrator, to help you. If you can't get a clear answer (you very well may not), perhaps hire a financial planner for at least a short consult.

✔ **Argue for better options.** Tell the human resources people (diplomatically, of course) if their plan is a dog. They should look for another plan that includes either ETFs or (sometimes just as good) low-cost index mutual funds. Not sure what to say or where to send them? Specific advice is coming in the next bullet point.

✔ **Check your statements.** It doesn't happen often, thank goodness, but yes, sometimes employers steal from their employees' retirement funds. Or give your employer the benefit of the doubt: Maybe they're just incompetent (and it's just a coincidence that mistakes seem always to reduce your account balance and never go in your favor). Check your statements with some regularity, and make certain that the money you are contributing is actually being credited to your account.

✔ **Plan your rollover.** If you leave your job, you may have the option of keeping your 401(k) plan right where it is. But 90 percent of the time, you will do much better by rolling your 401(k) into a self-directed IRA and then building yourself a well-diversified ETF portfolio.

One important caveat: You can't withdraw Traditional IRA money without penalty until you are 59½, whereas some (but not all) 401(k) plans allow you to withdraw your money penalty-free at age 55 if you decide to retire at that point. Don't be too quick to initiate a rollover if you think you may need to tap your funds in the years between 55 and 59½.

Chapter 10

Understanding Risk and Return

In This Chapter

▶ Understanding the relationship between risk and return

▶ Measuring risk

▶ Introducing Modern Portfolio Theory

▶ Addressing the assertion that "MPT is dead"

▶ Seeking a balanced portfolio

> *October. This is one of the peculiarly dangerous months to speculate in stocks. The others are July, January, September, April, November, May, March, June, December, August, and February.*
>
> —Mark Twain

A peculiarly good writer, but also a peculiarly bad money manager, Twain sent his entire fortune down the river on a few bad investments. A century and a half later, investing, especially in stocks, can still be a peculiarly dangerous game. But today we have low-cost indexed ETFs and a lot more knowledge about the power of diversification. Together, these two things can help lessen the dangers and heighten the rewards of the stock market. In this chapter, I hope to make you a better stock investor — at least better than Mark Twain.

Risk Is Not Just a Board Game

Well, okay, actually Risk *is* a board game, but I'm not talking here about *that* Risk. Rather, I'm talking about investment risk. And in the world of investments, risk means but one thing: volatility. Volatility is what takes people's nest eggs, scrambles them, and serves them up with humble pie. Volatility is what causes investors insomnia and heartburn. Volatility is the potential for financially crippling losses.

Ask people who had most of their money invested in stocks in 2008. For five years prior (just as the five years hence), the stock market had done pretty darned well. Investors were just starting to feel good again. The last market downfall of 2000–2002 was thankfully fading into memory. And then . . . *POW* . . . the U.S. stock market tanked by nearly 40 percent over the course of the year. Foreign markets fell just as much. Billions and billions were lost. Some portfolios (which may have dipped more than 40 percent, depending on what kind of stocks they held) were crushed. Many who had planned for retirement had to readjust their plans.

There was nothing pretty about 2008.

Is risk to be avoided at all costs? Well, no. Not at all. Risk is to be mitigated, for sure, but risk within reason can actually be *a good thing.* That is because risk and return, much like Romeo and Juliet or Coronas and lime, go hand in hand. Volatility means that an investment can go way down or way up. You hope it goes way up. Without some volatility, you resign yourself to a portfolio that isn't poised for any great growth. And in the process, you open yourself up to another kind of risk: the risk that your money will slowly be eaten away by inflation.

If you are ever offered the opportunity to partake in any investment scheme that promises you oodles and oodles of money with "absolutely no risk," run! You are in the presence of a con artist or a fool. Such investments do not exist.

The trade-off of all trade-offs (safety versus return)

If you look at different investments over the course of time, you find an uncanny correlation between risk (volatility risk, not inflation risk) and return. Safe investments — those that really do carry genuine guarantees, such as U.S. Treasury Bills, FDIC-insured savings accounts, and CDs — tend to offer very modest returns (often negative returns after accounting for inflation). Volatile investments — like stocks and "junk" bonds, the kinds of investments that cause people to lose sleep — tend to offer handsome returns if you give them enough time.

Time, then, is an essential ingredient in determining appropriate levels of risk. You would be wise to keep any cash you are going to need within the next six months to a year in a savings bank, or possibly in an ETF such as the iShares Barclays 1–3 Year Treasury Bond Fund (SHY), a short-term bond fund that yields an exceptionally modest return (currently yielding about 0.5 percent) but is very unlikely to lose value. You should *not* invest that portion of your money in any ETF that is made up of company stocks, such as the popular SPY or QQQ. True, SPY or QQQ can (and should), over time, yield much more than SHY, but they are also much more susceptible to sharp price swings. Unless you are not going to need your cash for at least a couple of years (and preferably not for six or seven or more years), you are best off avoiding any investment in the stock market, whether it be through ETFs or otherwise.

So just how risky are ETFs?

Asking how risky, or how lucrative, ETFs are is like trying to judge a soup knowing nothing about the soup itself, only that it is served in a blue china bowl. The bowl — or the ETF — doesn't create the risk; what's inside it does. Thus stock and real estate ETFs tend to be more volatile than bond ETFs. Short-term bond ETFs are less volatile than long-term bond ETFs. Small-stock ETFs are more volatile than large-stock ETFs. International ETFs often see more volatility than U.S. ETFs. And international "emerging-market" ETFs see more volatility than international developed-nation ETFs.

Figure 10-1 shows some examples of various ETFs and where they fit on the risk-return continuum. Note that it starts with bond ETFs at the bottom (maximum safety, minimum volatility) and nearer the top features the EAFE (Europe, Australia, Far East) Index and the South Korea Index Fund. (An investment in South Korean stocks involves not only all the normal risks of business but also includes currency risk, as well as the risk that some deranged North Korean dictator may decide he wants to pick a fight. Buyer beware.)

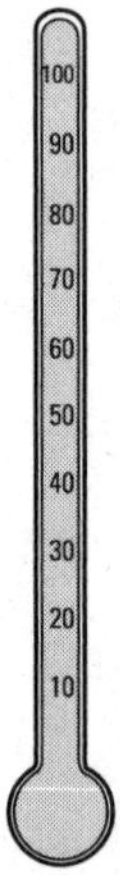

High Risk (and highest return potential)

100

90 iShares MSCI South Korea Index Fund (EWY)

80
70 iShares MSCI EAFE Index Fund (EFA)

60 Vanguard Mid Cap ETF (VO)
50

40 SPDR S&P 500 (SPY)

30
20 iShares Barclays 7-10 Year Treasury Bond Fund (IEF)

10 iShares Barclays 1-3 Year Treasury Bond Fund (SHY)

Low Risk (with more modest return potential)

© John Wiley & Sons, Inc.

Figure 10-1: The risk levels of a sampling of ETFs.

Keep in mind when looking at Figure 10-1 that I am segregating these ETFs — treating them as stand-alone assets — for illustration purposes. As I discuss later in this chapter (when I discuss something called Modern Portfolio Theory), stand-alone risk measurements are of limited value. The true risk of adding any particular ETF to your portfolio depends on what is already in the portfolio. (That statement will make sense by the end of this chapter. I promise!)

Smart Risk, Foolish Risk

There is safety in numbers, which is why teenage boys and girls huddle together in corners at school dances. In the case of the teenagers, the safety is afforded by anonymity and distance. In the case of indexed ETFs and mutual funds, safety is provided (to a limited degree only!) by diversification in that they represent ownership in many different securities. Owning many stocks, rather than a few, provides some safety by eliminating something that investment professionals, when they're trying to impress, call *nonsystemic risk.*

Nonsystemic risk is involved when you invest in any individual security, such as shares of HP, Martha Stewart Omnimedia, ImClone, (remember Martha and ImClone?), Enron, or General Motors. It's the risk that the CEO of the company will be strangled by his pet python, that the national headquarters will be destroyed by a falling asteroid, or that the company's stock will take a sudden nosedive simply because of some Internet rumor started by an 11th-grader in the suburbs of Des Moines. Those kinds of risks (and more serious ones) can be effectively eliminated by investing not in individual securities but in ETFs or mutual funds.

Nonsystemic risk contrasts with *systemic risk,* which, unfortunately, ETFs and mutual funds cannot eliminate. Systemic risks, as a group, simply can't be avoided, not even by keeping your portfolio in cash. Examples of systemic risk include the following:

- ✔ **Market risk.** The market goes up, the market goes down, and whatever stocks or stock ETFs you own will generally (though not always) move in the same direction.

- ✔ **Interest rate risk.** If interest rates go up, the value of your bonds or bond ETFs (especially long-term bond ETFs) will fall.

- ✔ **Inflation risk.** When inflation picks up, any fixed-income investments that you own (such as any of the conventional bond ETFs) will suffer. And any cash you hold will start to dwindle in value, buying less and less than it used to.

- ✔ **Political risk.** If you invest your money in the United States, England, France, or Japan, there's little chance that revolutionaries will overthrow the government anytime soon. When you invest in the stock or bond ETFs of certain other countries (or when you hold currencies from those countries), you'd better keep a sharp eye on the nightly news.

> ✔ **Grand scale risks.** The government of Japan wasn't over-thrown, but that didn't stop an earthquake and ensuing tsunami and nuclear disaster from sending the Tokyo stock market reeling in early 2011.

Although ETFs cannot eliminate systemic risks, don't despair. For while nonsystemic risks are a bad thing, systemic risks are a decidedly mixed bag. Nonsystemic risks, you see, offer no compensation. A company is not bound to pay higher dividends, nor is its stock price bound to rise simply because the CEO has taken up mountain climbing or hang gliding.

Systemic risks, on the other hand, do offer compensation. Invest in small stocks (which are more volatile and therefore incorporate more market risk), and you can expect (over the very long term) higher returns. Invest in a country with a history of political instability, and (especially if that instability doesn't occur) you'll probably be rewarded with high returns in compensation for taking added risk. Invest in long-term bonds (or long-term bond ETFs) rather than short-term bonds (or ETFs), and you are taking on more interest-rate risk. That's why the yield on long-term bonds is almost always greater.

In other words,

> Higher systemic risk = higher historical returns

> Higher nonsystemic risk = zilch

That's the way markets tend to work. Segments of the market with higher risks *must* offer higher returns or else they wouldn't be able to attract capital. If the potential returns on emerging-market stocks (or ETFs) were no higher than the potential returns on short-term bond ETFs or FDIC-insured savings accounts, would anyone but a complete nutcase invest in emerging-market stocks?

How Risk Is Measured

In the world of investments, risk means volatility, and volatility (unlike angels or love) can be seen, measured, and plotted. People in the investment world use different tools to measure volatility, such as standard deviation, beta, and certain ratios such as the Sharpe ratio. Most of these tools are not very hard to get a handle on, and they can help you better follow discussions on portfolio building that come later in this book. Ready to dig in?

Standard deviation: The king of all risk measurement tools

So you want to know how much an investment is likely to bounce? The first thing you do is look to see how much it has bounced in the past. Standard deviation measures the degree of past bounce and, from that measurement, gives us some notion of future bounce. To put it another way, standard deviation shows the degree to which a stock/bond/mutual fund/ETF's actual returns vary from its average returns over a certain time period.

Table 10-1 presents two hypothetical ETFs and their returns over the last six years. Note that both portfolios start with $1,000 and end with $1,101. But note, too, the great difference in how much they bounce. ETF A's yearly returns range from –3 percent to 5 percent while ETF B's range from –15 percent to 15 percent. The standard deviation of the six years for ETF A is 3.09. For ETF B, the standard deviation is 10.38.

Table 10-1	Standard Deviation of Two Hypothetical ETFs	
Balance, Beginning of Year	*Return (% Increase or Decrease)*	*Balance, End of Year*
ETF A		
1,000	5	1,050
1,050	–2	1,029
1,029	4	1,070
1,070	–3	1,038
1,038	2	1,059
1,059	4	1,101

(continued)

Table 10-1 *(continued)*

Balance, Beginning of Year	Return (% Increase or Decrease)	Balance, End of Year
ETF B		
1,000	10	1,100
1,100	6	1,166
1,166	−15	991
991	-8	912
912	15	1,048
1,048	5	1,101

Predicting a range of returns

What does the standard deviation number tell us? Let's take ETF A as an example. The standard deviation of 3.09 tells us that in about two-thirds of the months to come, we should expect the return of ETF A to fall within 3.09 percentage points of the mean return, which was 1.66. In other words, about 68 percent of the time returns should fall somewhere between 4.75 percent (1.66 + 3.09) and −1.43 percent (1.66 − 3.09). As for the other one-third of the time, anything can happen.

It also tells us that in about 95 percent of the months to come, the returns should fall within two standard deviations of the mean. In other words, 95 percent of the time you should see a return of between 7.84 percent [1.66 + (3.09 × 2)] and −4.52 percent [1.66 − (3.09 × 2)]. The other 5 percent of the time is anybody's guess.

Making side-by-side comparisons

The ultimate purpose of standard deviation, and the reason I'm describing it, is that it gives you a way to judge the relative risks of two ETFs. If one ETF has a 3-year standard deviation of 12, you know that it is roughly twice as volatile as another ETF with a standard deviation of 6 and half as risky as an ETF with a standard deviation of 24. A real-world example: The standard deviation for most short-term bond funds falls somewhere around 0.7. The standard deviation for most precious-metals funds is somewhere around 26.0.

Important caveat: Don't assume that combining one ETF with a standard deviation of 10 with another that has a standard deviation of 20 will give you a portfolio with an average standard deviation of 15. It doesn't work that way at all, as you will see in a few pages when I introduce Modern Portfolio Theory. The combined standard deviation will not be any greater than 15, but it could (if you do your homework and put together two of the right ETFs) be much less.

Beta: Assessing price swings in relation to the market

Unlike standard deviation, which gives you a stand-alone picture of volatility, beta is a relative measure. It is used to measure the volatility of something in relation to something else. Most commonly that "something else" is the S&P 500. Very simply, beta tells us that if the S&P rises or falls by x percent, then your investment, whatever that investment is, will likely rise or fall by y percent.

The S&P is considered the baseline, and it is assigned a beta of 1. So if you know that Humongous Software Corporation has a beta of 2, and the S&P shoots up 10 percent, Jimmy the Greek (if he were still with us) would bet that shares of Humongous are going to rise 20 percent. If you know that the Sedate Utility Company has a beta of 0.5, and the S&P shoots up 10 percent, Jimmy would bet that shares of Sedate are going to rise by 5 percent. Conversely, shares of Humongous would likely fall four times harder than shares of Sedate in response to a fall in the S&P.

In a way, beta is easier to understand than standard deviation; it's also easier to misinterpret. Beta's usefulness is greater for individual stocks than it is for ETFs, but nonetheless it can be helpful, especially when gauging the volatility of U.S. industry-sector ETFs. It is much less useful for any ETF that has international holdings. For example, an ETF that holds stocks of emerging-market nations is going to be volatile, trust me, yet it may have a low beta. How so? Because its movements, no matter how swooping, don't generally happen in response to movement in the U.S. market. (Emerging-market stocks tend to be more tied to currency flux, commodity prices, interest rates, and political climate.)

The Sharpe, Treynor, and Sortino ratios: Measures of what you get for your risk

 Back in 1966, a goateed Stanford professor named Bill Sharpe developed a formula that has since become as common in investment-speak as RBIs are in baseball-speak. The formula looks like this:

$$\frac{\text{Total portfolio return} - \text{Risk-free rate of return}}{\text{Portfolio standard deviation}} = \frac{\text{Sharpe measure}}{\text{(or Sharpe ratio)}}$$

The risk-free rate of return generally refers to the return you could get on a short-term U.S. Treasury bill. If you subtract that from the total portfolio return, it tells you how much your portfolio earned above the rate you could have achieved without risking your principal. You take that number and divide it by the standard deviation (discussed earlier in this section). And what *that* result gives you is the Sharpe ratio, which essentially indicates how much money has been made in relation to how much risk was taken to make that money.

Suppose Portfolio A, under manager Bubba Bucks, returned 7 percent last year, and during that year Treasury bills were paying 5 percent. Portfolio A also had a standard deviation of 8 percent. Okay, applying the formula,

$$\frac{7\% - 5\%}{8\%} = \frac{2\%}{8\%} = 0.25$$

That result wasn't good enough for Bubba's manager, so he fired Bubba and hired Donny Dollar. Donny, who just read *Investing in ETFs For Dummies,* takes the portfolio and dumps all its high-cost active mutual funds. In their place, he buys ETFs. In his first year managing the portfolio, Donny achieves a total return of 10 percent with a standard deviation of 7.5. But the interest rate on Treasury bills has gone up to 7 percent. Applying the formula,

$$\frac{10\% - 7\%}{7.5\%} = \frac{3\%}{7.5\%} = 0.40$$

The higher the Sharpe measure, the better. Donny Dollar did his job much better than Bubba Bucks.

The Treynor approach was first used by — you guessed it — a guy named Jack Treynor in 1965. Instead of using standard deviation in the denominator, it uses beta. The Treynor measure shows the amount of money that a portfolio is making in relation to the risk it carries relative to the market. To put that another way, the Treynor measure uses only systemic risk, or beta, while the Sharpe ratio uses total risk.

Suppose that Donny Dollar's portfolio, with its 10 percent return, had a beta of 0.9. In that case, the Treynor measure would be

$$\frac{10\% - 7\%}{0.9} = \frac{3\%}{0.9} = \frac{.03}{0.9} = 0.033$$

Is 0.033 good? That depends. It's a relative number. Suppose that the market, as measured by the S&P 500, also returned 10 percent that same year. It may seem like Donny isn't a very good manager. But when we apply the Treynor measure (recalling that the beta for the market is always 1.0),

$$\frac{10\% - 7\%}{1.0} = \frac{3\%}{1.0} = \frac{.03}{1.0} = 0.03$$

we get a lower number. That result indicates that while Donny earned a return that was similar to the market's, he took on less risk. Put another way, he achieved greater returns per unit of risk. Donny's boss will likely keep him.

Another variation on the Sharpe ratio is the Sortino ratio, which basically uses the same formula:

$$\frac{\text{Total portfolio return} - \text{Risk-free rate of return}}{\text{Portfolio standard deviation} \left(\text{downside only} \right)} = \text{Sortino ratio}$$

Note that instead of looking at historical ups and downs, it focuses only on the downs. After all, say members of the Sortino-ratio fan club, you don't lose sleep fretting about your portfolio rising in value. You want to know what your downside risk is. The Sortino-ratio fan club has been growing in size, but as yet, it is difficult to find Sortino-ratio calculations for any given security, including ETFs. I'm sure it will get easier over time, as comparing downside risk among various ETFs can be a helpful tool.

Meet Modern Portfolio Theory

For simplicity's sake, I've discussed the choice of one ETF over another (SHY or SPY) based on risk and potential return. In the real world, however, few people, if any, come to me or to any financial planner asking for a recommendation on a single ETF. More commonly, I'm asked to help build a portfolio of ETFs. And when looking at an entire portfolio, the riskiness of each individual ETF, although important, takes a back seat to the riskiness of the entire portfolio.

In other words, I would rarely recommend or rule out any specific ETF because it is too volatile. How well any specific ETF fits into a portfolio — and to what degree it affects the risk of a portfolio — depends on what else is in the portfolio. What I'm alluding to here is something called *Modern Portfolio Theory:* the tool I use to help determine a proper ETF mix for my clients' portfolios. I use this tool throughout this book to help you determine a proper mix for your portfolio.

Tasting the extreme positivity of negative correlation

Modern Portfolio Theory is to investing what the discovery of gravity was to physics. Almost. What the theory says is that the volatility/risk of a portfolio may differ dramatically from the volatility/risk of the portfolio's components. In other words, you can have two assets with both high standard deviations and high potential returns, but when combined they give you a portfolio with modest standard deviation but the same high potential return. Modern Portfolio Theory says that you can have a slew of risky ingredients, but if you throw them together into a big bowl, the entire soup may actually splash around very little.

The key to whipping up such pleasant combinations is to find two or more holdings that do not move in sync: One tends to go up while the other goes down (although both holdings, in the long run, will see an upward trajectory). In the figures that follow, I show how you'd create the fantasy ETF portfolio consisting of two high-risk/high-return ETFs with perfect negative correlation. It is a fantasy portfolio because perfect negative correlations don't exist; they simply serve as a target.

Figure 10-2 represents hypothetical ETF A and hypothetical ETF B, each of which has high return and high volatility. Notice that even though both are volatile assets, they move up and down at different times. This fact is crucial because combining them can give you a nonvolatile portfolio.

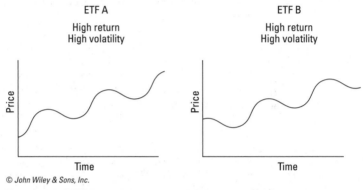

© *John Wiley & Sons, Inc.*

Figure 10-2: ETFs A and B each have high return and high volatility.

Figure 10-3 shows what happens when you invest in both ETF A and ETF B. You end up with the perfect ETF portfolio — one made up of two ETFs with perfect negative correlation. (If only such a portfolio existed in the real world!)

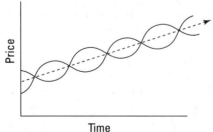

© *John Wiley & Sons, Inc.*

Figure 10-3: The perfect ETF portfolio, with high return and no volatility.

Settling for limited correlation

When the U.S. stock market takes a punch, which happens on average every three years or so, most U.S. stocks fall. When the market flies, most stocks fly. Not many investments regularly move in opposite directions. We do, however, find investments that tend to move independently of each other much of the time, or at least they don't move in the same direction all the time. In investment-speak, I'm talking about investments that have *limited* or *low correlation.*

Different kinds of stocks — large, small, value, and growth — tend to have limited correlation. U.S. stocks and foreign stocks tend to have even less correlation. But the lowest correlation around is between stocks and bonds, which historically have had almost no correlation.

Say, for example, you had a basket of large U.S. stocks in 1929, at the onset of the Great Depression. You would have seen your portfolio lose nearly a quarter of its value every year for the next four years. Ouch! If, however, you were holding high-quality, long-term bonds during that same period, at least that side of your portfolio would have grown by a respectable 5 percent a year. A portfolio of long-term bonds held throughout the growling bear market in stocks of 2000 through 2003 would have returned a hale and hearty 13 percent a year. (That's an unusually high return for bonds, but at the time the stars were in seemingly perfect alignment.)

During the market spiral of 2008, there was an unprecedented chorus-line effect in which nearly all stocks — value, growth, large, small, U.S., and foreign — moved in the same direction: down . . . depressingly down. At the same time, all but the highest quality bonds took a beating as well. But once again, portfolio protection came in the form of long-term U.S. government bonds, which rose by about 26 percent in value.

In August 2011, as S&P downgraded U.S. Treasurys, the stock markets again took a tumble, and — guess what? — Treasurys, despite their downgrade by S&P (but none of the other raters), spiked upward!

Reaching for the elusive Efficient Frontier

Correlation is a measurable thing, represented in the world of investments by something called the *correlation coefficient*. This number indicates the degree to which two investments move in the same or different directions. A correlation coefficient can range from –1 to 1.

A correlation of 1 indicates that the two securities are like the Rockettes: When one kicks a leg, so does the other. Having both in your portfolio offers no diversification benefit. On the other hand, if investment A and investment B have a correlation coefficient of –1, that means they have a perfect negative relationship: They always move in the opposite directions. Having both in your portfolio is a wonderful diversifier. Such polar-opposite investments are, alas, very hard to find.

Accusations that MPT is dead are greatly exaggerated

Since the market swoon of 2008, some pundits have claimed that Modern Portfolio Theory is dead. This claim is nonsense. As I mention, U.S. government bonds more than held their own during this difficult period. And even though all styles of stock moved down in 2008, they moved at different paces. And the degree to which they recovered has differed significantly. You see these differences in the charts in the upcoming sections "Filling in your style box" and "Buying by industry sector."

The investors who were hurt terribly in 2008 were those who sold their depressed stocks and moved everything into cash or "safe" bonds. Those bonds, at least long-term government bonds, then lost about 16 percent of their value in 2009. Those who flipped from stocks to bonds would have been doubly wounded. But those who kept the faith in MPT and rebalanced their portfolios would not have been so badly wounded. These investors would have been buying stock in 2008 instead of selling it. And any investor with a fairly well-balanced portfolio of stocks and bonds would have recouped her losses within two years after the market bottomed in March 2009.

A correlation coefficient of zero means that the two investments have no relationship to each other. When one moves,
the other may move in the same direction, the opposite direction, or not at all.

As a whole, stocks and bonds (not junk bonds, but high-
quality bonds) tend to have little to negative correlation.
Finding the perfect mix of stocks and bonds, as well as other
investments with low correlation, is known among financial
pros as looking for the *Efficient Frontier*. The Frontier represents the mix of investments that offers the greatest promise
of return for the least amount of risk.

Fortunately, ETFs allow us to tinker easily with our investments so we can find just that sweet spot.

Mixing and Matching Your Stock ETFs

Reaching for the elusive Efficient Frontier means holding both
stocks and bonds — domestic and international — in your
portfolio. That part is fairly straightforward and not likely to
stir much controversy (although, for sure, experts differ on
what they consider optimal percentages). But experts definitely don't agree on how best to diversify the domestic-stock
portion of a portfolio. Two competing methods predominate:

- ✔ One method calls for the division of a stock portfolio into
  domestic and foreign, and then into different styles: large
  cap, small cap, mid cap, value, and growth.

- ✔ The other method calls for allocating percentages of a
  portfolio to various industry sectors: healthcare, utilities,
  energy, financials, and so on.

My personal preference for the small to mid-sized investor, especially the ETF investor, is to go primarily with the
styles. But there's nothing wrong with dividing up a portfolio
by industry sector. And for those of you with good-sized
portfolios, a mixture of both, without going crazy, may be
optimal.

Filling in your style box

Most savvy investors make certain to have some equity in each of the nine boxes of the grid in Figure 10-4, which is known as the *style box* or *grid* (sometimes called the *Morningstar grid*).

Large cap value	Large cap blend	Large cap growth
Mid cap value	Mid cap blend	Mid cap growth
Small cap value	Small cap blend	Small cap growth

© *John Wiley & Sons, Inc.*

Figure 10-4: The style box or grid.

The reason for the style box is simple enough: History shows that companies of differing cap (capitalization) size (in other words, large companies and small companies), and value and growth companies, tend to rise and fall under different economic conditions. I define *cap size, value,* and *growth* in Chapter 3, and I devote the next few chapters to showing the differences among styles, how to choose ETFs to match each one, and how to weight those ETFs for the highest potential return with the lowest possible risk.

Table 10-2 shows how well various investment styles, per Morningstar, have fared in the past several years. Each figure represents the average annual return of all combined ETFs that represent a particular investment style.

Table 10-2	Recent Performance of Various Investment Styles				
	2010	*2011*	*2012*	*2013*	*2014*
Large cap growth ETFs	18.6	0.7	16.4	36.0	14.1
Large cap value ETFs	16.5	4.6	14.0	30.0	12.5
Small cap growth ETFs	10.7	0.5	14.5	41.3	2.5
Small cap value ETFs	25.9	-4.4	19.6	39.2	5.8

Buying by industry sector

The advent of ETFs has largely brought forth the use of sector investing as an alternative to the grid. Examining the two models toe-to-toe yields some interesting comparisons — and much food for thought.

One study on industry-sector investing, by Chicago-based Ibbotson Associates, came to the very favorable conclusion that sector investing is a potentially superior diversifier to grid investing because times have changed since the 1960s, when style investing first became popular. "Globalization has led to a rise in correlation between domestic and international stocks; large, mid, and small cap stocks have high correlation to each other. A company's performance is tied more to its industry than to the country where it's based, or the size of its market cap," concluded Ibbotson.

The jury is still out. For now, I invite you to do a little comparison of your own by comparing Tables 10-2 and 10-3. Note that by using either method of diversification, some of your investments should smell like roses in years when others stink. Also, recall what I state earlier about how all stocks crashed in 2008 but recovered at significantly different paces; this is true of various styles and sectors. And it is certainly true for various geographic regions. Modern Portfolio Theory is not dead!

Table 10-3 shows how well various industry sectors (as measured by their respective S&P indexes) fared in recent years. Yes, there are ETFs that track each of these industry sectors — and many more sectors.

Table 10-3   Recent Cumulative Return of Various Market Sectors, as of June 2015

	1-year return %	*3-year return %*	*5-year return %*	*10-year return %*
Healthcare	25.7	107.9	160.5	140.0
Energy	-17.8	19.6	43.8	75.8
Materials	2.5	48.6	70.7	85.9
Utilities	4.2	24.3	−55.3	48.0

Don't slice and dice your portfolio to death

One reason I tend to prefer the traditional style grid to industry-sector investing, at least for the nonwealthy investor, is that there are simply fewer styles to contend with. You can build yourself, at least on the domestic side of your stock holdings, a pretty well-diversified portfolio with but four ETFs: one small value, one small growth, one large value, and one large growth. With industry-sector investing, you would need a dozen or so ETFs to have a well-balanced portfolio, and that may be too many.

I hold a similar philosophy when it comes to global investing. Yes, you can, thanks largely to the iShares lineup of ETFs, invest in about 50 individual countries. (And in many of these countries, you can furthermore choose between large cap and small cap stocks, and in some cases, value and growth.) Too much! I prefer to see most investors go with larger geographic regions: U.S., Europe, Asia, emerging markets, and so forth.

You don't want to chop up your portfolio into too many holdings, or the transaction costs (especially with ETFs that require trading costs) can start to bite into your returns. Rebalancing gets to be a headache. Tax filing can become a nightmare. And, as many investors learned in 2008 — okay, I'll admit it, as *I* learned in 2008 — having a very small position in your portfolio, say less than 2 percent of your assets, in any one kind of investment isn't going to have much effect on your overall returns anyway.

As a rough rule, if you have $50,000 to invest, consider something in the ballpark of a 5- to 10-ETF portfolio, and if you have $250,000 or more, perhaps look at a 15- to 25-ETF portfolio. Many more ETFs than this won't enhance the benefits of diversification but will entail additional trading costs every time you rebalance your holdings.

Chapter 11

Exercising Patience and Learning Exceptions

- -

In This Chapter

▶ Peeking into the world of day-trading

▶ Treating time as your friend, not your enemy

▶ Rebalancing your ETF portfolio when the time is right

▶ Playing (or not playing) the ETF options game

- -

*M*any, if not most, day-traders (who just *love* ETFs, especially the really kooky ones) believe in something called *technical analysis:* the use of charts and graphs to predict movements in securities. The basic idea behind the charts, comes from a best-selling book on technical analysis.

 I once had the honor of interviewing one of the biggest names in technical analysis. This guy writes books, gives seminars, and tells everyone that he makes oodles and oodles of money by following charting patterns and buying and selling securities accordingly. At the time I interviewed him, I had been a journalist for 20 years, writing for many of the top U.S. magazines, covering many topics. If you develop one thing being a journalist for two decades, it is a very well-honed bullshit radar. I can tell you after spending an hour on the phone with this "expert" that he is perhaps making of oodles and oodles of money with his books and seminars, but he is *not* making oodles and oodles of money with his charts.

And neither will you.

The key to success in investing isn't to do a lot of trading based on secret formulas every bit as fruitless as alchemy. The key is to keep your investment costs low (ETFs will do that for you), diversify your portfolio (ETFs can do that, too), lose as little as possible to taxes (ETFs can help there, too), and exercise patience (that part's up to you).

In this chapter, I present the evidence to back up my contention that buying and holding, more or less, with regular rebalancing, is the thing to do. Yes, that's true even in today's uber-turbulent markets. You will see that the true champions of the investing world are those with the most patience. Here's a great quote that you may want to post next to your computer to look at the next time you contemplate swapping one ETF for another. It's from someone I admire quite a bit — someone who, I've heard, knows a little bit about investing.

> *The stock market is a method for transferring money from the impatient to the patient.*
>
> —Warren Buffet

In this chapter, you also discover the difference between hypothetical investing (the kind of investing where you allegedly get rich overnight) and investing in the real world in which Warren Buffet invests. The difference is huge.

The Tale of the Average Investor (A Tragicomedy in One Act)

I talk a bit in this book about *correlation,* the tendency for two things (such as two ETFs or other investments) to move in the same direction. A correlation of 1.0 indicates a *perfect* correlation: think Lucille Ball in the mirror imitating Harpo Marx. Another perfect correlation is the correlation between stock prices and the public's willingness to purchase those stocks.

For some strange reason, the market for stocks (and stock funds, such as ETFs) does not work the same way as, say, the market for cars, shoes, or pineapples. With most products, if the seller drops the price, the public is likely to increase consumption. With stocks and stock funds, when the price *rises,* the public increases consumption.

For example, after tech stocks had their fabulous run in the 1990s, only then — in the latter part of the decade — did money start pouring into tech stocks. After the bubble had burst and tech stocks were selling cheaper than tarnished dirt, people were selling right and left, and no one was buying. As I write these words, the same kind of buying frenzy has been seen more recently in social-media stocks and China stocks. As soon as the bubble bursts on these, well, it'll be red-tag-sale day once again.

Returns that fall way short of the indexes

Every year, the investment research group Dalbar compares the returns of indexes to the returns that mutual fund investors see in the real world. In their 2014 study, the Dalbar research crew found that the average stock mutual fund investor for the 20 years prior to December 31, 2013 earned but 5.02 percent a year. This compares to the more than 9.22 percent that someone would have earned just plunking his money in an S&P 500 index fund for those two decades and leaving it put. Bond fund investors did just as poorly in relation to the bond indexes.

How to explain such lackluster investor returns? In part, the culprit is the average investor's inclination to invest in pricey and poor-performing mutual funds. Another problem is that the average investor jumps ship too often, constantly buying when the market is hot, selling when it chills, and hopping back on board when the market heats up again. He is forever buying high and selling low — not a winning strategy, by any means.

ETFs can solve the first part of the problem. They are, as long as you pick the right ones, not pricey. In fact, they cost very little. Most ETFs are also guaranteed not to underperform the major indexes because they mirror those indexes. As for the jumping-ship problem, however, I fear that ETFs can actually *exacerbate* the problem.

ETFs can make failure even easier!

ETFs were brought into being by marketing people from the Toronto Stock Exchange who saw a way to beef up trading volume. Unlike mutual funds, which can be bought and sold only at day's end, ETFs trade throughout the day. In a flash, you can plunk a million in the stock market. A few seconds later, you can sell it all.

Yipeee!

In other words, the next time Dalbar does a 20-year return study, after ETFs have really caught on with the average investor, I fear that their findings, if they include ETFs, may be even more dismal. Remember: Just because ETFs can be traded throughout the day doesn't mean you *have* to or that you *should* trade them!

The vast majority of ETF trades are made by institutional investors: managers of mutual funds or hedge funds, multibillion-dollar endowments, pension funds, and investment banks. These are highly trained, incredibly well-paid professionals who do nothing all day but study the markets.

When you go to buy, say, the Financial Select Sector SPDR ETF (XLF) which represents stocks in the financial sector, you are betting that the price is going to go up. If you are day-trading, you are betting that the price will go up that day. If you are selling, you are betting that the price will fall that day. Someone, most likely a highly educated financial professional with an army of researchers and computers more powerful than the FBI's, someone who does nothing but study financial stocks 80 hours a week (for which reason his wife is about to leave him) is on the other end of your transaction. As you sell, he — we'll call him Chad — is buying. Or, as you buy, he is selling. Obviously, Chad's vision of the next few hours and days is different from yours. Chad may not know that his wife Barbie is about to leave him for a professional hockey player, but if either of you has any idea which way financial stocks are headed, well . . . let me put it this way: Do you really think that you know something Chad doesn't? Do you really think that you're going to get the better end of this deal?

Obviously, lots of ETF traders think they are pretty smart because ETFs are among the most frequently traded of all securities. But that's not necessarily a good thing. Read on.

The lure of quick riches

If you jump onto the Internet, as I just did, and type in the words "Market timing success," you will see all kinds of websites and newsletters offering you all kinds of advice (much of it having to do with reading charts) that's sure to make you rich. Add the initials "ETF" to your search, and you'll quickly see that an entire cottage industry has formed to sell advice to wannabe ETF day-traders.

According to these websites and newsletters, following their advice has yielded phenomenal returns in the past (and they'll give you specific BIG numbers proving it). And following their advice in the future (after you've paid your hefty subscription fee) will likewise yield phenomenal returns.

If you're wondering, by the way, who regulates investment websites and newsletters and the performance figures they publish, wonder no more. No one does. The U.S. Supreme Court decided in 1985 that, just as long as a newsletter is providing general and not personal advice, the publisher is protected by the free-speech provisions of the First Amendment.

John Rekenthaler, a VP at Morningstar, once told me (and I love how he put it): "Investment newsletter publishers have the same rights as tabloid publishers. There's nothing illegal about a headline that reads 'Martian Baby Born with Three Heads!' and there's nothing illegal about a headline that reads 'We Beat the Market Year In and Year Out!'" Both should be read with equal skepticism.

Caveat emptor: ETF-trading websites for suckers

One way to make sure you don't end up a player in an investment horror story is to be on the lookout for ridiculous claims. Market timing services are popping up all over the Internet. Why not? ETFs are hot. They are in the news. They sound so impressive. And there is a sucker born every minute.

Please, please, don't fork over your money assuming that you're going to get the secrets to instant wealth by trading ETFs. It won't happen.

Following are just a few examples of the countless websites hoping to lure you in with big promises. I can't possibly list them all, so be wary:

www.stockmarkettiming.com

Cost: $359/year for the "Platinum Plan"

Direct from the website: *StockMarketTiming.com, LLC is a financial service for investors and traders who want to increase their portfolios in the most non-stressful and effective way possible in both bullish and bearish markets! We have developed a market timing system that uses technical analysis for trading the popular Exchange Traded Funds (ETFs) — DIA, SPY, and QQQ, which has produced outstanding gains!*

Russell says: Outstanding gains for whom?

We are the home of the most honest, concise, credible (unbiased and zero-hype), low-risk, and one of the most effective financial Web sites on the Internet today!

Russell says: I'm glad that the hype is unbiased. I hate biased hype.

www.marketpolygraph.com

Cost: $713.00/month for investment professionals, but "only" $45.65/month for U.S. private investors.

Direct from the website: *Marketpolygraph provides proprietary market timing research to private and professional investors who receive decisive trading signals for specific exchange traded funds (ETFs). Our simple and direct market timing research entails only minutes of follow-up effort every month and represents the singular requirement for realizing exceptional investment returns.*

Russell says: Only minutes a month, eh? It takes me longer than that each day just to boot up my computer.

www.kt-timing.com/rydex

Cost (from the website): *Yearly subscription is USD 200 for each of the OPEN and CLOSE model signals. If you opt for the OPEN and CLOSE signals, both services are available for USD 300 and are needed to utilize the Combined OPEN/CLOSE strategy.*

Russell says: Don't ask me what any of the above means; I have no idea, and I refuse to risk hurting my brain by trying to find out.

Direct from the website: *The objective of all our short term trading models is to achieve unsurpassed all weather performance.*

Russell says: Good objective.

Patience Pays, Literally

The flip side of flipping ETFs is buying and holding them, which is almost certain, in the long run, to bring results far superior to market timing. It's the corollary to choosing ETFs over stocks. Study after study shows that the markets are, by and large, *efficient.* What does that mean? So many smart players are constantly buying and selling securities, always on the lookout for any good deals, that your chances of beating the indexes, whether by market timing or stock picking, are very slim.

One of but many studies on the subject, "The Difficulty of Selecting Superior Mutual Fund Performance" by Thomas P. McGuigan, appeared in the *Journal of Financial Planning.* McGuigan found that only 10 to 11 percent of actively managed mutual funds outperform index funds over a 20-year period. (*Active managers* are professionals who try to pick stocks and time the market.)

We can probably safely assume that the professionals do better than the amateurs, and even the professionals fail to beat the market 90 percent of the time.

It is not unusual for the stock market to lose or gain several percentage points in a week. With every blip, a good number of investors feel a tightening in their chest. And yet, history has seen huge losses, and somehow, eventually, the market has always recovered.

Remember September 11, 2001? Following the destruction of the World Trade Center towers, the Dow immediately dropped more than 7 percent. Six months later, the Dow was up by 10.5 percent. On September 24, 1955, President Eisenhower's heart attack led to a one-day drop of 6.5 percent. Six months later, the Dow was up 12.5 percent. I could give example after example.

In 2008, the market had its worst dip since the Great Depression; the S&P 500 tumbled nearly 37 percent for the year. But it came back, gaining 26 percent in 2009 and about 15 percent in 2010. Had you rebalanced in 2008, shaving off bonds and buying up stock at rock-bottom prices, your portfolio (provided it was well-diversified) would likely have fully recovered in just two years . . . and then continued to rise for the next four years . . . and counting. . . . That's not to say that the market will *always* come back. One of these days . . . well, even Rome eventually fell. But history shows that the stock market is a mighty resilient beast. I suggest that you build a portfolio of ETFs — including stock and bond ETFs — and hang tight. Sooner or later (barring some truly major economic upheaval), you will very likely be rewarded.

Exceptions to the Rule (Ain't There Always)

A buy-and-hold approach to ETF investing doesn't mean that you should purchase a bunch of ETFs and *never* touch them.

In certain circumstances, it makes sense to trade ETFs rather than buy and hold. For example, you need to rebalance your portfolio, typically on an annual basis, to keep risk in check, and on occasion you may want to swap ETFs to harvest taxes at year end. Or life changes may warrant tweaking a portfolio.

Rebalancing to keep your portfolio fit

Few investors walked away from 2008 smelling like a rose. But those who were slammed, truly slammed, were those who had more on the stock side of their portfolios than they should have. It happens, and it happens especially after bull markets, such as we saw in the several years prior to 2008.

Let's take the case of Samantha. In 2003, when she was 50 years old, she sat down and looked at her financial situation and goals. She determined that she warranted a 60/40 (60 percent stock/40 percent bond) portfolio and duly crafted a darned good one. But then she got lazy. She held that portfolio without touching it through the stock market boom years of 2003 through 2007. As a result, her portfolio morphed from a 60/40 mix to a 70/30 mix by the start of 2008.

Uh oh.

In other words, just when the market tanked, just when she could have really used the ballast that bonds provide, her lopsided portfolio, due to neglect, was primed for disaster. The stock market fell by about 37 percent, and her 70 percent stock portfolio fell by about a quarter. That's a big fall. And to add insult to injury, just when stocks hit rock bottom, she had no "dry powder" (cash) with which to reload her stock portfolio.

It is in large part to prevent such big falls, and lack of "dry powder," that you need to rebalance. That is, on a regular basis, you need to do exactly the opposite of what most investors do: You need to sell off some of your winners and buy up the losers.

By doing so, not only do you cap your risk, but studies show that you will juice your returns. By systematically buying low and selling high, you may, over the long run, increase your average annual returns by as much as 1.5 percent. That's not a bad return at all for an exercise that shouldn't take you more than a couple hours! (***Note:*** I say "as much as 1.5 percent" because the profitability of rebalancing will depend on how many asset classes you own and the correlations they have to each other.)

How rebalancing works

Samantha actually hurt herself in two ways. In 2008, she was 55 years old: five years closer to retirement than she was when she established her "ideal" 60/40 portfolio. It would have been reasonable at that point for Samantha to adjust her mix to, say, 50/50 to reflect the need for a bit more protection against market losses as retirement neared. Had Samantha started off 2008 with a proper portfolio, whether it was 60/40 after rebalancing or 50/50 after reassessing and then rebalancing, she would have been in a much better position to weather the storm that was coming.

 Prepare yourself for the next market storm! How? The answer is fairly simple: Don't allow any one slice of your portfolio to overtake the rest. Periodically pull your portfolio back into balance.

To illustrate, I'll use a simple middle-of-the-road ETF portfolio. At the start of the year, the portfolio is just where you want it to be: 60 percent diversified stocks, 40 percent bonds. But it turns out to be a banner year for stocks, and especially for small cap U.S. stocks. At the end of the year, as you can see in Table 11-1, the portfolio looks quite different.

 What to do? Bring things back into balance, starting with the bond position. That's because the split between stocks and bonds has the greatest impact on portfolio risk. In this example, you need to increase the bond allocation from 31 percent back up to 40 percent. If you have a year-end portfolio of $100,000, that means you'll buy $9,000 of BND and TIP to bring up your bond allocation by 9 percentage points.

Where will the $9,000 come from? That depends. You could sell off part of your stock position, which may be necessary given that things are pretty seriously out of balance. But do keep in mind that selling off winning positions in a taxable account will require you to pay capital gains — and possibly a small commission on the ETF trades. So to the extent possible, try to rebalance by shoring up your losing positions with fresh deposits or with dividends and interest earned on your portfolio.

Table 11-1   A Shifting Portfolio Balance

Beginning of Year One (In Balance)

ETF	Percent of Portfolio
Vanguard Mega Cap 300 ETF (MGC)	16 percent
Vanguard Small Cap ETF (VB)	14 percent
Vanguard FTSE All-World ex-US ETF (VEU)	16 percent
Vanguard FTSE All-World ex-US Small Cap Index ETF (VSS)	14 percent
Vanguard Total Bond Market ETF (BND)	30 percent
iShares Barclays TIPS Bond Fund (TIP)	10 percent

End of Year One (Out of Balance)

ETF	Percent of Portfolio
Vanguard Mega Cap 300 ETF (MGC)	17 percent
Vanguard Small Cap ETF (VB)	19 percent
Vanguard FTSE All-World ex-US ETF (VEU)	18 percent
Vanguard FTSE All-World ex-US Small Cap Index ETF (VSS)	15 percent
Vanguard Total Bond Market ETF (BND)	22 percent
iShares Barclays TIPS Bond Fund (TIP)	9 percent

How often to rebalance

The question of how often to rebalance has been studied and restudied, and most financial professionals agree that once a year is a good time frame, at least for those still in the accumulation phase of their investing careers. Anything less frequent than that increases your risk as positions get more and more out of whack. Anything more frequent than annually and you may lower your returns by interrupting rallies too often and increasing your "friction" costs (trading commissions, spreads, and possible taxes).

Keep these costs in mind as you rebalance. Tweaking a portfolio by a few dollars here and there to achieve "perfect" balance may not make financial sense.

A rule I give myself is never to pay more than one-half of 1 percent to make a trade for rebalancing purposes. In the example in the previous section, if a trade of $8,000 for BND will cost you $10, you are forking out only 0.125 percent to make the trade . . . so, by all means, make the trade.

If, however, to get your portfolio in perfect balance, you were faced with making a $1,000 trade that would cost you $10 (1 percent of the amount you're trading), I don't think I'd opt to spend the $10. I'd rather wait another year (or perhaps less if I sensed that a major shift had occurred) before acting.

Another way to approach rebalancing is to seek to address any allocations that are off by more than 10 percent, and don't sweat anything that's off by less. In other words, if BND is given an allocation in the portfolio of 30 percent, I wouldn't worry too much about rebalancing unless that percentage falls to 27 percent, or rises to 33 percent.

Rebalancing for retirees

If you are in the *decumulation* phase of your investing career (that's a fancy way of saying that you are living off of your savings), you may want to rebalance every 6 months instead of 12. The reason: Rebalancing has a third purpose for you, in addition to risk-reduction and performance-juicing. For you, rebalancing is a good time to raise whatever cash you anticipate needing in the upcoming months. In times of super-low interest rates on money market and saving accounts, such as we've seen in recent years, it can be profitable to rebalance more often so that you don't need to keep as much cash sitting around earning squat.

Contemplating tactical asset allocation

Astute readers — such as you — now may be wondering this: If you can juice your returns by rebalancing (systematically buying low and selling high), can you perhaps juice your returns even more by *over*-rebalancing? In other words, suppose you design a 60/40 portfolio, and suddenly stocks tank. Now you have a 50/50 portfolio. Might you consider not only buying enough stock to get yourself back to a 60/40 portfolio, but also (because stocks are so apparently cheap) buying even *more* stocks than you need for simple rebalancing purposes?

Investment professionals call this kind of maneuver "tactical asset allocation." It is the art of tilting a portfolio given certain economic conditions. Tactical asset allocation is different than market timing only in the degree to which action is required. With tactical asset allocation, you make a gentle and unhurried shift in one direction or another, whereas market timing entails a more radical and swift shifting of assets. While tactical asset allocation, done right, may add to your bottom line, market timing will almost always cost you. The division between the two can be a fine line, so proceed with caution.

Understanding the all-important P/E ratio

I talk about reversion to the mean in Chapter 9. If a certain asset class has been seeing returns much, much lower than its historical average, you may want to very slightly overweight that asset class. If, for example, you are considering over-weighting U.S. stocks, it makes more sense to do it when U.S. stocks are selling relatively cheaply. Typically, but not always, an asset class may be "selling cheap" after several years of underperforming its historical returns.

But is there any way to find a more objective measure of "selling cheap"? Investment legend Benjamin Graham liked to use something called the P/E ratio. The P stands for price; the E stands for earnings. When the market price of a stock (or all stocks) is high, and the earnings (or profits for a company or companies) are low, then you have a high P/E ratio; conversely, when the market price is down but earnings are up, you have a low P/E ratio. Graham, as well as his student Warren Buffett, preferred to buy when the P/E ratio was low.

Throughout much of this book, I urge you to consider tilting your entire stock portfolio, on a permanent basis, toward lower P/E stocks, otherwise known as *value stocks*. Here, I'm talking not about a permanent tilt but a mild, temporary one. It stands to reason that if value stocks outperform other stocks — and historically they have done just that — if the entire stock market appears to be a value market, then that market may outperform in the foreseeable future.

Recent work by Yale University economist Robert J. Shiller has lent credence to the notion that buying when the P/E ratio is low raises your expected returns. In fact, Shiller has tinkered with the way the P/E ratio is defined so that the earnings part of the equation looks back over a decade (rather than the typical one year) and then factors in inflation. Shiller's research, based on tracking market returns with varying P/E ratios over the decades, indicates that when his adjusted P/E ratio is low, the stock market is more likely to produce gains over the following decade. When the P/E ratio is high (it reached an all-time high of about 44 in 1999, for example), you may be looking forward to a decade of very low (or no) returns.

Applying the ratio to your portfolio

Although Shiller's theories have been hotly debated, it stands to reason that, if they are applied carefully, you may just do yourself a favor to slightly overweight all stocks when the P/E ratio is low and to underweight all stocks when the P/E ratio is high. But against the probability that Shiller's formula holds, you need to weigh the very real transaction costs involved in shifting your portfolio. On balance, I wouldn't suggest engaging in tactical asset allocation very often . . . and then only if the numbers seem to be shouting at you to act.

One very quick way to check the P/E ratio for the entire stock market would be to look up an ETF that tracks the entire market, such as the Vanguard Total Stock Market ETF (VTI), on Vanguard's website (www.vanguard.com) or on just about any financial website (such as www.morningstar.com) to see the P/E ratio. Or, to see Shiller's newfangled P/E calculations, go to www.multpl.com. (The P/E ratio is sometimes called the "multiple.")

The historical average for Shiller's adjusted P/E over the past 50 years is 19.5. As I'm writing these words, the P/E for the market is 27.2. Warm. If stock prices should continue to race ahead of earnings, and you start to see an adjusted P/E of, say, 30 or more — or, conversely, 10 or less — you may want to gently — very gently — tweak your portfolio in one direction or another.

Did I remember to say gently?

If, all things being equal, you determine that you should have a portfolio of 60 percent stocks, and if the adjusted P/E falls to the low teens, consider adding 2 to 3 percentage points to your stock allocation, and that's all. If the market P/E falls to 10, then maybe, provided you can stomach the volatility, consider adding yet another percentage point or two, or even three, to your "neutral" allocation. If the adjusted P/E rises to 30 or so, you may want to lighten up on stocks by a few points. Please, keep to these parameters. Tilting more than a few percentage points — particularly on the up side (more stocks than before) — increases your risks beyond the value of any potential gain.

Buying unloved assets

Ever notice how weeds grow so much faster than the plants that you *want* to see grow? For years, Morningstar has advocated, and continues to advocate with varying levels of enthusiasm, something called "Buy the Unloved." It calls not for overweighting asset classes that sport low P/E ratios, but for overweighting asset classes that investors (being the lemmings that they are) have abandoned in droves. In other words, you are encouraged to buy "weeds."

As I'm writing this, for example, Morningstar is listing U.S. growth stocks as being among the weediest of asset classes . . . despite high performance in past years. According to the strategy, now might be a good time to buy U.S. growth stocks, and a not-so-good time to buy the more popular investment categories of large blend stocks and conservative allocation funds.

If you shift from the "loved" to the "unloved" (in other words, you allocate tactically), history shows you will do quite well. According to Morningstar, holding unloved categories of funds for three to five years would have seen annual average returns of 10.3 percent over the past 20 years, versus 6.4 percent for loved funds.

Investing the SweetSpot way

A few years ago, I encountered a man named Neil Stoloff, a wealth manager outside Detroit, Michigan, who calls his shop SweetSpot Investments LLC. Just as Robert Shiller crunched historical data to come up with a new-and-improved way of measuring P/E, Stoloff crunched historical data and came up with a new-and-improved way of defining "unloved."

Each January, Stoloff examines more than 600 ETFs and mutual funds that track about 100 different U.S. and global industry sectors (from energy to financials to healthcare), as well as entire foreign markets (such as France, South Africa, and Malaysia). He calculates the flow of money into and out of each sector and market over the year that just ended, looking for the greatest outflows. And that's where he invests: into the areas that most investors have decided they wouldn't touch with the proverbial 10-foot pole. These are the weediest weeds Stoloff can find. A year later he repeats the process, and while he's at it he sells whatever was bought three years prior.

Given that he tinkers just once a year, I would classify Stoloff as a professional tactical asset allocator rather than a market timer.

How has SweetSpot performed? Exceptionally well. For the latest performance figures, go to Stoloff's website, www. sweetspotinvestments.com. (Disclosure time: Neil and I have become good friends. At my urging, Neil had his return figures audited by an independent accounting firm, and I believe I'm being objective in saying that this guy may be on to something.)

Stoloff's strategy is not one that do-it-yourselfers can easily employ. Finding and making sense of the data on flows for each of 600 funds isn't nearly as easy as finding market-sector P/E ratios. To tap into the SweetSpot methodology, you would need to become a SS subscriber.

Tell Stoloff that you learned of his methodology through this book, and he'll give you a discounted subscription. For details, write neil@sweetspotinvestments.com. (Disclosure #2: In exchange for this endorsement — ringing or not — I stand to receive zero compensation from Neil or anyone else associated with SweetSpot Investments.)

Even if SweetSpot isn't your cup of tea, you can still benefit from the wisdom of investing contrarily. Often you can get a sense of the direction in which the herd is running simply by keeping your ears open at cocktail parties. Just move opposite the crowd — slowly — and you'll likely outperform over time. As with any other kind of tactical asset allocation, I urge you to always consider your total allocation and make certain that you remain well diversified.

Revamping your portfolio with life changes: Marriage, divorce, and babies

Rebalancing to bring your portfolio back to its original allocations, making tactical adjustments, and harvesting losses for tax purposes aren't the only times it may make sense to trade ETFs. Just as you may need a new suit if you lose or gain weight, sometimes you need to tailor your portfolio in response to changes in your life.

As I discuss in Chapter 9, the prime consideration in portfolio construction is whether you can and should take risks in the hope of garnering high returns or whether you must limit your risk with the understanding that your returns will likely be modest. (Diversification can certainly help to reduce investment risk, but it can't eliminate it.) Certain events may occur in your life that warrant a reassessment of where you belong on the risk/return continuum.

If a single person of marrying age walks into my office and asks me to help build a portfolio, I will want to know if wedding bells will be ringing in the near future. A married couple walks into my office, and one of the first things I take note of is how close they sit together. And if the woman has a swollen belly, I really take notice.

No, I'm not being nosy. Marriage, divorce, and the arrival of babies are major life changes and need to be weighed heavily in any investment decisions. So too are the death of a spouse or parent (especially if that parent has left a hefty portfolio to the adult child); a child's decision to attend college; any major career changes; or the imminent purchase of a new house, new car, or Fabergé egg.

Betsy and Mark: A fairly typical couple

Betsy and Mark are engaged to be married. They don't have a lot of money. But both are young (early 30s), in good health, gainfully employed, and without debt. They plan to merge their savings of roughly $37,500 and asked me to help them invest it for the long haul.

The first thing we do is to decide how much money to take out to cover emergencies. Given their monthly expenses of roughly $3,500, we decide to earmark five months' of living expenses — $17,500 — and plunk that into an online savings account. That leaves us with $20,000 to invest.

Normally, I wouldn't consider an ETF portfolio for $20,000, but this is money they tell me they aren't going to touch until retirement. I urge them both to open a Roth IRA. (Any money you put into a Roth IRA grows tax-free for as long as you wish, and withdrawals are likewise tax-free.) I ask them to divide the $20,000 between the two accounts. Since each of them can contribute $5,000 per year, I have them both make double contributions — one for the past year (for example, you can make your 2015 contribution until April 15, 2016), and one for the current year.

To save on transaction costs and keep things simple for now, I limit the number of investments and give each partner a "partial" portfolio. Neither account alone is well-diversified, but together, they are.

Betsy's Roth IRA:

Vanguard Mega Cap 300 ETF (MGC)	$4,000
Vanguard FTSE All-World ex-US Small Cap Index ETF (VSS)	$3,000
Vanguard Total Bond Market ETF (BND)	$3,000

Mark's Roth IRA:

Vanguard FTSE All-World ex-US ETF (VEU)	$4,000
Vanguard Small Cap ETF (VB)	$3,000
Vanguard Total Bond Market ETF (BND)	$3,000

As Betsy and Mark's portfolio grows, I would plan to add other asset classes (real estate investment trusts, natural resource stocks, inflation-protected securities, and so on) and other accounts.

One year later

Betsy is pregnant with twins! The couple is saving up for their first home, with a goal of making that purchase within 18 months. Although IRAs are normally not to be touched (without stiff penalty) before age 59½, an exception is made for first-time home purchases. Betsy and Mark could take out as much as $10,000 without penalty.

I'd rather that they leave their Roth IRA money untouched, but the couple informs me that they think the money may need to be tapped. At this point, the money in the Roth IRA has grown from $20,000 to $22,000 (for illustration purposes, I'm pretending that each investment grew by an equal amount), and Betsy and Mark can each contribute another $5,000 in fresh money, bringing the total of both accounts to $32,000. Since there is a possibility that $10,000 will need to be yanked in one year, I decide to earmark any fresh money to a fairly nonvolatile short-term bond ETF.

Betsy's Roth IRA:

Vanguard Mega Cap 300 ETF (MGC)	$4,400
Vanguard FTSE All-World ex-US Small Cap Index ETF (VSS)	$3,300
Vanguard Total Bond Market ETF (BND)	$3,300
Vanguard Short-Term Bond ETF (BSV)	$5,000

Mark's Roth IRA:

Vanguard FTSE All-World ex-US ETF (VEU)	$4,400
Vanguard Small Cap ETF (VB)	$3,300
Vanguard Total Bond Market ETF (BND)	$3,300
Vanguard Short-Term Bond ETF (BSV)	$5,000

Yet one year later

The twins (Aiden and Ella) have arrived! Much to their surprise, Betsy's parents have gifted the couple $10,000 for the purchase of the home. The Roth IRA money needn't be touched. At this point, I would sell the short-term bond fund and add to their other positions. Also, provided the couple had another $5,000 each to contribute, I'd begin adding asset classes to the mix, perhaps starting with the iShares

Barclays TIPS Bond Fund (TIP), the SPDR S&P Global Natural Resources ETF (GNR), the Vanguard REIT ETF (VNQ), and the Vanguard Global ex-US Real Estate ETF (VNQI).

Hopefully, Betsy and Mark (and Aiden and Ella) will have many happy years together. And with each major life event, I would urge them to adjust their portfolio appropriately.

Are Options an Option for You?

Beyond the world of exchange-traded funds, an entirely different universe is filled with things called *exchange-traded derivatives*. A *derivative* is a financial instrument that has no real value in and of itself; rather, its value is directly tied to some underlying item of value, be it a commodity, a stock, a currency, or an ETF.

The most popular derivative is called an *option*. Think of an option as sort of a movie ticket. You give the cashier $8.50 to see the movie, not to hold some dumb little piece of cardboard. Certainly the ticket itself has no intrinsic value. But the ticket gives access (the option) to see the movie.

 Most options in the investment world give you the right either to buy or sell a security at a certain price (the *strike price*) up to a certain specified date (the *expiration date*). Options are a prime example of a *leveraged* investment. In other words, if you buy an option, you're leveraging the little bit of money that you pay for the option — the *premium* — in hopes of winning big money. If you're an option seller, you stand to make the amount of the small premium, but you risk losing big money. For the system to work, the sellers have to win much more often than the buyers . . . and they do.

Lately, options on ETFs have been hot, hot, hot . . . and growing hotter. Options on certain ETFs, most notably the SPY (which represents the S&P 500) and the QQQ (which represents the 100 largest company stocks traded on the NASDAQ), typically trade just as many shares on an average day as the ETFs themselves. On most days, options on ETFs like the QQQ and SPY trade more shares than any other kind of options, including options on individual stocks, commodities, and currencies.

You see, ETFs provide traders with the opportunity to trade the entire stock market, or large pieces of it, rather than merely individual securities. In the past, this was doable but difficult. You cannot trade a mutual fund on the options market as you can an ETF.

Much of this often frenetic trading in ETF options, at least on the buying side, is being done by speculators, not investors. If you have an itch to gamble in the hopes of hitting it big, options may be for you. In that case, I'll refer you to *Futures & Options For Dummies* by Joe Duarte, M.D. (Wiley). Dr. Duarte will warn you, as I am warning you, that successful option trading takes an iron gut, a lot of capital, and a lot of expertise. And even if you have all that, you may still end up getting hurt.

Part IV
The Part of Tens

Peek into the world's emerging markets by visiting www.dummies.com/extras/investinginetfs.

In this part . . .

✔ Dig into common questions about ETFs, like whether they're risky and how to choose among the hundreds of ETFs available.

✔ Find out how to avoid common mistakes, like buying too much of the same thing.

Chapter 12

Ten FAQs about ETFs

In This Chapter

▶ Assessing risk

▶ Considering professional help

▶ Figuring out which ETFs make sense for you

*O*ften when someone asks me what I'm working on, and I say, *"Investing in ETFs For Dummies,"* I see the eyes glaze over, and then, if the topic isn't immediately steered in a new direction, I'm inevitably asked what the heck an ETF is. And so I explain (essentially quoting, from memory, a few lines from this book's Introduction). The *next* question I'm asked is invariably one of the following.

Are ETFs Appropriate for Individual Investors?

You bet they are. Although the name *exchange-traded funds* sounds highly technical and maybe a little bit scary, ETFs are essentially friendly index mutual funds with a few spicy perks. They are *more* than appropriate for individual investors. In fact, given the low expense ratios and high tax efficiency of most ETFs, as well as the ease with which you can use them to construct a diversified portfolio, these babies can be the perfect building blocks for just about any individual investor's portfolio.

Are ETFs Risky?

That all depends.

Some ETFs are way riskier than others. It's a question of what kind of ETF we're talking about. Most ETFs track stock indexes, and some of those stock indexes can be extremely volatile, such as individual sectors of the U.S. economy (technology, energy, defense and aerospace, and so on) or the stock markets of emerging-market nations. Other ETFs track broader segments of the U.S. stock market, such as the S&P 500. Those can be volatile, too, but less so. Commodity ETFs can be more jumpy than stocks.

But other ETFs track bond indexes. Those tend to be considerably less volatile (and less potentially rewarding) than stock ETFs. One ETF (ticker symbol SHY) tracks short-term Treasury bonds, and as such is only a little bit more volatile than a money market fund.

Many of the newer generation ETFs are *leveraged,* using borrowed money or financial derivatives to increase volatility (and potential performance). Those leveraged ETFs can be so wildly volatile that you are taking on risk of Las Vegas proportions.

 When putting together a portfolio, a diversity of investments can temper risk. Although it seems freakily paradoxical, you can sometimes add a risky ETF to a portfolio (such as an ETF that tracks the price of a basket of commodities, or the stocks of foreign small companies) and lower your overall risk! How so? If the value of your newly added ETF tends to rise as your other investments fall, that addition will lower the volatility of your entire portfolio. (Financial professionals refer to this strange but sweet phenomenon as *Modern Portfolio Theory.*)

Do I Need a Financial Professional to Set Up and Monitor an ETF Portfolio?

Do you need an auto mechanic to service your car? I don't know. It depends on both your particular skills and your inclination to spend a Sunday afternoon getting greasy under the hood. Setting up a decent ETF portfolio, with the aid of this book, is very doable. You can certainly monitor such a portfolio as well. A professional, however, has special tools and (I hope) objectivity to help you understand investment risk and construct a portfolio that fits you like a glove, or at least a sock. A financial planner can also help you properly estimate your retirement needs and plan your savings accordingly.

Do be aware that many investment "advisors" out there are nothing more than salespeople in disguise. Don't be at all surprised if you bump into a few who express their disgust of ETFs! ETFs make no money for those salespeople, who make their living hawking expensive (often inferior) investment products. Your best bet for good advice is to find a *fee-only* (takes no commissions) financial planner. If you are more or less a do-it-yourselfer but simply wish for a little guidance, try to find a fee-only planner who will work with you on an hourly basis.

How Much Money Do I Need to Invest in ETFs?

You can buy one share of any number of ETFs for as low as the price of a share. But since you usually pay a commission to trade (I'd say the average trading commission is about $10), buying one $20 share (and thus paying a 50 percent commission) would hardly make good sense. Starting at about $3,000 perhaps, it may be worth investing in ETFs, but only if you plan to keep that money invested for at least several years. Smaller amounts are perhaps better invested in mutual funds (preferably low-cost index mutual funds), money markets, or other instruments that incur no trading costs.

If you wish to invest in an ETF at a brokerage house that doesn't charge trading commissions for that particular ETF (Vanguard, for example, doesn't charge you to trade Vanguard ETFs; and Charles Schwab doesn't charge you to trade Schwab ETFs), then you can buy one share at a time with impunity.

With Hundreds of ETFs to Choose from, Where Do I Start?

The answer depends on your objective. If you are looking to round out an existing portfolio of stocks or mutual funds, your ETF should complement that. Your goal is always to have a well-diversified collection of investments. If you are starting to build a portfolio, you want to make sure to include stocks and bonds and to diversify within those two broad asset classes.

There is not much in the world of stocks, bonds, and commodities that can't be satisfied with ETFs. Try to have both U.S. and international stock ETFs. And within the U.S. stock arena, aim to have large cap growth, small cap growth, large cap value, and small cap value. (I explain these terms in Chapters 3 and 4.) You can also diversify your stock ETFs by industry sector: consumer staples, energy, financials, and so on. (See Chapter 6 for a discussion of sector diversification.) Generally, I wouldn't attempt to use separate ETFs to accomplish both grid diversification and sector diversification; doing so would require an unwieldy number of holdings.

On the bond side of your portfolio, you want both government-issued bonds and corporate bonds, and if you're in a higher tax bracket, you want municipal bonds as well. For more conservative portfolios in which bonds play a major role, foreign bonds may offer added diversification.

Although most ETFs are somewhat reasonably priced, some are more reasonably priced than others. If you are going to pay 0.50 percent a year in operating expenses for a certain ETF, you should have a good reason for doing so. Many ETFs are available for under 0.20 percent, and some for even less than 0.10 percent.

Where Is the Best Place for Me to Buy ETFs?

I suggest setting up an account with a financial supermarket such as Fidelity, Vanguard, T. Rowe Price, Schwab, or TD Ameritrade. Each of these allows you to hold ETFs, along with other investments — such as mutual funds or individual stocks and bonds — in one account. (You probably don't need or want individual securities. I'm just saying. . . .)

Different financial supermarkets offer different services and charge different prices depending on how much you have to invest, how often you trade, and whether you do everything online or by phone. You need to do some shopping around to find the brokerage house that works best for you. I provide more suggestions for shopping financial supermarkets in Chapter 2, where you'll also find contact information.

Is There an Especially Good or Bad Time to Buy ETFs?

Nope, not really, at least not that can be determined in advance. Studies show rather conclusively that the stock and bond markets (or any segment of the stock or bond markets) is just about as likely to go up after a good day as it is after a bad day (week, month, year, or any other piece of the calendar). Trying to time the market tends to be a fool's game — or, just as often, a game that some like to play with other people's money.

Do ETFs Have Any Disadvantages?

Because most ETFs follow an index, you probably won't see your ETF (or any of your index mutual funds) winding up number one on *Wise Money* magazine's list of Top Funds for the Year. (But you probably won't find any of your ETFs at the bottom of such a list, either.) The bigger disadvantage of ETFs — compared with mutual funds — is the cost of trading them, although that cost should be minimal.

Building a well-diversified portfolio of ETFs — stocks, bonds, large cap, small cap, U.S., international — may also seem to have the disadvantage that in any given year, some of your ETFs are going to do poorly. Just remember that *next* year those particular investments, the ones that look so disgustingly dull (or worse) right now, may be the shiniest things in your portfolio.

Does It Matter Which Exchange My ETF Is Traded On?

No. Most ETFs are traded on the NYSE Arca (Archipelago) exchange, but plenty of others are traded on the NASDAQ. It doesn't matter in the slightest to you, the individual investor. The cost of your trade is determined by the brokerage house you use. The *spread* (the difference between the price a buyer pays and the price the seller receives) is determined in large part by the share volume of the ETF being traded. Regardless of the exchange, if the volume is small (such as would be the case for, say, the Global X Nigeria ETF), you may want to place a *limit order* rather than a *market order.*

Which ETFs Are Best in My IRA, and Which Are Best in My Taxable Account?

Generally, investments that generate income — whether interest, dividends, or capital gains — are best kept in a tax-advantaged retirement account, such as your IRA or 401(k) plan. That would include any bond, REIT, or high-dividend paying ETF. You'll eventually need to pay income tax on any money you withdraw from those accounts, but it is generally better to pay later than sooner. In the case of a Roth IRA, which is often the best case of all, you will never have to pay taxes on the earnings, the principal, what is in the account, or what you withdraw. Try to put your ETFs that have the greatest potential for growth — REIT ETFs are great candidates — into your Roth IRA.

Because retirement accounts generally penalize you if you take money out before age 59½, anyone younger than that would want to keep all emergency money in a non-retirement account.

Chapter 13

Ten Mistakes Most Investors (Even Smart Ones) Make

In This Chapter

▶ Paying and risking too much

▶ Trading too frequently

▶ Saving too little and expecting too much from the market

▶ Ignoring inflation and IRS rules

*R*emember that personal investing course you took in high school? Of course you don't! Your high school never offered such a course. Chances are that you've never taken such a course. Few of us middle-agers have. And that lack of education — combined with a surfeit of cheesy and oft-advertised investment industry products, plus an irresponsible and lazy financial press — leads many investors to make some very costly mistakes.

Paying Too Much for an Investment

Most investors pay way, way too much to middlemen who suck the lifeblood out of portfolios, leaving too many folks with too little to show for their investments. By investing primarily in ETFs, you can spare yourself and your family this tragic fate. The typical ETF costs a fraction of what you would typically pay in yearly management fees to a mutual fund company. You never pay any *loads* (high commissions). And trading fees, as long as you're not dealing in dribs and drabs, and being charged for each drib and drab, should be minimal.

Failing to Properly Diversify

Thou shalt not put all thy eggs in one basket is perhaps the first commandment of investing, but it is astonishing how many sinners there are among us. ETFs allow for easy and effective diversification. By investing in ETFs rather than individual securities, you have already taken a step in the right direction. Don't blow it by pouring all your money into one ETF in a single hot sector! You want to invest in both stock and bond ETFs, and both U.S. and international securities. You want diversification on all sides. Invest, to the extent possible, mostly in *broad* markets: value, growth, small cap, large cap. On the international side of your portfolio, aim to invest more in regions than in individual countries. ETFs make such diversification easy.

Taking on Inappropriate Risks

Some people take on way too much risk, investing perhaps everything in highly volatile technology or biotech stocks. But many people don't take enough risk, leaving their money to sit in secure but low-yielding money market funds or, worse, in the vault of their local savings and loan. If you want your money to grow, you may have to stomach some volatility. In general, the longer you can tie your money up, and the less likely you are to need to tap into your portfolio anytime soon, the more volatile your portfolio can be. A portfolio of ETFs can be amazingly fine-tuned to achieve the levels of risk and return that are appropriate for you.

Selling Out When the Going Gets Tough

It can be a scary thing, for sure, when your portfolio's value drops 10 or 20 percent . . . never mind the 40 percent that an all-stock portfolio would have lost in 2008 (demonstrating graphically why you shouldn't have an all-stock portfolio). Keep in mind that if you invest in stock ETFs, that scenario is going to happen. It has happened many times in the past; it will happen many times in the future. That's just the nature of the beast. If you sell when the going gets tough (as many investors do), you lose the game. The stock market is resilient. Hang tough. Bears are followed by bulls (think 2009 and 2010). Your portfolio — as long as you are well diversified — will almost surely bounce back, given enough time.

Paying Too Much Attention to Recent Performance

Many investors make a habit of bailing out of whatever market segment has recently taken a dive. Conversely, they often look for whatever market segment has recently shot through the roof, and that's the one they buy. Then, when *that* market segment tanks, they sell once again. By forever buying high and selling low, their portfolios dwindle over time to nothing.

When you build your portfolio, don't overload it with last year's ETF superstars. You don't know what will happen next year. Stay cool. You may notice that in this book, I do not include performance figures for any of the ETFs discussed (except in one or two circumstances to make a specific point). That omission was intentional. Many of the ETFs I discuss are only a few years old, and a few years' returns tell you *nothing*. On the other hand, the indexes tracked by certain ETFs go back decades. In those cases, I often do provide performance figures.

Not Saving Enough for Retirement

Compared to spending, saving doesn't offer a whole lot of joy. But you can't build a portfolio out of thin air. If your goal is one day to be financially independent, to retire with dignity, you probably need to build a nest egg equal to about 20 times your yearly budget. Doing so won't be easy. It may mean saving 15 percent of your paycheck for several decades. The earlier you start, the easier it will be.

Savings come from the difference between what you earn and what you spend. Remember that both are adjustable figures. One great way to save is to contribute at least enough to your 401(k) plan at work to get your employer's full match, if any. Do it! Another is to remember that material goodies, above and beyond the basics, do not buy happiness and fulfillment. Honest. Psychologists have studied the matter, and their findings are rather conclusive.

Having Unrealistic Expectations of Market Returns

One reason many people don't save enough is that they have unrealistic expectations; they believe fervently that they are going to win the lottery or (next best thing) earn 25 percent a year on their investments. The truth: The stock market, over the past 86 years, has returned about 10 percent a year before inflation and 7 percent a year after inflation. Bonds have returned about 5 percent before inflation and 2 to 3 percent after inflation. A well-balanced portfolio, therefore, may have returned 7 or 8 percent before inflation and maybe 5 percent or so after inflation.

Five percent growth after inflation — with interest compounded every year — isn't too shabby. In 20 years time, an investment of $10,000 growing at 5 percent will turn into $26,530 in constant dollars. Most of us in the investment field expect future returns to be more modest. But with a very well-diversified, ultra-low-cost portfolio, leaning toward higher-yielding asset classes, you may be able to do just as well as Mom and Dad did. If you want to earn 25 percent a year, however, you are going to have to take on inordinate risk. And even then, I wouldn't bank on it.

Discounting the Damaging Effect of Inflation

No, a dollar certainly doesn't buy what it used to. Think of what a candy bar cost when you were a kid. Think of what you earned on your first job. Are you old enough to remember when gas was 32 cents a gallon? Now look into the future, and realize that your nest egg, unless it's wisely invested, will shrivel and shrink. Historically, certain investments do a better job of keeping up with inflation than others. Those investments, which include stocks, tend to be somewhat volatile. It's a price you need to pay, however, to keep the inflation monster at bay. The world of ETFs includes many ways to invest in stocks, but if you find the volatility hard to take, you might temper it with a position in Treasury Inflation-Protected Securities (TIPS). The iShares Barclays TIPS Bond Fund (TIP) tracks an index of TIPS. You can read about TIPS in Chapter 7.

Not Following the IRS's Rules

When they leave their jobs, many employees cash out their 401(k) accounts, thereupon paying the IRS a stiff penalty and immediately losing the great benefit of tax deferral. The government allows certain tax breaks for special kinds of accounts, and you really need to play by the rules or you can wind up worse off than if you had never invested in the first place.

People over 70½ must be especially careful to take the Minimum Required Distributions (MRDs) from their IRAs or 401(k) plans. Calculators are available online; simply type "MRD calculator" into your favorite search engine. Unlike a retirement calculator, based on all kinds of assumptions, the MRD is a straightforward equation. Any online calculator can take you there, or ask your accountant or the institution where you have your IRA.

Failing to Incorporate Investments into a Broader Financial Plan

Have you paid off all your high-interest credit card debt? Do you have proper disability insurance? Do you have enough life insurance so that, if necessary, your co-parent and children could survive without you? A finely manicured investment portfolio is only part of a larger picture that includes issues such as debt management, insurance, and estate planning. Don't spend too much time tinkering with your ETF portfolio and ignoring these other very important financial issues.

Index

• Numerics •

20x Rule, 166–168
401(k), 179–180, 181, 182–183, 234, 239
529 college plans, 180

• A •

accounts, creating for ETFs, 30–34
active ETFs, 158–160
active investing, compared with passive investing, 22–25
active management, 24
active managers, 211
ADRs, 94
all-in-one ETFs, 120–122
allocation, calculating, 146–147
amateur investors, compared with professional investors, 20–22
ask price, 33–34
assessing price swings, 193
asset allocation, tactical, 216–219
average investors, 206–211

• B •

Barclays Capital Aggregate Bond Index, 49
Barclays Global Investors, 41
Baskets of Listed Depositary Receipts (BLDRS), 94
Bear Stearns, 158
beneficiary designation, 31
beta, 193
bid price, 33–34
BlackRock, Inc., 15–16, 94
BlackRock iShares, 41–42

BLDRS (Baskets of Listed Depositary Receipts), 94
BLDRS Asia 50 ADR (ADRA), 99
BLDRS Emerging Markets 50 ADR (ADRE), 100, 158
BLDRS Europe 100 ADR (ADRU), 97
blend, 15, 58
bond ETFs
    about, 123–124
    buying, 126–129
    corporate, 133–135
    costs of, 128–129
    history of, 124–126
    options for, 129–136
    Treasury, 130–132
Bond Investing For Dummies (Wild), 129
bonds, adding, 121–122
book value, 66–67
bounce factor, as a global ETF consideration, 93
brokerage houses
    about, 30, 34
    Charles Schwab, 37–38
    Fidelity Investments, 37
    miscellaneous, 39
    price structure, 35–36
    SIPC coverage, 35
    T. Rowe Price, 38
    TD Ameritrade, 38
    Vanguard Group, 36–37
    what to look for, 34–35
broker-dealer, 30
Buffett, Warren (investor), 68
buy, placing orders to, 31–32
buy-and-hold approach, 212
buying
    ETFs, 232–233
    by industry sector, 202–203

• C •

calculating
  allocation, 146–147
  commissions, 25–26
  optimal mix, 107
  risk, 190–195
capital gains taxes, ETFs and,
  17–19
Capital One Investing/
  ShareBuilder, 39
capitalization (cap), 55
cash account, 31
Charles Schwab, 28, 37–38, 47
Cheat Sheet (website), 4
children, portfolio changes and,
  221–224
choosing
  between classic and new indexes,
    9–11
  ETFs, 68–71, 232
  ETFs for large value, 68–71
  global ETFs, 93–104
  Real Estate Investment Trusts
    (REITs), 147–148
commissions, calculating, 25–26
commodities
  about, 148–149
  gold, 149–151
  oil and gas, 152–156
  playing indirectly, 155–158
  silver, 151–152
commodity pool, 152
commodity-rich countries, 157–158
contango, 154
contrarian investing, 172
corporate bond ETFs, 133–135
correlation
  defined, 206
  with domestic and international
    ETFs, 89
  as a global ETF consideration, 92
  limited, 198
  low, 198
  negative, 196–197

Real Estate Investment Trusts
  (REITs) and, 145
seeking low, 108–109
correlation coefficient, 199–200
Correlation Tracker tool, 43
cost advantage, of ETFs, 14–16
costs
  active ETFs and, 159
  bond ETFs and, 128–129
  minimizing, 170–171
  mistakes with paying too much,
    235–236
creating accounts for ETFs, 30–34
currency, volatility of, 88
current yield, 129

• D •

derivative, 224
DIAMONDS Trust Series, 8
DIAMONDS Trust Series 1
  (DIA), 64
'The Difficulty of Selecting Superior
  Mutual Fund Performance'
  (McGuigan), 211
Dinky Town (website), 137
Direxion Daily Technology Bear 3x
  (TECS), 118
diversification
  about, 19–20
  bonds and, 127
  correlations and, 108–109
  global ETFs and, 87–88
  mistakes with, 236
dividend funds
  about, 112
  arguments for and against,
    113–116
  high dividend options, 112–113
dividends
  distributions of, 67
  Real Estate Investment Trusts
    (REITs) and, 145
divorce, portfolio changes and,
  221–224

Dodd, David (author)
  Security Analysis, 66
Dow Jones, 48
DSI (iShares KLD 400 Social Index ETF), 111
Duarte, Joe (author)
  Futures & Options For Dummies, 225
Dummies (website), 4

• *E* •

earnings growth, 67
economic self-sufficiency, aiming for, 178–182
Efficient Frontier, 200
efficient market, 171–172
Eisenhower, Dwight (US president), 212
emergency funds, 181
emerging-market bonds, 140–141
emerging-market stock ETFs, 99–101
energy sector, 109
Energy Select Sector SPDR (XLE), 153, 156
ETF (exchange-traded fund). *See also* bond ETFs; global ETFs
  about, 1, 7–9
  active, 158–160
  all-in-one, 120–122
  benefits of, 13–20
  buying, 232–233
  choosing, 9–11, 232
  choosing between classic and new indexes, 9–11
  corporate bond, 133–135
  creating accounts for, 30–34
  disadvantages of, 233
  distinguishing from mutual funds, 12–13
  drawbacks of, 25–26
  emerging-market stock, 99–101
  FAQs, 229–234
  foreign-stock, 181–182
  high dividend options, 112–113

  inverse, 118
  materials, 156–157
  mining, 156
  national municipal, 137
  natural resources, 156–157
  not recommended, 64–65
  preferring over individual stocks, 11–12
  risks of, 187–188
  selecting for large value, 68–71
ETF-trading websites, 209–211
ETNs (exchange-traded notes), 118
eTrade, 39
European stock ETFs, 96–98
exchanges, 234
exchange-traded derivatives, 224
exchange-traded fund (ETF). *See also* bond ETFs; global ETFs
  about, 1, 7–9
  active, 158–160
  all-in-one, 120–122
  benefits of, 13–20
  buying, 232–233
  choosing, 9–11, 232
  choosing between classic and new indexes, 9–11
  corporate bond, 133–135
  creating accounts for, 30–34
  disadvantages of, 233
  distinguishing from mutual funds, 12–13
  drawbacks of, 25–26
  emerging-market stock, 99–101
  FAQs, 229–234
  foreign-stock, 181–182
  high dividend options, 112–113
  inverse, 118
  materials, 156–157
  mining, 156
  national municipal, 137
  natural resources, 156–157
  not recommended, 64–65
  preferring over individual stocks, 11–12
  risks of, 187–188
  selecting for large value, 68–71

exchange-traded notes (ETNs), 118
expectations, mistakes with, 238
expiration date, 224

• F •

failure, 208–209
Fama, Eugene (economist), 55
FAQs, 229–234
fees, for global ETFs, 88–89
Fidelity Investments, 28, 37, 47
Fidelity Magellan Fund, 19–20
financial plans, mistakes with, 239
financial professionals, 20–22,
    230–231
Financial Select Sector SPDR ETF
    (XLF), 208
First Trust IPOX-100 Index Fund
    (FPX), 116
First Trust Morningstar Dividend
    Leaders Index Fund (FDL), 113
529 college plans, 180
fixed-income diversification,
    foreign bonds for, 138–140
Folio Investing, 39
food timeline (website), 149
foolish risk, 188–190
foreign bonds
    about, 137
    for fixed-income diversification,
        138–140
foreign stocks. *See* global ETFs
foreign taxes, 104
foreign-stock ETFs, 181–182
Forum for Sustainable and
    Responsible Investment
    (website), 112
401(k), 179–180, 181, 182–183, 234,
    239
French, Kenneth (economist), 55
FTSE China 25 Index (FXI), 87
Futures & Options For Dummies
    (Duarte), 225

• G •

gas, 152–156
global ETFs
    about, 85–86
    choosing, 93–104
    considerations for, 92–93
    diversification in, 87–88
    mixing domestic and
        international, 88–91
    world markets, 86
Global X Brazil Financials ETF
    (BRAF), 106
Global X China Materials ETF
    (CHIM), 106
Global X Nigeria ETF, 234
Global X Silver Miners ETF (SIL),
    156
gold, 149–151
Graham, Benjamin (author)
    influence of, 55
    P/E ratio (price to earnings ratio),
        217–219
    Security Analysis, 66
grand scale risk, 190
Greed Alert icon, 4
growth, compared with value, 56
Guggenheim, 45–46
Guggenheim Solar ETF (TAN), 112
Guggenheim S&P 600 Small Cap
    Pure Growth ETF (RZG), 79
Guggenheim S&P 600 Small Cap
    Pure Value (RZV), 83

• H •

Hershey bars, 149
high-risk/high-return ETF
    portfolios, 174–175
history, of bond ETFs, 124–126
home market, as a global ETF
    consideration, 92
Hurd, Mark (CEO), 11

• I •

Ibbotson Associates, 202
icons, explained, 3–4
ImClone, 11
Index Investing For Dummies
    (Wild), 158, 171
indexes
  about, 47
  Barclays, 49
  Dow Jones, 48
  MSCI, 48
  returns falling short of the, 207
  Russell, 49
  Standard & Poor's, 47–48
Individual 401(k), 179–180
individual investors, ETFs and, 229
industry, buying by, 202–203
industry sector, 67
inflation
  global ETFs and, 88
  mistakes with, 238–239
inflation risk, 189
inflation-protected securities,
    132–133
interest rate risk, 189
international stocks. *See* global
    ETFs
Internet resources
  Barclays Capital Aggregate Bond
    Index, 49
  Baskets of Listed Depositary
    Receipts (BLDRS), 94
  BlackRock iShares, 41, 94
  Capital One Investing/
    ShareBuilder, 39
  Charles Schwab, 47
  Cheat Sheet, 4
  Dinky Town, 137
  Dow Jones, 48
  Dummies, 4
  ETF-trading, 209–211
  eTrade, 39
  Fidelity Investments, 47
  Folio Investing, 39
  food timeline, 149
  Forum for Sustainable and
    Responsible Investment, 112
  Guggenheim, 46
  Invesco PowerShares, 44
  Investing in Bonds, 129
  kt-timing.com/rydex, 211
  marketpolygraph, 210
  Money Chimp, 171
  Morningstar, 129
  MSCI, 48
  multpl, 218
  ProShares, 47
  REIT ETFs, 148
  Russell 1000, 49
  Schwab, 95
  Scottrade, 39
  Standard & Poor's, 48
  State Street Global Advisers
    (SSgA) SPDRs, 43
  stockmarkettiming, 210
  SweetSpot Investments LLC, 220
  TIAA-CREF, 39
  TradeKing, 39
  Vanguard, 43, 94, 218
  WisdomTree, 45, 95
  Yahoo! Finance, 10, 20
inverse ETFs, 118
Invesco PowerShares, 15, 44
investing. *See also* sector investing
  in IPOs, 116–118
  timing, 171–172
  tips for optimal, 169–172
Investing in Bonds (website), 129
investment professionals, 20–22,
    230–231
investors, average, 206–211
IPOs, investing in, 116–118
IRA, 104, 234, 239
IRS, mistakes with, 239
iShares Barclays 1-3 Year Treasury
    Bond Fund (SHY), 130–131,
    188

iShares Barclays 7-10 Year Treasury Bond ETF Fund (IEF), 127, 131
iShares Barclays 20+ Year Treasury Bond Fund (TLT), 131–132
iShares Barclays Aggregate Bond Fund (AGG), 136
iShares Barclays TIPS Bond Fund ETF (TIP), 132, 133, 173, 215, 239
iShares COMEX Gold Trust (IAU), 150, 151
iShares Dow Jones U.S. Basic Materials (IYM), 157
iShares Dow Jones U.S. Energy Index (IYE), 156
iShares Dow Jones U.S. Oil Equipment & Services Index Fund (IEZ), 156
iShares Dow Jones U.S. Total Market ETF (IYY), 59
iShares iBoxx $ Investment Grade Corporate Bond Fund (LQD), 133–134, 180
iShares JP Morgan USD Emerging Markets Bond Fund (EMB), 141
iShares KLD 400 Social Index ETF (DSI), 111
iShares Morningstar Large Growth ETF (JKE), 60, 63–64
iShares Morningstar Large Value ETF (JKF), 68, 70
iShares Morningstar Small Core (JKJ), 76, 77
iShares Morningstar Small Growth Index ETF (JKK), 79
iShares Morningstar Small Value Index (JKL), 82–83
iShares MSCI ACWI (All Country World Index) ex US Index (ACWEX), 95
iShares MSCI ACWI Index Fund (ACWI), 95, 121

iShares MSCI All Peru Capped (EPU), 158
iShares MSCI Brazil (EWZ), 157
iShares MSCI Chile Investable Market (ECH), 158
iShares MSCI EAFE Growth Index (EFG), 101, 102
iShares MSCI EAFE Index Fund (EFA), 188
iShares MSCI EAFE Small Cap Index (SCZ), 103–104
iShares MSCI EAFE Value Index (EFV), 101
iShares MSCI Emerging Markets (EEM), 100–101, 158
iShares MSCI Japan Index Fund (EWJ), 87, 99
iShares MSCI Malaysia (EWM), 157
iShares MSCI South Africa (EZA), 157
iShares MSCI South Korea Index Fund (EWY), 188
iShares MSCI USA ESG Select (KLD), 111
iShares Russell 1000 ETF (IWB), 60, 62
iShares Russell 1000 Value ETF (IWD), 68, 69–70
iShares Silver Trust (SLV), 151
iShares S&P 500 Growth Index Fund (IVW), 87
iShares S&P 500 Value Index Fund (IVE), 87
iShares S&P Aggressive Allocation Fund (AOA), 121
iShares S&P Conservative Allocation Fund (AOK), 121
iShares S&P Europe 350 (IEV), 97–98
iShares S&P Global Energy Index Fund (IXC), 156
iShares S&P Moderate Allocation Fund (AOM), 121

iShares S&P National Municipal
  Bond Fund (MUB), 138
iShares S&P North American
  Natural Resources (IGE), 157
iShares S&P Small Cap 600 (IJR),
  76, 77
iShares S&P Small Cap 600 Growth
  ETF (IJT), 79, 87
iShares S&P Small Cap 600 Value
  Index (IJS), 83, 87
iShares S&P/Citigroup
  International Treasury Bond
  Fund (IGOV), 139
iShares value and growth, 101–102
iUnits, 41

• J •

Japan, 88
Journal of Financial Planning, 211
Journal of Indexes, 155

• K •

K-2 forms, 154–155
kt-timing.com/rydex (website), 211

• L •

large caps
  about, 55
  blended options, 60–62
  growth and value options, 60
  options for, 58–65
large growth companies, 57–58
large growth stocks
  about, 53, 54
  large growth companies, 57–58
  options for large cap ETFs, 58–65
  styles, 55–57
large value stocks
  about, 53, 65–67

best buys, 67–71
buying the index, 68
selecting ETFs, 68–71
leveraged funds, 119–120
leveraged investment, 224
life changes, portfolio and,
  221–224
limit orders, 33–34, 234
limited correlation, 198
load, 12

• M •

Malkiel, Burton G. (author)
  A Random Walk Down Wall Street,
  155
management fees
  BlackRock iShares, 41
  Guggenheim, 46
  State Street Global Advisers
    (SSgA) SPDRs, 43
  Vanguard ETFs, 42
margin account, 31
market makers, 18–19
market orders, 33–34, 234
market risk, 189
Market Vectors Global Alternative
  Energy ETF (GEX), 112
Market Vectors Gold Miners ETF
  (GDX), 156
Market Vectors Solar Energy ETF
  (KWT), 112
market-neutral funds, 89
marketpolygraph (website), 210
marriage, portfolio changes and,
  221–224
materials ETFs, 156–157
Materials Select Sector SPDR
  (XLB), 157
McGuigan, Thomas (author)
  'The Difficulty of Selecting
  Superior Mutual Fund
  Performance,' 211

measuring
  allocation, 146–147
  commissions, 25–26
  optimal mix, 107
  risk, 190–195
Mencken, H.L. (journalist), 122
micro cap, 55
mid cap, 55
middle of the road ETF portfolios, 175–176
minimizing costs, 170–171
Minimum Required Distributions (MRDs), 239
mining ETFs, 156
mistakes, common, 235–239
mixing and matching
  stock ETFs, 200–204
  suppliers, 40–41
mixing domestic and international, 88–91
Modern Portfolio Theory (MPT)
  about, 196, 230
  correlation coefficient, 199–200
  current status of, 199
  incorporating, 170
  limited correlation, 198
  negative correlation, 196–197
Money Chimp (website), 171
money requirements, 231
Morningstar (website), 129
Morningstar grid. *See* style box/grid
MPT (Modern Portfolio Theory)
  about, 196, 230
  correlation coefficient, 199–200
  current status of, 199
  incorporating, 170
  limited correlation, 198
  negative correlation, 196–197
MRDs (Minimum Required Distributions), 239
MSCI, 48
MSCI EAFE, 89

multiple. *See* P/E ratio (price to earnings ratio)
multpl (website), 218
municipal bonds
  about, 130, 137
  tax-free income and, 137–138
mutual funds, distinguishing ETFs from, 12–13

• *N* •

nano cap, 55
NASDAQ-100 Index, 118, 119
NASDAQ-100 Trust Series 1, 8
national municipal ETFs, 137
natural resources ETFs, 156–157
negative correlation, 196–197
nonsystemic risk, 189
NYSE Arca (Archipelago) exchange, 234

• *O* •

oil, 152–156
optimal mix, calculating, 107
options, 224–225
orders, placing to buy, 31–32

• *P* •

Pacific region stock ETFs, 98–99
passive investing, compared with active investing, 22–25
patience, importance of, 211–212
P/B (price to book value) ratio, 66–67
P/E ratio (price to earnings ratio), 56, 66, 93, 217–219
perfect correlation, 23, 206
performance, mistakes with, 237
PIMCO, 159
placing orders to buy, 31–32

political risk, 189
portfolios
about, 163–164
adding P/E ratio to, 218–219
aiming for economic self-sufficiency, 178–182
finding a good fit, 172–178
401(k), 179–180, 181, 182–183, 234, 239
high-risk/high-return, 174–175
life changes and, 221–224
middle of the road, 175–176
rebalancing, 213–216
risk questions, 164–169
safe, 176–178
simple, 173–174
tips for optimal investing, 169–172
PowerShares Dividend Achievers Portfolio (PFM), 113
PowerShares Dynamic Energy Exploration & Production (PXE), 156
PowerShares Dynamic Large Cap Growth (PWB), 65
PowerShares Global Clean Energy (PBD), 112
PowerShares High Growth Rate Dividend Achievers Portfolios (PHJ), 113
PowerShares High Yield Equity Dividend Achievers Portfolio (PEY), 113
PowerShares QQQ Trust Series 1, 8
PowerShares S&P SmallCap Health Care Portfolio ETF (PSCH), 106
PowerShares S&P SmallCap Industrials Portfolio ETF (PSCI), 106
predicting range of returns, 192
premium, 26, 224
price structure, comparing for brokerage houses, 35–36

price swings, assessing, 193
price to book value (P/B) ratio, 66–67
professionals, financial, 20–22, 230–231
ProShares, 46–47
ProShares Short Dow30 (DOG), 118
ProShares Short MidCap400 (MYY), 118
ProShares Short QQQ fund (PSQ), 46, 118
ProShares Short S&P500 (SH), 118
ProShares Ultra Dow30 (DDM), 119
ProShares Ultra MidCap400 (MVV), 119
ProShares Ultra QQQ (QLD), 46, 119, 120
ProShares Ultra S&P500 (SSO), 119
ProShares UltraShort Consumer Goods ETF (SZK), 118
publications
Bond Investing For Dummies (Wild), 129
Futures & Options For Dummies (Duarte), 225
Index Investing For Dummies (Wild), 158, 171
Journal of Financial Planning, 211
Journal of Indexes, 155
A Random Walk Down Wall Street (Malkiel), 155
Security Analysis (Graham and Dodd), 66

• Q •

quick riches, 209

• R •

R squared, 23
A Random Walk Down Wall Street (Malkiel), 155

Real Estate Investment Trusts (REITs)
about, 108, 144
benefits of, 144–146
calculating allocation, 146–147
choosing, 147–148
website, 148
rebalancing portfolios, 213–216
REITs (Real Estate Investment Trusts)
about, 108, 144
benefits of, 144–146
calculating allocation, 146–147
choosing, 147–148
website, 148
Rekenthaler, John (VP), 209
Remember icon, 3
Renaissance IPO ETF (IPO), 118
resources, Internet
Barclays Capital Aggregate Bond Index, 49
Baskets of Listed Depositary Receipts (BLDRS), 94
BlackRock iShares, 41, 94
Capital One Investing/ShareBuilder, 39
Charles Schwab, 47
Cheat Sheet, 4
Dinky Town, 137
Dow Jones, 48
Dummies.com, 4
ETF-trading, 209–211
eTrade, 39
Fidelity Investments, 47
Folio Investing, 39
food timeline, 149
Forum for Sustainable and Responsible Investment, 112
Guggenheim, 46
Invesco PowerShares, 44
Investing in Bonds, 129
kt-timing.com/rydex, 211
marketpolygraph, 210
Money Chimp, 171

Morningstar, 129
MSCI, 48
multpl, 218
ProShares, 47
REIT ETFs, 148
Russell 1000, 49
Schwab, 95
Scottrade, 39
Standard & Poor's, 48
State Street Global Advisers (SSgA) SPDRs, 43
stockmarkettiming, 210
SweetSpot Investments LLC, 220
TIAA-CREF, 39
TradeKing, 39
Vanguard, 43, 94, 218
WisdomTree, 45, 95
Yahoo! Finance, 10, 20
retirees, rebalancing for, 216
retirement, mistakes with, 237–238
return. See also risk
about, 185
falling short of the indexes, 207
predicting range of, 192
relationship with risk, 166
safety versus, 187
reversion to the mean, 172
risk. See also return
about, 185–186
beta, 193
ETFs and, 187–188, 230
measuring, 190–195
mistakes with, 236
relationship with return, 166
safety versus return, 187
seeking adjustment, 107
Sharpe ratio, 194–195
small value stocks, 81–82
smart compared with foolish, 188–190
Sortino ratio, 194–195
standard deviation, 191–193
Treynor ratio, 194–195

risk questionnaires, limitations of, 168–169
risk tolerance, as a global ETF consideration, 92–93
rollover, 183
Roth IRA, 104, 180, 181
Russell 1000, 49

• S •

safe ETF portfolios, 176–178
sample portfolio menus
about, 163–164
aiming for economic self-sufficiency, 178–182
finding a good fit, 172–178
401(k), 179–180, 181, 182–183, 234, 239
risk questions, 164–169
tips for optimal investing, 169–172
Schwab, contact information for, 95
Schwab International Equity ETF (SCHF), 95
Schwab U.S. Broad Market ETF (SCHB), 59
Schwab U.S. Large-Cap ETF (SCHX), 60, 62
Schwab U.S. Large-Cap Growth ETF (SCHG), 60, 64
Schwab U.S. Large-Cap Value ETF (SCHV), 68, 70–71
Schwab U.S. Small-Cap (SCHA), 76, 78
SCHX (Schwab U.S. Large-Cap ETF), 60, 62
Scotttrade, 39
sector investing
about, 105
options for, 109–110
selecting stocks by sector, 106–109
types of sectors, 109–110

Securities Investor Protection Corporation (SIPC), 35
Security Analysis (Graham and Dodd), 66
selecting
between classic and new indexes, 9–11
ETFs, 68–71, 232
ETFs for large value, 68–71
global ETFs, 93–104
Real Estate Investment Trusts (REITs), 147–148
selling out, 236–237
SEP-IRA, 179–180
September 11 terrorist attacks, 212
ShareBuilder, 36
Sharpe, Bill (professor), 194
Sharpe ratio, 194–195
Shiller, Robert J. (economist), 217–218
shorting ETFs, 14
side-by-side comparisons, 192–193
silver, 151–152
SIMPLE plan, 181
SIPC (Securities Investor Protection Corporation), 35
small cap, 55
small cap blend funds, 76–78
small cap growth funds, 78–80
small cap international, 103–104
small growth stocks
about, 73–74
options for, 75–80
start-ups and, 74–75
small value stocks
about, 73–74, 80–81
recommended, 82–83
risk of, 81–82
smart risk, 188–190
social investing, options for, 111–112
social issues, ETFs focused on, 111–112
Sortino ratio, 194–195

sovereign bond, 130
S&P 500, 89
S&P 500 Pure Value ETF (RPV), 45, 46
SPDR Barclays Capital High Yield Bond ETF (JNK), 127
SPDR Barclays Capital TIPS ETF (IPE), 132
SPDR Dividend ETF (SDY), 112
SPDR Gold Shares (GLD), 150
SPDR Nuveen Barclays Capital Municipal Bond (TFI), 138
SPDR S&P 500 (SPY), 8, 43, 65
SPDR S&P Global Natural Resources ETF (GNR), 157
SPDR S&P Metals and Mining ETF (XME), 156
specialized stocks
   about, 105, 110–111
   options for, 111–112
   performance history of, 111
spread, 32, 234
SRI funds, 110–111
SSgA (State Street Global Advisers) SPDRs, 43
standard deviation, 191–193
Standard & Poor's, 47–48
start-ups, small growth stocks and, 74–75
State Street Global Advisers, 150
State Street Global Advisers (SSgA) SPDRs, 43
static, 121
status, Real Estate Investment Trusts (REITs) and, 145–146
Stewart, Martha (celebrity), 11
stock ETFs, mixing and matching, 200–204
stockmarkettiming (website), 210
stocks, 11–12 *See also* global ETFs
stocks, large growth
   about, 53, 54
   large growth companies, 57–58

options for large cap ETFs, 58–65
styles, 55–57
stocks, large value
   about, 53, 65–67
   best buys, 67–71
   buying the index, 68
   selecting ETFs, 68–71
stocks, small growth
   about, 73–74
   options for, 75–80
   start-ups and, 74–75
stocks, small value
   about, 73–74, 80–81
   recommended, 82–83
   risk of, 81–82
stocks, specialized
   about, 105, 110–111
   options for, 111–112
   performance history of, 111
Stoloff, Neil (wealth manager), 219–220
strike price, 224
style
   active ETFs and, 159
   as a global ETF consideration, 92
   of large growth stocks, 55–57
style box/grid
   filling in, 201–202
   large growth stocks in, 54
   large value stocks, 65–66
   small growth stocks, 74–75
   small value stocks, 80–81
   using, 108
style drift, 19–20
style investing, 108
suppliers
   about, 40
   BlackRock iShares, 41–42
   Guggenheim, 45–46
   Invesco PowerShares, 44
   miscellaneous, 47
   mixing and matching, 40–41
   ProShares, 46–47

State Street Global Advisers
(SSgA) SPDRs, 43
Vanguard ETFs, 42–43
WisdomTree, 45
SweetSpot Investments LLC
(website), 220

● **T** ●

T. Rowe Price, 28, 38, 159
T. Rowe Price Emerging Markets
Bond Fund (PREMX), 140
tactical asset allocation, 216–219
tangible property, Real Estate
Investment Trusts (REITs)
and, 146
tax-deferred vessels, 179–180
taxes
consequences of selling
securities, 33
efficiency with, 171
ETFs and taxable accounts, 234
foreign, 104
for global ETFs, 89
gold, 151
oil and gas, 154–155
Real Estate Investment Trusts
(REITs) and, 145
tax-free income, municipal bonds
and, 137–138
tax-free vessels, 180
TD Ameritrade, 35, 38
technical analysis
about, 205–206
average investors, 206–211
Technical Stuff icon, 4
TIAA-CREF, 39
timing
for buying ETFs, 233
investments, 171–172
risk and, 187
Tip icon, 3
TIPS (U.S. Treasury Inflation-
Protected Securities), 132–133

titling, 31
total market capitalization, 54
tracking error, 26
tracking performance history of
SRIs, 111
TradeKing, 39
trading ETFs in large lots, 13–14
traditional IRA, 179–180
transparency, 20, 158
Treasury bond ETFs, 130–132
Treasury Inflation-Protected
Securities (TIPS), 239
Treynor, Jack (investor), 195
Treynor ratio, 194–195
20x Rule, 166–168

● **U** ●

United States Natural Gas Fund
(UNG), 154
United States Oil Fund (USO),
152–154
unloved assets, 219
U.S. bond market, 135–136
U.S. Treasury Inflation-Protected
Securities (TIPS), 132–133

● **V** ●

value, compared with growth, 56
Vanguard, 28, 36–37, 42–43, 94, 218
Vanguard (website), 218
Vanguard Dividend Appreciation
ETF (VIG), 112
Vanguard Emerging Markets
Government Bond (VWOB),
141
Vanguard Energy ETF (VDE), 153,
156
Vanguard FTSE All-World ex-US
ETF (VEU), 95, 173, 215
Vanguard FTSE All-World ex-US
Small Cap Index (VSS), 103,
215

Vanguard Growth ETF (VUG), 60, 63
Vanguard Index Trust 500 Portfolio, 42
Vanguard Large Cap ETF (VV), 60–61
Vanguard Materials ETF (VAW), 157
Vanguard Mega Cap 300 ETF (MGC), 60, 61, 172, 173, 215
Vanguard Mega Cap 300 Value Index ETF (MGV), 68, 69
Vanguard Mega Cap Growth ETF (MGK), 60, 63
Vanguard Mid Cap ETF (VO), 188
Vanguard MSCI Emerging Market ETF (VWO), 100, 158
Vanguard MSCI Europe ETF (VGK), 97
Vanguard Pacific ETF (VPL), 98
Vanguard REIT Index ETF (VNQ), 145
Vanguard Short-Term Bond (BSV), 136
Vanguard Short-Term Corporate Bond Index (VCSM), 134–135
Vanguard Small Cap (VB), 76–77, 172, 173, 215
Vanguard Small Cap Growth ETF (VBK), 78
Vanguard Small Cap Value ETF (VBR), 82
Vanguard Total Bond Market (BND), 135–136, 173, 215
Vanguard Total International Bond ETF (BNDX), 139–140
Vanguard Total Stock Market ETF (VTI), 59, 145, 218
Vanguard Total World Stock ETF (VT), 95, 121
Vanguard Value ETF (VTV), 68, 69
versatility, of ETFs, 14
Vinik, Jeffrey (fund manager), 19–20

volatility
about, 186
of currency, 88
of sectors, 107

• W •

Warning! icon, 3
Water Resources ETF (PHO), 44
websites
Barclays Capital Aggregate Bond Index, 49
Baskets of Listed Depositary Receipts (BLDRS), 94
BlackRock iShares, 41, 94
Capital One Investing/ ShareBuilder, 39
Charles Schwab, 47
Cheat Sheet, 4
Dinky Town, 137
Dow Jones, 48
Dummies, 4
ETF-trading, 209–211
eTrade, 39
Fidelity Investments, 47
Folio Investing, 39
food timeline, 149
Forum for Sustainable and Responsible Investment, 112
Guggenheim, 46
Invesco PowerShares, 44
Investing in Bonds, 129
kt-timing.com/rydex, 211
marketpolygraph, 210
Money Chimp, 171
Morningstar, 129
MSCI, 48
multpl, 218
ProShares, 47
REIT ETFs, 148
Russell 1000, 49
Schwab, 95
Scottrade, 39

Standard & Poor's, 48
State Street Global Advisers
(SSgA) SPDRs, 43
stockmarkettiming, 210
SweetSpot Investments LLC, 220
TIAA-CREF, 39
TradeKing, 39
Vanguard, 43, 94, 218
WisdomTree, 45, 95
Yahoo! Finance, 10, 20
Wild, Russell (author)
Bond Investing For Dummies, 129
Index Investing For Dummies, 158,
171
WilderHill Clean Energy Fund
(PBW), 44
WisdomTree, 45, 95

WisdomTree currency hedged
funds, 102
WisdomTree Europe Hedged
Equity ETF (HEDJ), 102
WisdomTree Europe Small-Cap
Hedged Equity ETF (EUSC),
102
WisdomTree Japan Hedged Real
Estate ETF (DXJR), 106
Workplace Equality ETF (EQLT),
111
world markets, 86, 121

Yahoo! Finance (website), 10, 20

Notes

Notes

Notes

Notes

Notes

Notes

Notes

Notes

About the Author

Russell Wild is a NAPFA-certified financial advisor and principal of Global Portfolios, an investment advisory firm based in Philadelphia, Pennsylvania. He is one of only a handful of wealth managers in the nation who is both fee-only (takes no commissions) and welcomes clients of both substantial *and* modest means. He calls his firm Global Portfolios to reflect his ardent belief in international diversification — using exchange-traded funds to build well-diversified, low-expense, tax-efficient portfolios.

Wild, in addition to the fun he has with his financial calculator, is also an accomplished writer who helps readers understand and make wise choices about their money. His articles have appeared in many national publications, including *AARP The Magazine, Consumer Reports, Details, Men's Health, Men's Journal, Parade, Reader's Digest, The Saturday Evening Post,* and *Real Simple.* And he has also contributed to numerous professional journals, such as *Financial Planning, Financial Advisor,* and the *NAPFA Advisor Magazine.*

The author or coauthor of two dozen nonfiction books, he also wrote two other Dummies titles in addition to this one: *Bond Investing For Dummies* and *Index Investing For Dummies.* No stranger to the mass media, Wild has shared his wit and wisdom on such shows as *Oprah, The View, CBS Morning News,* and *Good Day New York,* and in hundreds of radio interviews.

Wild holds a Master of Business Administration (MBA) degree with a concentration in finance from The Thunderbird School of Global Management, in Glendale, Arizona (consistently ranked the #1 school for international business by both *U.S. News & World Report and The Wall Street Journal*); a Bachelor of Science (BS) degree in business/economics *magna cum laude* from American University in Washington, D.C.; and a graduate certificate in personal financial planning from Moravian College in Bethlehem, Pennsylvania (America's sixth-oldest college). A member of the National Association of Personal Financial Advisors (NAPFA) since 2002, Wild is also a long-time member and past president of the American Society of Journalists and Authors (ASJA).

The author grew up on Long Island and now lives in the West Mt. Airy section of Philadelphia. His son Clayton lives in Washington, D.C., where he is pursuing a career in politics. His daughter Adrienne attends Pennsylvania's Kutztown University. His dogs Norman, a standard poodle, and Zoey, a mysterious mix of breeds, protect their 1924 home from murderous squirrels. His website is www.globalportfolios.net.

Dedication

To the small investor, who has been bamboozled, bullied, and beaten up long enough.

Author's Acknowledgments

Although I've written many books, the first edition of this book was my first *Dummies* book, and writing a first *Dummies* book is a bit like learning to ride a bicycle — on a very windy day. If it weren't for Joan Friedman, project editor, who kept a steady hand on the back of my seat, I would surely have fallen off a curb and been run over by a pickup truck flying a Confederate flag. Joan, hands down, is one of the best editors I've ever worked with. She's a very nice person too.

Other nice people that I'd also like to tip my bicycle helmet to include Marilyn Allen of Allen O'Shea Literary Agency (she calls me "babe," just like agents do in movies; I love that) and Stacy Kennedy, acquisitions editor at Wiley. If these two gals hadn't gotten together, I wouldn't have had a bicycle to ride.

Thanks, too, to Paul Justice, CFA, editor of Morningstar's ETFInvestor newsletter. Paul, who knows a heck of a lot about ETFs, was the official technical editor on this book, and he checked every chapter to make certain that this remained strictly a work of nonfiction. Fellow fee-only financial advisor and good friend Neil Stoloff then double checked. You da man, Neil.

I'd like to thank Morningstar — all the folks there aside from Paul — for extreme generosity in providing fund industry data and analysis. Additional good data came from the various ETF providers, such as Vanguard, State Street, BlackRock, and T. Rowe Price, as well as a few non-ETF providers, such as Dimensional and the U.S. Treasury. Thanks, all.

I'd also like to thank Donald Bowles, my old professor of economics at American University, for showing me that supply and demand curves can be fun. Sorry we lost touch, but I haven't forgotten you.

And finally, I'd like to thank my old man, attorney Lawrence R. Wild, both my most beloved and most difficult client, who, if he told me once, told me a thousand times: "Rich or poor, it's good to have money." It took me years, Dad, to discover the profound wisdom in that statement.

Publisher's Acknowledgments

Acquisitions Editor: Stacy Kennedy

Compiler: Traci Cumbay

Project Editor (previous edition): Joan Friedman

Project Editor: Tim Gallan

Art Coordinator: Alicia B. South

Production Editor: Antony Sami

Cover Image: © jannoon028/Shutterstock

Apple & Mac

iPad For Dummies, 6th Edition
978-1-118-72306-7

iPhone For Dummies, 7th Edition
978-1-118-69083-3

Macs All-in-One For Dummies,
4th Edition
978-1-118-82210-4

OS X Mavericks For Dummies
978-1-118-69188-5

Blogging & Social Media

Facebook For Dummies,
5th Edition
978-1-118-63312-0

Social Media Engagement
For Dummies
978-1-118-53019-1

WordPress For Dummies,
6th Edition
978-1-118-79161-5

Business

Stock Investing For Dummies,
4th Edition
978-1-118-37678-2

Investing For Dummies,
6th Edition
978-0-470-90545-6

Personal Finance For Dummies,
7th Edition
978-1-118-11785-9

QuickBooks 2014 For Dummies
978-1-118-72005-9

Small Business Marketing Kit
For Dummies, 3rd Edition
978-1-118-31183-7

Careers

Job Interviews For Dummies,
4th Edition
978-1-118-11290-8

Job Searching with Social Media
For Dummies, 2nd Edition
978-1-118-67856-5

Personal Branding For Dummies
978-1-118-11792-7

Resumes For Dummies,
6th Edition
978-0-470-87361-8

Starting an Etsy Business
For Dummies, 2nd Edition
978-1-118-59024-9

Diet & Nutrition

Belly Fat Diet For Dummies
978-1-118-34585-6

Mediterranean Diet For Dummies
978-1-118-71525-3

Nutrition For Dummies,
5th Edition
978-0-470-93231-5

Digital Photography

Digital SLR Photography
All-in-One For Dummies,
2nd Edition
978-1-118-59082-9

Digital SLR Video & Filmmaking
For Dummies
978-1-118-36598-4

Photoshop Elements 12
For Dummies
978-1-118-72714-0

Gardening

Herb Gardening For Dummies,
2nd Edition
978-0-470-61778-6

Gardening with Free-Range
Chickens For Dummies
978-1-118-54754-0

Health

Boosting Your Immunity
For Dummies
978-1-118-40200-9

Diabetes For Dummies,
4th Edition
978-1-118-29447-5

Living Paleo For Dummies
978-1-118-29405-5

Big Data

Big Data For Dummies
978-1-118-50422-2

Data Visualization For Dummies
978-1-118-50289-1

Hadoop For Dummies
978-1-118-60755-8

Language & Foreign Language

500 Spanish Verbs For Dummies
978-1-118-02382-2

English Grammar For Dummies,
2nd Edition
978-0-470-54664-2

French All-in-One For Dummies
978-1-118-22815-9

German Essentials For Dummies
978-1-118-18422-6

Italian For Dummies, 2nd Edition
978-1-118-00465-4

Available in print and e-book formats.

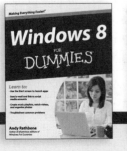

Available wherever books are sold.

For more information or to order direct visit www.dummies.com

Take Dummies with you everywhere you go!

Whether you are excited about e-books, want more from the web, must have your mobile apps, or are swept up in social media, Dummies makes everything easier.

For Dummies is the global leader in the reference category and one of the most trusted and highly regarded brands in the world. No longer just focused on books, customers now have access to the For Dummies content they need in the format they want. Let us help you develop a solution that will fit your brand and help you connect with your customers.

Advertising & Sponsorships

Connect with an engaged audience on a powerful multimedia site, and position your message alongside expert how-to content.

Targeted ads • Video • Email marketing • Microsites • Sweepstakes sponsorship

21 Million Monthly Page Views & 13 Million Unique Visitors

# of For Dummies

Custom Publishing

Reach a global audience in any language by creating a solution that will differentiate you from competitors, amplify your message, and encourage customers to make a buying decision.

Apps • Books • eBooks • Video • Audio • Webinars

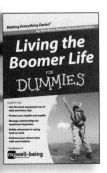   

Brand Licensing & Content

Leverage the strength of the world's most popular reference brand to reach new audiences and channels of distribution.

For more information, visit www.Dummies.com/biz

FOR DUMMIES

A Wiley Brand

Dummies products make life easier!

- DIY
- Consumer Electronics
- Crafts
- Software

- Cookware
- Hobbies
- Videos

- Music
- Games
- and More!

For more information, go to **Dummies.com** and search the store by category.

FOR DUMMIES

A Wiley Brand